BY THE MINISTERING OF ANGELS

BY THE MINISTERING OF ANGELS

Heavenly Visitations in LDS Church History

Marlene Bateman Sullivan

Horizon Publishers
Springville, Utah

ISBN 13: 978-0-88290-795-4
ISBN 10: 0-88290-795-4

Published by Horizon Publishers, an imprint of Cedar Fort, Inc.,
925 N. Main, Springville, UT, 84663
Distributed by Cedar Fort, Inc. www.cedarfort.com

Cover design by Nicole Williams
Cover design © 2006 by Lyle Mortimer
Printed in the United States of America

10 9 8 7 6 5 4 3 2 1

Printed on acid-free paper

Dedication

To my dear daughter Tiffany,
who had a dream and the courage to follow it through.

Wherefore, by the ministering of angels, and by every word which proceedeth forth out of the mouth of God, men began to exercize faith in Christ; and thus by faith, they did lay hold upon every good thing.

—Moroni 7:25

Table of Contents

Chapter 1

Angelic Visitations through Dreams and Visions

When the gospel was restored, God once again began communing with His chosen prophets, just as He had in ancient times. Joseph Smith, the first prophet of this dispensation, received many revelations and visions for the benefit and guidance of the Saints, as has every prophet who has directed the Church since Joseph's death in 1844.

However, prophets are not the only ones entitled to receive revelation. Communication has always been open between heaven and earth, and it is the privilege of Saints in all ages to receive the spiritual gift of personal revelation. Through all periods of time and in all dispensations, God has helped His children on earth by giving them guidance, inspiration, comfort, and help through personal revelation. "And now, he imparteth his word by angels unto men, yea, not only men but women also. Now this is not all; little children do have words given unto them many times" (Alma 32:23).

Through the holy scriptures, we are given much knowledge and direction. Heavenly Father has also given us the presence of the Holy Ghost, which can lead us in the paths of righteousness. Another way God can communicate with mortals is through dreams and visions. Elder James E. Talmage said, "Visions and dreams have constituted a means of communication between God and men in every dispensation of the priesthood."[1]

President Wilford Woodruff taught two of the most important ways God uses to communicate with mortals are through the scriptures and the mouth of His prophets. Then he added, "The Lord has other ways of communicating His mind and will. . . . Frequently, as has been the case in every age, truths, principles, warnings, etc., are communicated to the children of men by means of dreams and visions."[2]

As a means of personal revelation, dreams and visions were given to people in ancient times. They continue today provided we have sufficient faith. "I would ask of you, have all these things passed, of which I have spoken? . . . Behold I say unto you, Nay; and God has not ceased to be a God of miracles. . . . And the reason why he ceaseth to do miracles among the children of men is because that they dwindle in unbelief, and depart from the right way" (Mormon 9:15, 20).

God will never turn away from us. Revelation will never cease unless people turn away from God. In the Book of Mormon, whenever people were indifferent about following God, revelation decreased accordingly. "And because of their iniquity the church had begun to dwindle; and they began to disbelieve in the spirit of prophecy and in the spirit of revelation" (Helaman 4:23).

When he spoke in general conference, Elder Boyd K. Packer emphasized the fact that revelation continues today as it did anciently. "Revelation continues with us today," he observed. "The promptings of the Spirit, the dreams, the visions and the visitations, and the ministering of angels all are with us now. And the still, small voice of the Holy Ghost 'is a lamp unto [our] feet, and a light unto [our] path'" (Psalm 119:105).[3]

President Harold B. Lee had this to say about revelation:

> I bear you my solemn testimony that the Church today is guided by revelation. Every soul in it who has been blessed to receive the Holy Ghost has the power to receive revelation. When we begin to understand that beyond sight, as Brigham Young said, the spirit world is right here round about us, and if our spiritual eyes could be open, we could see others visiting with us, directing us. And if we will learn not to be so sophisticated that we rule out that possibility of impression from those who are beyond sight, then we too may have a dream that may direct us as a revelation.[4]

This idea is reinforced in the scriptures. In the Doctrine and Covenants, we read, "And your minds in time past have been darkened because of unbelief, and because you have treated lightly the things you have received" (D&C 84:55).

The Millennial Star was an early Church periodical used to keep Church members informed about official Church doctrine with editorials usually written by one of the Twelve Apostles. In one issue of *The Millennial Star,* Elder H. Ricks wrote:

> We often pray for the gifts of God, and when He bestows them upon us, we are sometimes unaware, it seems to me, that we are in possession of them. We do not try to make ourselves understand the whisperings of the Spirit, nor do we always endeavor to distinguish between dreams in which there is an inspired meaning, and others to which there is no such importance attached. . . . We should be very careful not to lightly esteem the gifts of God.[5]

When speaking of communication between heaven and earth, President Harold B. Lee said:

> Now there's one more way by which revelations may come, and that is by dreams. Oh, I'm not going to tell you that every dream you have is a direct revelation from the Lord—it may be fried liver and onions that have been responsible for an upset or disorder. But I fear that in this age of sophistication there are those of us who are prone to rule out all dreams as of no purpose, and of no moment. And yet all through the scriptures there were recorded incidents where the Lord, by dreams, has directed His people.[6]

As God's children, we are entitled to our Heavenly Father's counsel. Dreams are one of the ways He can use to advise and help us as we travel through mortality. While speaking during general conference, Elder David A. Bednar spoke of a young man who learned through a dream that the Lord was aware of him. In his address, Elder Bednar explained that the young man's priesthood leader had a dream. He related:

"In the dream, he saw the young man dressed in a white shirt and wearing a missionary name tag. With a companion seated at his side, the young man was teaching a family. The young man held the Book of Mormon in his hand, and he looked as if he were testifying of the truthfulness of the book. The priesthood leader then awoke from his dream.

"At an ensuing priesthood gathering, the leader approached the young man he had seen in his dream and asked to talk with him for a few minutes. The leader then said, 'I am not a dreamer. I have never had a dream about a single member of this stake, except for you. I am going to tell you about my dream, and then I would like you to help me understand what it means.' The priesthood leader recounted the dream and asked the young man about its meaning. . . . Choking with emotion, the young man simply replied, 'It means God knows who I am.'"

Elder Bednar declared, "That young man received the Lord's tender mercies through an inspired priesthood leader." He added, "I testify that the tender mercies of the Lord are available to all of us and that the Redeemer of Israel is eager to bestow such gifts upon us. . . . Faithfulness and obedience enable us to receive these important gifts."[7]

All of the spiritual gifts that come from God can be used for our benefit and salvation. Elder George F. Richards, father of LeGrand Richards, was president of the Quorum of the Twelve Apostles when he said:

> I believe in dreams, brethren. . . . The Lord has given me dreams which to me are just as real and as much from God as was the dream of King Nebuchadnezzar, which was the means of saving a nation from starvation, or the dream of Lehi who through a dream led his colony out of the old country across the mighty deep to this promised land, or any other dreams that we might read in the scriptures. . . . The Lord has revealed to men by dreams something more than I ever understood or felt before. It is not out of place for us to have important dreams.[8]

Historical Aspects

Dreams and visions have been a source of knowledge in every dispensation of time. In ancient Greece, dreams were greatly respected. The Greeks believed dreams came from Jupiter, the king of gods. In ancient Egypt and Babylon, a college of wise men was set apart to interpret the dreams of monarchs. In Greek and Roman culture, it was common, after the performance of sacred rites, to sleep in the temple so any information sought for could be made known to the dreamer.

Ancient philosophers wrote many treatises upon dreams. Aristotle considered them a reality represented as ripples of water that only needed to be straightened out. Ancient Jews, American Indians, and many other cultures had a deep respect for dreams, which they used as guides for their lives.

Nowadays, different cultures regard dreams in various ways. While many cultures still respect dreams, others consider them of no importance. While it may be true that significant dreams are rare, it is not prudent to automatically dismiss all dreams as unimportant.

Every man of righteousness in the scriptures believed in angels, dreams, visions, and miracles. God is no respecter of persons, and He does not change. Since we know He values people in this day just as much as those who lived in previous dispensations, we know He continues to use visions, angels, and dreams as a method of communication today. The scriptures confirm this belief. "And if there were miracles wrought then, why has God ceased to be a God of miracles and yet be an unchangeable Being? And behold, I say unto you he changeth not; if so he would cease to be God; and he ceaseth not to be God, and is a God of miracles" (Mormon 9:19).

We find many instances of communication through dreams in the scriptures. In the Old Testament, Jacob saw angels of God ascending and descending on a ladder that reached into heaven (see Genesis 28:12). An angel told Jacob in a dream that he should return to Canaan (see Genesis 31:11). God warned Laban in a dream when he was pursuing his son-in-law, Jacob (see Genesis 31:24). And God spoke to Israel "in the visions of the night" (see Genesis 46:2).

Joseph, the son of Jacob, roused the anger of his brothers when he related his dreams, which testified he would be in a position of power over them (see Genesis 37:5–11). Although his brothers scornfully called Joseph a dreamer (see Genesis 37:19), his dreams came true, and he eventually became a powerful leader.

While in prison, Joseph correctly interpreted the dreams of the Pharaoh's butler and baker. Later, when Pharaoh had a perplexing dream, Joseph was released from prison so he could give its interpretation. Because he was able to correctly interpret the Pharaoh's highly symbolic dream, Joseph was made a ruler over the people of Egypt, warded off starvation for Egypt, and was able to save his father's household (see Genesis 41:40–43).

After listening to a man's dream and learning its interpretation, Gideon became a hero when he delivered Israel from the Midianites (see Judges 7:13–15).

When Solomon prayed to be blessed with the gift of discernment and to have an understanding heart so he could correctly judge the people, the Lord appeared to him in a dream. In the dream, the Lord not only granted Solomon's request but also gave him riches and honor and lengthened out his days (see 1 Kings 3:5–15).

Most of the book of Ezekiel describes the countless visions and revelations this prophet received from God. One of the things Ezekiel saw was the resuscitation of dry bones, which symbolized the restoration of the favor of the Lord to the house of Israel and the coming forth of the stick of Ephraim in the last days. Ezekiel also saw the union of the house of Israel with the house of Judah and the effect this joining would have on turning the hearts of the children to their ancestors (see Ezekiel 37:15–28).

Daniel was favored of the Lord to receive much personal revelation. The scriptures tell us, "Daniel had understanding in all visions and dreams" (Daniel 1:17). Because he was able to interpret Nebuchadnezzar's dream, Daniel was raised from captivity to preside over governors and presidents of more than one hundred provinces (see Daniel 2).

Later, Daniel had a vision of tremendous magnitude, where he saw the imposing events of the future, including the rise and fall of kingdoms and the persecution and final triumph of the Saints (see Daniel 7–8). We can see the fulfillment of Daniel's vision by tracing the history of the world down to our present day.

God spoke to both Job "in thoughts from the visions of the night" (Job 4:13) and to Jeremiah, who recorded, "Moreover the word of the Lord came unto me, saying, Jeremiah, what seest thou?" (Jeremiah 1:11). Habakkuk also had visions, saying, "And the Lord answered me, and said, Write the vision " (Habakkuk 2:2). Zechariah was similarly blessed to receive dreams and visions (see Zechariah 1:8–11, 18–21; 2:1–2; 6:1–8).

Dreams and their interpretations have always helped open the future for God's people. In the New Testament, Joseph was reassured in a dream that Mary had conceived through the power of the Holy Ghost and he should proceed with his marriage plans. "But while he thought on these things, behold, the angel of the Lord appeared unto him in a dream" (Matthew 1:20).

After the wise men visited the newborn baby Jesus, they were given lifesaving counsel in a dream. "And being warned of God in a dream that they should not return to Herod, they departed into their own country another way" (Matthew 2:12).

While Jesus was still young, Joseph was warned that he, Mary, and Jesus should flee to Egypt. "Behold, the angel of the Lord appeareth to Joseph in a dream, saying, Arise, and take the young child and his mother, and flee into Egypt, and be thou there until I bring thee word: for Herod will seek the young child to destroy him" (Matthew 2:13).

Joseph was also told in a dream when it was safe for the family to return home. "But when Herod was dead, behold, an angel of the Lord appeareth in a dream to Joseph in Egypt" (Matthew 2:19). Later, Joseph was told not go to Judea but to Galilee instead, being "warned of God in a dream" (Matthew 2:22).

After the crucifixion of Jesus Christ, the apostles had many dreams and visions to direct them during their ministry. Peter was shown in a vision that the Gentiles were entitled to the blessings of the gospel (see Acts 10:9–16). Saul saw Ananias in a vision and knew that this faithful follower of Christ would restore his sight. Likewise, Ananias was told by the Lord in a dream to heal Saul. "And there was a certain disciple at Damascus, named Ananias; and to him said the Lord in a vision . . . enquire in the house of Judas for one called Saul, of Tarsus: for, behold, he prayeth" (Acts 9:10–11).

In Acts, we read how the Lord directed Paul to go to Macedonia: "And a vision appeared to Paul in the night" (Acts 16:9). Later, the Lord reassured Paul: "Then spake the Lord to Paul in the night by a vision, be not afraid" (Acts 18:9). A few chapters later, Paul writes about a vision he received while in the temple. He recalled, "Even while I prayed in the temple, I was in a trance" (Acts 22:17).

In the beginning of the Book of Mormon, we learn Lehi had dreams that instructed him to leave Jerusalem so he and his family could escape the destruction that would soon come to that city. "And it came to pass that the Lord commanded my father, even in a dream, that he should take his family and depart into the wilderness" (1 Nephi 2:2).

Lehi also had one of the most significant dreams in the Book of Mormon that, when interpreted, gives us a greater understanding of the plan of salvation. In this dream, Lehi saw a rod of iron beside a straight and narrow path that led to the tree of life. Many people who tried to reach the tree lost their way, while others watching from a great and spacious building mocked those who reached the tree (see 1 Nephi 8:2–38).

Later in the Book of Mormon, God used a dream to communicate with Omer. "And the Lord warned Omer in a dream that he should depart out of the land" (Ether 9:3).

The Lord also showed a powerful vision to the brother of Jared. "And when the Lord had said these words, he showed unto the brother of Jared all the inhabitants of the earth which had been, and also all that would be" (Ether 3:25).

One of the few Lamanite believers at one point in the Book of Mormon, Abish was converted because of a vision (see Alma 19:16). Through a vision, Amulek was instructed to welcome Alma. "And I know that thou art a holy prophet of God, for thou art the man whom an angel said in a vision: Thou shalt receive" (Alma 8:20).

In modern ages, the last dispensation of time was opened through a miraculous vision received by Joseph Smith, who saw the Father and the Son. As a chosen prophet of God, Joseph Smith received numerous visions and revelations that enabled him to restore the gospel on earth.

What Is the Purpose of Dreams?

Our Father in Heaven is a loving Father who watches over His children on earth carefully. He communicates with us as often as we desire. Divine communication comes when we invite God into our lives and is usually initiated by our prayers, especially when we ask for guidance or assistance. Heavenly Father can use dreams as one way to communicate with us in order to guide or comfort us, testify of the truth, or teach us principles of the gospel.

The editor of the *Millennial Star* wrote:

> It is a glorious privilege of the Saints of God in all ages to receive knowledge and intelligence from God, by means of dreams, visions, tongues, &c. The Saints of old received intelligence through these channels. Prophets and righteous men have sought information from the eternal worlds, and in dreams and visions of the night, and by the out-pouring of the Holy

> Spirit, have had unfolded to them scenes of the past, the present, the future, have had their minds enveloped in the glory and sublimity of eternal realties, and have been cheered, refreshed, strengthened, and prepared for the emergencies of life.
>
> Whether mankind realizes the matter or not, still it is true that these gifts and blessings—these channels of instruction, and communication with inhabitants of other worlds, are appointed of God for the benefit of those who wish to be instructed of Him. And although a majority of mankind ridicule such things, still it is on record that in these "last days" in which we live, men are not to be denied or deprived of these blessings, where they are sought for from a fervent desire of learning of the things of God.[9]

Personal revelation can be a significant guiding force in our lives. In order to receive this blessing, we must strive to obey God's commandments. Speaking about how to receive divine help to guide us in our lives, President Brigham Young said, "How shall we know what to do? By being obedient to every requirement of the Gospel. Brother Hooper has stated that I promised him the assistance of the Almighty [in his calling]. I did. I laid my hands upon him and blessed him, and told him that he should have dreams and visions, and power with God to know what to do, if he lived his religion; but if he did not, I promised him nothing."[10]

We must have faith and be believing in order to receive revelation. We must not expect signs or revelations to create our faith. Faith comes *before* revelations and signs. "But, behold, faith cometh not by signs, but signs follow those that believe. Yea, signs come by faith, not by the will of men, nor as they please, but by the will of God. Yea, signs come by faith, unto mighty works, for without faith no man pleaseth God" (D&C 63:9–11).

We know from the preceding comment that we must live worthy if we are to receive the blessings that come from personal revelation. President Heber C. Kimball stated:

> Brethren and sisters, I exhort you above all things to hold fast to your integrity, seek for righteousness and cleave unto it, and if you see anything that is contrary to these holy principles among this people, you may know that it is not good. There is no person in this Church who can increase in the knowledge of God, in the spirit of revelation, in the gift of prophecy, in visions or in dreams,

unless they cleave unto God with full purpose of heart, but by being faithful these gifts will be multiplied unto the Saints.[11]

Why Does the Lord Use Dreams to Communicate with Us?

Why would God use dreams as a means of communication rather than speak to our minds when we are awake? Perhaps one reason lies in the very nature of dreams. Dreams occur when we are at rest. Sleep may be the only time when we are not preoccupied with the rush of everyday activities and when we are quiet enough to allow the Spirit to penetrate our thoughts.

The Holy Ghost has a difficult time reaching us when we are stressed, worried, or busy. It is much easier to receive personal revelation when we are tranquil and at peace. Since night is a time of rest and relaxation, it is a time when we are naturally more receptive to divine communication.

Parley P. Pratt observed, "In all ages and dispensations God has revealed many important instructions and warnings to men by means of dreams. When the outward organs of thought and perception are released from their activity, the nerves unstrung, the whole of mortal humanity lies hushed in quiet slumbers in order to renew its strength and vigor, it is then that the spiritual organs are at liberty in a certain degree to assume their wanted functions, to recall some faint outline, some confused and half defined recollections of that heavenly world, and those endearing scenes of their former estate from which they have descended in order to obtain and mature a tabernacle of flesh."

Elder Pratt continued, talking about how night is a quiet time when angels can reach mortals. He says that at night, "their kindred spirit, their guardian angels, then hover about them with the fondest affection, the most anxious solicitude. Spirit communes with spirit, thought meets thought, soul blends with soul, in all the raptures of mutual pure and eternal love. In this situation the spiritual organs . . . are susceptible of converse with Deity, or of communion with angels, and the spirits of just men made perfect. In this situation we frequently hold communion with our departed father, mother, brother, sister, son or daughter."[12]

The editor of *The Millennial Star* wrote about dreams as a form of divine communication, declaring "the fact is, spirit ministers to spirit, and so *we dream revelations,* because the angels inform our spirits what to dream; and the eyes of our understandings see it: and the ears of our perception conceive; and lo, there is a line of communication from heaven to earth!"[13]

If we desire divine communication, we must have quiet time to allow the Spirit into our lives. Many of us live in a fast-paced world where every waking moment is spent rushing from one task to another. If the TV is not blaring, the radio is, and if we are not speaking, others are. During the day we are absorbed in our jobs, taking care of children, or doing any one of a hundred other things. Is there any quiet time in our lives—other than at night—when we give the Spirit a chance to communicate with us?

The Spirit has a still, small voice. We cannot expect it to speak to us during our child's soccer game, while buying tomatoes at the grocery store, or when we are standing in line at the bank. When we are asleep, our bodies are finally free from physical activity and, if we can still our minds as well, the Spirit will be able to commune with us.

True and False Dreams

While dreams can be a form of divine personal revelation, truly inspired dreams are rare, and we must remember that false dreams can come from Satan. We must guard against being deceived by false revelations, such as those that come through clairvoyants, mystics, astrologers, palms readers, and board games that use the powers of darkness. Such revelations originate from Satan, and it is wise to avoid such things at all times.

Satan will use any method possible to lead people astray and can give us dreams that appear to be from God but are intended to direct us off course. Because of this, it is our responsibility to discern which dreams are from God and which are not.

In *The Millennial Star*, an early Church leader wrote:

> Dreams are of different kinds and are given for various purposes; each true one, however, being applicable to the situation and requirements of the individual receiving it, or, of the people about whom it contains directions. Dreams must be divided into two kinds or classes, true and false; the former are given for a definite purpose, either as warnings of judgments to come, or telling of duties to perform in the present or the future; the

> latter are delusive, treacherous and not to be counted as proceeding from a good source. Those beneficial to us and productive of happiness and joy are from a good and holy source, and are given for the purpose of strengthening our determinations and confirming our faith, or of warning us of difficulties which will be presented before us by the Adversary, to daunt our courage and lure us on to destruction.[14]

Another writer noted, "Saints may at all times seek the Holy Spirit to understand and know when true principle is communicated. They should possess sufficient of the Spirit to know whether this dream is true or not, or the parts of it that are true, and those which are not."[15]

Elder Boyd K. Packer taught that as a method of revelation, dreams and visions can be susceptible to evil influences. He said, "The evil one has the power to tap into those channels of revelation and send conflicting signals which can mislead and confuse us. There are promptings from evil sources which are so carefully counterfeited as to deceive even the very elect (see Matthew 24:24). Nevertheless, we can learn to discern these spirits."[16]

Satan is constantly laying snares in order to deceive, and we must use wisdom and caution when considering dreams, for the devil will try to influence us for ill. Elder Vaughn J. Featherstone noted that people should constantly be on guard so as not to be deceived. He warned that some people have dreams they believe are from God but which are actually from Satan. Such dreams, he observed, are meant to destroy a person's testimony when they don't come true. "God bless us to have vision," he added, "and dream the right kinds of dreams and to be able to discern them."[17]

Joseph Smith gives us four keys that we can use to determine whether communication comes from God or Satan. First, the Prophet Joseph said, revelation from God will be sent in order to further His work on earth, while Satan's communication will often be confusing. If "all the intelligence that can be obtained from someone claiming to have the power of the Spirit . . . is some incoherent expression . . . such a heterogeneous mass of confusion never can enter into the kingdom of heaven."[18]

Joseph said that the second key is that the Spirit has dignity and will not cause individuals to behave strangely, such as speaking in an unnatural voice or distorting bodies, while Satan causes people to have "strange fits, as in tremblings and faintings, which make them stretch out their legs and arms, as in a swoon; . . . trances, and coming out of them., . . . (and) twitchings, tumblings."[19]

The third key is that there is nothing unnatural about the Spirit of God. Acting wildly out of character indicates that a person is communing with Satan rather than God. Joseph Smith said, "Soon after the Gospel was established . . . many false spirits were introduced, many strange visions were seen, and wild, enthusiastic notions were entertained; men ran out of doors under the influence of this spirit, and some of them got upon the stumps of trees and shouted. . . . One man pursued a ball that he said he saw flying in the air."[20]

The fourth key is that Satan is quite willing to teach a measure of truth in order to promote false ideas. Joseph said, "There have also been ministering angels in the Church which were of Satan appearing as an angel of light."[21] Joseph reminded people that no angel sent from God would ever contradict a former revelation, as Satan's angels were doing.

By using these keys and developing the spirit of discernment, a person can decide whether a dream is meaningful or not. How do we do this? By paying attention to how we feel after the dream and to what ideas we receive in the dream. In talking about personal revelation, the Prophet Joseph said, "A person may profit by noticing the first intimation of the spirit of revelation; for instance, when you feel pure intelligence flowing into you, it may give you sudden strokes of ideas, so that by noticing it you may find it fulfilled the same day or soon; (i.e.) those things that were presented unto your minds by the Spirit of God will come to pass; and thus by learning the spirit of God and understanding it you may grow into the principle of revelation, until you become perfect in Christ Jesus."[22]

Discerning which dreams are inspired and meaningful has always been a matter of concern. Elder Joseph G. Romney outlines a few more guidelines, noting, "a good dream from the Spirit of God is very easily told; it will make persons wiser, more humble and more obedient than they have ever been before."[23] In other words, a good dream will draw us closer to God.

Dreams that come from God will also be impressive and give people a deeper sense of understanding than they had before. Frequently, a dream from God will strike individuals with such emotional force and power that they intuitively know it is important and from God.

President Wilford Woodruff said that a person who has the Spirit of God can identify true dreams from false ones. "We have had a great many dreams—I have had in my life, and I suppose you have more or less—which amount to nothing," he said. "A man may go to bed half-worried to death, tired and dream about something that will never take place. . . . Yet I have had dreams of a very different character. . . . There are a great many things taught us in dreams that are true, and if a man has the spirit of God he can tell the difference between what is from the Lord and what is not."[24]

The perplexing thing about dreams is that many of them do not seem to make sense and are confusing. This is because almost all dreams are highly symbolic, which means the people, places, objects, and activities in them represent something else. Unless you ponder your dream carefully and are able to discover what the various elements represent, you will not be able to understand it.

In the Old Testament, Nebuchadnezzar had a highly symbolic dream. He saw an image whose head was made of gold, whose arms were of silver, whose belly was of brass, whose legs were of iron, and whose feet were part iron and part clay. In Nebuchadnezzar's dream, the image was destroyed by a stone that had been cut without hands (see Daniel 2:31–34). Although Pharaoh knew his dream was important, he was utterly confused by it until Daniel, through the power and inspiration of the Lord, explained what it meant (see Daniel 2:38–45).

Another earmark of an inspired dream is that the message will be clear, easily remembered, and leave a distinct emotional impression for good. Dreams that are troubling, disturbing, or cause undue grief are most likely not from God.

The editor of *The Millennial Star* wrote, "Now one mark of a dream from God is that it is distinguished for the clearness and simplicity of the impression that it makes upon the mind of him that dreams. . . . The Lord does not suffer wicked spirits to foul and blot and mar a dream, when he wants to communicate His mind and will. . . . The Angel of God guards the dreamer till a clear and a distinct impression is made. And that impression is of an unmistakable character; it cannot be misunderstood, any more than the light of the sun can be mistaken for the darkness of midnight."[25]

One final and important factor to remember is true dreams will always be consistent with and adhere strictly to doctrines of the Church. While dreams are commonplace, the dream that comes from God is a rare jewel—not often seen and treasured all the more when it is.

A Word of Caution

Although it is the right of all Latter-day Saints to receive revelation, we must always remember that such revelation will only be given in regard to our own personal realm of responsibility. We are entitled to revelation regarding our own lives and our own families, but no member of the Church will ever receive revelation from God regarding the actions of those who he or she has no responsibility for.

"Revelation comes in an orderly way in the Church," Elder Packer reminds us. "We are entitled to personal revelation. However, unless we are set apart to some presiding office, we will not receive revelations concerning what others should do."[26]

Other teachings confirm this. The editor of *The Millennial Star* wrote, "It is the privilege of the Saints to have dreams and visions for edification, comfort, instruction, and warning; but the Lord does not make known matters of doctrine and principle, for the guidance of his Church, through the members thereof; he has an appointed and ordained channel through which such knowledge is imparted."[27]

We should also note that those who receive dreams that guide them—telling them what they need to start or stop doing—do not become puffed up in their hearts or lose the spirit of humility, which is so essential for any true follower of Christ. The gift of revelation is not bestowed upon us so we can boast but to help us during our mortal lives.

Those who receive revelation through dreams must treat such inspiration sacredly. We should only talk about these happenings in certain places and on special occasions, and we should always maintain a respectful attitude. The audience must be appropriate. Reveal important dreams only to those who believe as you believe. Jesus said, "Give not that which is holy unto dogs, neither cast ye your pearls before swine, lest they trample them under their feet, and turn again and rend you" (Matthew 7:6).

"Dreams oftentimes burst like an empty bubble, yet the Lord uses dreams," Elder Featherstone observed. "I suppose that they may be motivation or prophetic, as I mentioned. And I suppose also, the Lord trusts us with some dreams of visions that have to do with our own personal lives. . . . Now, I have had dreams. . . that I have never divulged, not to a living soul. And they're just as clear in my mind as when I had them. And I will not tell them. . . . I hold them sacred."[28]

Visions vs. Dreams

One of the main differences between dreams and visions is that the physical body is asleep during a dream. Elder James E. Talmage said, "In general, visions are manifested to the waking sense whilst dreams are given during sleep. In the vision, however, the senses may be so affected as to render the person practically unconscious, at least oblivious to ordinary occurrences while he is able to discern the heavenly manifestation. In the earlier dispensations, the Lord frequently communicated through dreams and visions, oftentimes revealing to prophets the events of the future even to the latest generations."[29]

Visions occur when people or events are seen through the eyes of our spirit. Joseph Smith's vision of the Father and the Son in the Sacred Grove marked the opening of the last dispensation of time and paved the way for the restoration of the gospel. Joseph Smith continued to have many visions to help establish and lead The Church of Jesus Christ of Latter-day Saints.

Joseph states that during a vision, one sees with spiritual rather than mortal eyes. He said, "By the power of the Spirit our eyes were opened and our understandings were enlightened, so as to see and understand the things of God" (D&C 76:12). When he had a vision of the Savior in the temple at Kirtland, Joseph observed, "The veil was taken from our minds, and the eyes of our understanding were opened. We saw the Lord standing upon the breastwork of the pulpit, before us; and under his feet was a paved work of pure gold, in color like amber" (D&C 110:1–2).

Erastus Snow talked about what constitutes a vision when he explained, "It is simply the spirit within us enjoying a higher privilege of conversing with spirits, seeing spiritual things and conversing with spirits or immortal beings."[30]

Visions and dreams from God are alike in that both make the recipients feel as if they are removed from earthly matters. Some dreams are so vivid and real that people describe what they've seen as visions, while others have described their visions as having dream-like qualities. Occasionally, while under the influence of the Spirit, individiuals can be so overwhelmed that it can be hard to tell where they are in regard to their physical bodies. On 21 January 1836, while at the Kirtland Temple, the Prophet Joseph Smith had a vision and was not sure if he was still in his mortal body or not. He said, "The heavens were opened upon us, and I beheld the celestial kingdom of God, and the glory thereof, whether in the body or out I cannot tell."[31]

One of the most remarkable visions the Church has received in the latter days was given to President Joseph F. Smith and is called the Vision of the Redemption of the Dead. It is recorded as scripture as section 138 of the Doctrine and Covenants.

As the time approaches for the Lord's second coming, we can be sure that the flow of communication between heaven and earth will continue and most likely increase. The scriptures tell us, "And it shall come to pass in the last days, saith God, I will pour out my Spirit upon all flesh: and your sons and your daughters shall prophesy and your young men shall have visions, and your old men shall dream dreams" (Acts 2:17).

Chapter 2

Angelic Visits to Prophets and Church Leaders

As God's chosen servants and leaders of the faithful, prophets throughout the ages have been blessed with a special closeness to God. An important and necessary function of a prophet is to receive spiritual communication from heaven, so God can guide and direct His children here on earth. By virtue of their holy calling, prophets are given dreams and visions to further God's purposes for mankind.

In the scriptures, we are told there has never been a prophet who has *not* received revelations from God through visions and dreams. The Lord said, "Hear now my words: If there be a prophet among you, I the Lord will make myself known unto him in a vision, and will speak unto him in a dream" (Numbers 12:6).

Since the restoration of the gospel in these latter days, revelation has continued to be a cornerstone of The Church of Jesus Christ of Latter-day Saints. "Some have thought the day of revelation is long past, but I want to bear my witness that that day is not past," President Harold B. Lee testified. "The Church is being guided by revelation today. Brother [John A.] Widtsoe used to tell us about a group who gathered round him between meetings at a stake conference and said, 'Oh, Brother Widtsoe, how long has it been since the Church received a revelation?' And Brother Widtsoe stroked his chin for a moment and said, 'Oh, probably since last Thursday.'"[1]

Speaking in general conference, Elder Charles A. Callis, president of the Southern States Mission, said, "In this Church we are . . . guided by the compass of divine revelation which is in the possession of the leaders of this Church, even the revelations of God, the gift of the Holy Ghost, which God pours into every believing heart, and as we follow the direction of this compass we shall be guided safely into the harbor of eternal life."[2]

When President Woodruff received his patriarchal blessing in the Kirtland Temple on 15 April 1837, he was promised many blessings—one of which was the gift of visions. President Woodruff wrote, "The Patriarch also said I should be wrapt in the visions of heaven, and an angel of God should teach me many things. This was literally fulfilled."[3]

President John Taylor was also guided by the Spirit. A lesson in the *Young Woman's Journal* talks about how God's Spirit often rested upon President Taylor, saying, "Manifestations of its presence were frequent, not only in the expansion of his mind to understand doctrines and principles, but also in dreams and visions."[4]

The learned apostle James E. Talmage declared that God reveals His desires and plans to Church leaders. He wrote, "Under circumstances best suiting the divine purposes, through the dreams of sleep or in waking visions of the mind, by voices without visional appearance or by actual manifestations of the Holy Presence before the eye, God makes known His designs, and instructs His revelators."[5]

Melvin J. Ballard

Melvin J. Ballard was born in Logan, Utah, on 9 February 1873. He served two missions and, in 1909, was set apart as president of the Northwestern States Mission. On 7 January 1919, Elder Ballard was called to be one of the Twelve Apostles. He helped prepare the Latter-day Saint hymnbook for publication and actively worked to establish the Boy Scout program in the Church.

One of the most thrilling events of Elder Ballard's life was when he received a glorious dream about the Savior. This incident has touched the hearts of many who heard Elder Ballard relate it and others who read his account. This sacred encounter occurred while he was serving as a missionary at the Fort Peck Reservation. Elder Ballard first related his experience to a group of young people because he felt this vision of Jesus Christ would impress his audience with "the reality of His death, of His crucifixion, and His resurrection."

Elder Ballard loved to testify of Christ. He declared, "I know that He lives, and I know that through Him men must find their salvation, and that we cannot ignore this blessed offering that He has given to us as the means of our spiritual growth to prepare us to come to Him and be justified." Elder Ballard then related his experience:

> I was doing missionary work with some of our brethren, laboring among the Indians, seeking the Lord for light to decide certain matters pertaining to our work there, and receiving a witness from Him that we were doing things according to His will, I found myself one evening in the dreams of the night, in that sacred building, the Temple. After a season of prayer and rejoicing, I was informed that I should have the privilege of entering into one of those rooms, to meet a glorious Personage, and as I entered the door, I saw, seated on a raised platform, the most glorious Being my eyes ever have beheld, or that I ever conceived existed in all the eternal worlds.
>
> As I approached to be introduced, he arose and stepped towards me with extended arms, and he smiled as he softly spoke my name. If I shall live to be a million years old, I shall never forget that smile. He took me into his arms and kissed me, pressed me to His bosom, and blessed me, until the marrow of my bones seemed to melt! When He had finished, I fell at His feet, and as I bathed them with my tears and kisses, I saw the prints of the nails in the feet of the Redeemer of the world. The feeling that I had in the presence of Him who hath all things in His hands, to have His love, His affection, and His blessings was such that if I ever can receive that of which I had but a foretaste, I would give all that I am, all that I ever hope to be, to feel what I then felt.[6]

In 1917, Ballard had another dream that he initially did not understand. However, later that year, he was able to discover the meaning.

The account states that "he [Elder Ballard] dreamed that he was crossing a great desert, when he came upon the remains of a Pony Express rider. As he looked around, he discovered some leather pouches, kicked them, and they broke open and out fell nuggets of tarnished gold. He picked up some of them and rubbed them together with his hands until they became brilliant."[7]

In explaining this dream, Elder Ballard noted that at the end of 1917 he became interested in reactivating boys who had drifted away from the Church. His efforts began when he began talking with a couple of boys who were no longer active. Elder Ballard became their friend and encouraged the boys to come back into full fellowship with the Church. When he heard about some other boys in the same situation, Elder Ballard went to talk to them as well, in an attempt to bring them back into the Church.

From that time on, Elder Ballard actively sought out boys who had fallen away. He was friendly, visited them as frequently as he could, and urged them to return to The Church of Jesus Christ of Latter-day Saints and to live by its teachings.

By the end of the year, Elder Ballard had rounded up over one hundred boys. Because of their renewed activity, a number of new branches were established. Many years later, one of the boys Elder Ballard fellowshipped was called to be the president of the Northwestern States Mission.

Relating this to his dream, Elder Ballard felt that the boys who had fallen away from the Church were the pieces of tarnished gold he had found on the ground. He believed that, like the gold, the boys only needed a little personal care and attention to become bright and shining once more.

George Q. Cannon

George Q. Cannon was born on 11 January 1827 in Liverpool, England. He was serving as chief executive of the Church's emigration effort when he was called to the Quorum of the Twelve Apostles. He later served as president of the European Mission and as a private secretary to President Brigham Young. Elder Cannon helped organize the Sunday School program and began publishing The Juvenile Instructor. *He also served five terms as a U.S. Congressman. Elder Cannon served under four presidents of the Church as a counselor in the First Presidency.*

In 1850, Elder Cannon was called to go on a mission to Hawaii, or the Sandwich Islands as they were called at that time. In the company of nine other missionaries, he traveled to San Francisco where they bought their tickets for the voyage. Although the elders boarded the ship, they could not leave the harbor for a full week because of contrary winds. While the ship was stuck in harbor, Elder Cannon had a dream. He states:

> One night, after we had been one week on board, I dreamed that I was on board a vessel, and that the Elders who were my companions and myself were amidships and were turning a windlass for the purpose of lifting the anchor which seemed to be fast in the mud. The cable that we were trying to wind on the windlass ran forward to the forecastle and over the bow. All our efforts, however, did not appear to have any effect on the anchor.
>
> While we were engaged in this labor I thought that the Prophet Joseph came walking forward from the quarter deck and as he came up to where I stood he told me to accompany him. He was dressed in white. He walked forward to the forecastle on which he climbed, and I followed him. He knelt down and prayed a few minutes aloud that the anchor might be loosened.
>
> After he finished his prayer, I thought he told me to take hold of the rope and pull the anchor up. To my great surprise it was pulled up with the greatest ease. After witnessing this I spoke to him, and said, "I wish I was in possession of such faith."
>
> He replied that it was my privilege, and that I ought to have it; that I would need it to preserve me from pestilence and the judgments that were about to be sent forth on the nations. Many other instructions of this character he gave me, but the lesson that he taught was, that great works could be accomplished through the means of faith and prayer. I certainly learned in this instance that faith and prayer had more effect than the windlass.
>
> That day we left San Francisco on our voyage. It is a great many years since I had that dream; but I have never forgotten it; and during the years that have since elapsed, I have proved to my entire satisfaction that the lesson taught by the Prophet Joseph on that occasion is a true one, and that all of us, young and old, should exercise faith and have "recourse" to prayer.[8]

Vaughn J. Featherstone

Vaughn J. Featherstone was born 26 March 1931 in Stockton, Utah. From 1965 to 1967, Elder Featherstone served on the Church General Missionary Committee. He was called in October 1970 to be president of the Boise North Stake. Elder Featherstone served in that capacity until 1972, when he was called to the First Quorum of the Seventy, serving as the new second counselor in the Presiding Bishopric.

Elder Featherstone believes that dreams are sacred and that many of them should not be divulged. However, he did have one dream that he shared—but only after it came true eight years later. At the time of the dream, Elder Featherstone was on the missionary committee of the Church and did a great deal of traveling. Often, he was accompanied by General Authorities. The brethren he traveled with had ecclesiastical authority, while Elder Featherstone's main job was to train the people in various fields.

Elder Featherstone said, "I had a dream that I was sitting in the Granite Stake Tabernacle on 20th South and 9th East: and that not only was I sitting there, but I was presiding over the meeting and directing it. And not only that, but as I got up, I was speaking as the presiding authority.

"I was awakened out of a sound sleep and I thought about that, and (thought) 'there's no way that could happen.' I couldn't see how that could possibly happen. In the first place, I was not in an authoritative position. I knew that I may be invited to a stake conference in that building, but I wouldn't be the authority in that conference."

Elder Featherstone continued to ponder the dream but dismissed the idea that it was from God. He said that further proof that the dream was *not* inspired was the fact that even if he were to be released from his present calling and called to a stake position, his stake did not even meet in that particular building on 20th South.

Still, Elder Featherstone kept having the same dream over and over—even when he was transferred to Boise, Idaho, and was called to be in the stake presidency there.

Years later, Elder Featherstone was transferred back to Salt Lake City, Utah. Once again, he was called to be in the stake presidency.

Elder Featherstone said, "And do you know where they meet? Twentieth South and Ninth East. As I went to the meeting that morning, I could see in my mind's eyes the dream I'd had sometime before, maybe eight years before, as clear as a bell—where I was sitting and all the things that were taking place. And as I stood at the pulpit I could see that in my mind's eyes also. There are some dreams like that that we don't know. No one heard about that until that morning. And then I shared with them the dream that I'd had that one day that might take place. Hold your dreams, some dreams are sacred."[9]

Heber J. Grant

Heber J. Grant, the seventh president of the Church, was born on 22 November 1856 in Salt Lake City, Utah. He was called to be a stake president when he was twenty-four years old and an apostle when he was twenty-six. Elder Grant opened and presided over a mission in Japan and later presided over the European Mission. In November 1916, Heber J. Grant became president of the Quorum of the Twelve Apostles and two years later became president of The Church of Jesus Christ of Latter-day Saints. One of President Grant's most enduring legacies was establishing the Church welfare program.

After President Heber J. Grant's wife, Lucy Stringham, died in January 1893, President Grant thought it might ease the sorrow of his three little daughters if he took them on a trip to several prominent eastern cities, including New York, Chicago, Boston, Philadelphia, and Washington. While President Grant and his three daughters were in Washington, his oldest daughter, Rachel, became ill. When a doctor was called in to examine her, he diagnosed Rachel with diphtheria.

President Grant said, "In those days . . . diphtheria was almost sure death. I have known more than one family in which six, seven, or eight children have died of diphtheria. It was an alarming disease. Very soon thereafter my second daughter (Lutie) came down with it, and they were both sick nigh until death."

Lutie's condition became more serious than Rachel's, and President Grant recollected, "I heard the doctor say to the nurse regarding my second daughter, 'If you miss giving that child a stimulant every fifteen minutes—if you miss just once—she will die.'

"I stayed up all night to see that she did not miss giving the stimulant, and the next morning the child was no better. I went into my room and shed some bitter tears at the thought that in all probability I should have to take that little girl home in a coffin. Kneeling down, I pleaded with the Lord to spare her life, for the very joy I was giving to my girls added to and intensified my own sorrow; and I asked that I be not obliged to have an additional sorrow in taking that little girl, whom I had brought away from home to give her pleasure in order that she might forget the death of her mama, back to her home in a coffin.

"I begged that that might not come into my life. The testimony of the Spirit came to me: 'The power of the Priesthood is here on the earth. Send for the elders and rebuke the power of the destroyer and that girl shall live.' Immediately I thanked the Lord for the whisperings of this Spirit and I shed tears of gratitude and thanksgiving . . . .

"George Q. Cannon was in Washington at the time and also Bishop Hiram R. Clawson, the father of Elder Rudger Clawson of the Council of the Twelve. I sent at once for them to come and administer to my children.

"President Clawson anointed her and Brother Cannon confirmed the anointing. In that confirmation he said something that I have never heard before or since, in my life. He said, (speaking to Lutie) 'The adversary, the destroyer, has decreed your death and made public announcement of his decree, but by the authority of the Priesthood of God which we hold as his servants, and in the name of Jesus Christ, our Redeemer, we rebuke the decree of the destroyer and say, you shall live.'"

It was as the Spirit had whispered to President Grant. Both children recovered. However, it was not until the girls were almost well enough to travel that President Grant found out the meaning of Brother Cannon's unusual statement during Lutie's blessing. President Grant and his daughters were staying in a boarding house run by a husband and his wife. One day the man told President Grant that he wanted to share a joke about his wife.

The man said, "She [his wife] believes in spiritualistic mediums and in communication through the mediums, and when the little girls were taken down sick in the house, she went to a medium, who told her . . . 'I see in your home two little girls; I see that the older one of the two little girls is taken sick. I see that she is very sick. I now see that the next little girl is taken sick. I now see that she is very sick. I now see that both of them are sick nigh unto death. I now see the older of the two girls recover. I now see the second little girl die.' Then she described the journey of that body in a coffin from Washington to Salt Lake in great detail, from each city, over the mountains, and finally being lowered into the ground."

President Grant then said, "I knew then the meaning of the inspiration of the living God to George Q. Cannon when he said 'The adversary has decreed your death, and made public announcement of it. . . . It was rebuked and instead of the little girl being buried as the spiritualistic medium said she would be because the devil himself has inspired her to do so . . . she is alive, healthy and strong. She is the mother of seven beautiful children."[10]

President Grant also saw his departed wife, Lucy, who had died two years before, in a dream. This occurred when President Grant was extremely worried about his seven-year-old son, Heber. Little Heber had been suffering from a hip disease for four years and was now gravely ill. President Grant said that when his son was a baby, he had great hopes for the infant, because he was his only living son. When doctors told him that there was no hope of recovery and that his son would soon die, President Grant was devastated. He related:

> The dream was that while I was sleeping, a messenger came in company with my wife, and she instructed him to carefully take Heber out of the bed, that she had come for him, and she wanted him to go with her, and the messenger was to take him so quietly that I would not be disturbed.
>
> In my dream, I jumped up out of bed immediately, and took hold of my boy. The messenger who was acting under Lucy's instructions to take him away had a struggle with me, and I succeeded in wrenching Heber away from him. But in doing so, I fell, and I fell upon him, and very seriously injured his limb, from which he had been suffering so long with hip disease. His cries of agony pierced my very soul, and I got to thinking, "What if I have injured him, and made him lame for all the days of his life? It would have been better to have let his mother take him. . . ."
>
> I felt quite sad to think I had not consented to my boy being taken by his mother. I walked out of the house and wandered around the streets, and happened to meet Brother Joseph

E. Taylor. I told him of Lucy coming to the house to try and get her boy, and of the struggle that I had had with the messenger.

He spoke of the fact that a mother has to offer her life upon the altar of sacrifice to bring her children into the world, and he said to me, "Brother Grant, much as I like to keep my children on this earth, I believe if the mother of any of my children were to come for her child, I certainly would raise no objections. I do not think there should be any family quarrels over a matter of this kind."[11]

In the dream, President Grant humbly replied:

I believe you are right, Brother Taylor, and if she comes again, she shall have the boy without any protest on my part.

After coming to that conclusion, I was awakened by my brother, B. F. Grant, who was staying that night with us. He came into the room and told me that the child was dying. I went into the front room and sat down. There was a vacant chair between me and my wife who is now living, and I felt the presence of that boy's deceased mother sitting in that chair.

I did not tell anybody what I felt, but I turned to my wife and said, "Do you feel anything strange?"

"Yes," she said. "I feel assured that Heber's mother is sitting between us, waiting to take him away."[12]

President Grant's son died a short time later.

Alonzo Hinckley

Alonzo Hinckley, an uncle of President Gordon B. Hinckley, was born on 23 April 1870 in Cove Fort, Utah. He was called to be a stake president in 1902 and then a mission president in 1932. In 1934, he was called by President Heber J. Grant to serve as an apostle.

When Elder Hinckley was called to go on a mission, he and his wife were expecting their second child. He was in the Netherlands when his wife gave birth to their son in November 1897. Anxious about the impending birth, Elder Hinckley said that he had never received better news than when he was notified that all was well and that mother and baby were fine.

After receiving a letter telling him about the birth, Elder Hinckley wrote a letter to his wife. He said in part, "I am so happy and relieved of anxiety that I actually am beside myself. I cannot keep from laughing when I meet any one, and tell them of my good fortune. I am the most thankful man in Holland; and I tell you, it did not take me long to get on my knees and pour out my heart in gratitude to God for his mercies unto us. . . .

"I have had such a lovely dream. I have been with you all—seen you, my dear wife, and the little newcomer, and all those kind ones who have surrounded you. I saw you made comfortable and happy. It seemed that I was in a hurry to get off again for Holland. But I first thanked all, with my heart so full of love that I gathered you all in my arms and embraced you, and then took one more peek in the door at Rose and the children, and then landed back in Holland. Was this not a beautiful dream for one in my mood?"[13]

Amazingly, in a far-off land, President Hinckley knew the very day and hour that his son was born.

Heber C. Kimball

Heber C. Kimball was born on 14 June 1801 in Sheldon, Vermont. After his conversion, he went on eight missions in eight years. In 1834, Elder Kimball became one of the original members of the Quorum of the Twelve Apostles. After coming west with the Saints, Elder Kimball was chief justice of the State of Deseret and served in the legislature for seven years. He supervised all temple work, helped colonize the Great Basin, and was devoted to developing Utah politically, socially, and culturally.

While on his first mission to England, Elder Kimball became downcast after contemplating the affairs of the Church, which were gloomy at that time. Men who had once been close friends of Joseph Smith had become his enemies. These men were increasingly vocal as they criticized the Prophet and actively worked to turn people against him. In addition, Elder Kimball was deeply worried about his family, who was poverty stricken; many family members were also ill.

During this time, Elder Kimball had the following dream. Although the dream was symbolic, once Elder Kimball understood it, he was greatly comforted. He records:

> I was in a great water, swimming, and had swam away, trying to make land, although I saw no land, until I had become

> weary and tired, when I began to sink; then an angel came to me and placed his hand under my chin, for some time keeping me from sinking, until I had rested and gained strength; he blessed me and said, "Brother Heber, you shall now have strength to swim ashore."
>
> I again began to swim, and it appeared as though every time I stretched forth my arms and feet, I would move rods at each stroke, and continued doing so until I reached land.[14]

Elder Kimball felt the dream meant that he would soon have success preaching the word of God. He was inspired to go to Preston, which was near Liverpool. While there, Elder Kimball did experience great success. During the eleven months he spent in the area, Elder Kimball and his companions baptized nearly fifteen hundred people. He and the other missionaries organized many branches and also opened the European Mission.

On another occasion, Elder Kimball received a symbolic dream that, once interpreted, let him know where the missionaries would be successful—and unsuccessful—in teaching the gospel. Elder Kimball states:

> Having great anxiety for the welfare of the small branch which we had raised in London, I retired to rest and had the following dream. I thought that we dug a well on high ground in order to obtain water, and after digging some considerable time, we came to an excellent spring; we then commenced to back it up, but before it was finished, we had occasion to leave for a short time and when we returned to complete it, we found it carefully filled up with sand, and all attempts to remove it proved unavailing, we thought it better to choose another spot on lower ground, where we were successful. When we returned to London, we experienced a perfect fulfillment of my dream—having to open a new preaching place at Barrett's Academy, King Square, Goswell Road, our former place being closed against us.[15]

Although at first, Elder Kimball did not understand this particular dream, which was reminiscent of one that Lehi had in the Book of Mormon, he knew it held personal significance for him. Elder Kimball writes:

"I dreamed that I was traveling with a companion, and we came to a powerful, rapid stream of water like the Niagara River. The waves were rolling very high and increasing in size. They had been muddy, but were getting clear. As we came to this rushing stream, we did not know how we should get out over it. I turned my eyes a few moments from my companion, and when I looked back I saw him on the other side of the river and climbing a steep hill. I did not know how he got there.

"I wanted to cross, so I called to him as loud as I could to stop and wait for me, but he paid no attention to me, but went on as fast as he could. Then a person came to me and said you have an iron rod in your hand, which I perceived I had. It was several feet long. The angel said to me: 'You must use this rod and feel your way over the river.'

"Then I awoke."

Elder Kimball had this dream two weeks before his companion Jedediah M. Grant died. As he pondered on it, the meaning gradually became clear. He explained, "My companion (in the dream) was J. M. Grant, who had suddenly died and left me, and was on the other side of the veil. The waters mean the people. They are increasing in strength and growing better and clearer. The iron rod is the word of God, which I must cling to till I get through life."[16]

David O. McKay

David O. McKay was born 8 September 1873 in Huntsville, Utah. After serving a mission to Great Britain, he was called to serve in the Weber Stake Sunday School presidency. In April 1906, Elder McKay was ordained an apostle. Elder McKay presided over the Church Education Program, wrote the first Sunday School manual, and recommended that seminaries and institutes be placed adjacent to public schools. President McKay became the ninth president of The Church of Jesus Christ of Latter-day Saints in 1951. Under his direction, membership of the Church tripled, the missionary force grew sixfold, and temples were built in Switzerland and New Zealand.

On a beautiful day in May 1921, Elder McKay and his companion, Elder Cannon, left the United States of America to sail to their assigned mission in Apia, Samoa. That night Elder McKay noticed the sunset, which seemed unusually beautiful. The setting sun colored the sky pink, while the clouds around the horizon were tinted in various hues of crimson and orange. As Elder McKay lay in his berth that night, he thought about how lovely the sunset had been but said that it didn't stir his soul with nearly as much emotion as his children and other loved ones did. He then fell asleep.

Elder McKay stated that in his dream, he "beheld in vision something infinitely sublime. In the distance I beheld a beautiful white city. Though it was far away, yet I seemed to realize that trees with luscious fruit, shrubbery with gorgeously tinted leaves, and flowers in perfect bloom abounded everywhere. The clear sky above seemed to reflect those beautiful shades of color.

"I then saw a great concourse of people approaching the city. Each one wore a white flowing robe and a white headdress. Instantly my attention seemed centered upon their leader, and though I could see only the profile of his features and his body, I recognized him at once as my Savior! The tint and radiance of his countenance were glorious to behold. There was a peace about him which seemed sublime—it was divine! The city, I understood, was his. It was the City Eternal; and the people following him were to abide there in peace and eternal happiness."

As Elder McKay wondered to himself who the people were, he said, "As if the Savior read my thoughts, he answered by pointing to a semicircle that then appeared above them, and on which were written in gold the words:

> *"These Are They Who Have Overcome the World—*
> *Who have Truly Been Born Again!"*[17]

On another occasion, President McKay was speaking in Tonga on 13 January 1955. "Do you know what I saw today, in vision?" he asked those in attendance. "A temple on one of these islands where the members of the Church may go and receive the blessings of the temple of God. You are entitled to it."[18]

At that time, only a very few temples were on the earth. However, only three years later, President McKay dedicated the New Zealand Temple. Shortly after that dedication, he told the people that the General Authorities had approved a plan to build beautiful but inexpensive temples in various parts of the world so more people could receive the blessings that come from being a member of The Church of Jesus Christ of Latter-day Saints.

Parley P. Pratt

Parley P. Pratt was an influential leader in the early Church. He was born in Burlington, New York, on 12 April 1807. He served many missions, was founding editor of The Millennial Star, *and composed many hymns. In 1835, he was called to be one of the original members of the Quorum of the Twelve Apostles.*

In the early years of The Church of Jesus Christ of Latter-day Saints, many leaders were thrown into prison without justifiable cause and without receiving due process of law. Such was the case with Parley P. Pratt. However, on one occasion as he sat languishing in prison, Elder Pratt was visited in a dream by an angel and told that he would soon be freed. It was fitting that the angel's promise of freedom was realized on July fourth. On that day, aided by others, Elder Pratt was able to escape.

Elder Pratt's experience is briefly mentioned in a eulogy written for his son, Nathan, who died when he was five years old. The eulogy states, "On the grand national Anniversary of American independence, the glorious 4th of July, his father [Parley] being [illegible writing] and warned, by an Angel of the Lord, in a vision of the night, burst his chains, threw open his prison doors, and emerged forth from his prison: and after wandering for near a week, night and day, almost without food, he avoided all pursuit and arrived at the residence of his family."[19]

Franklin D. Richards

Franklin D. Richards was born on 2 April 1821 in Richmond, Massachusetts. He served four missions to England, compiled the Pearl of Great Price, and helped establish the Perpetual Emigration Fund. Elder Richards was called to be an apostle in 1849 and became president of the Quorum of the Twelve Apostles in 1889.

While serving on a mission to England, Elder Richards learned in a dream that he would be called to an important position in the Church.

On 13 August, 1847, Elder Richards wrote in his diary:

> This morning I awoke from a dream in which I seemed to have been with President Brigham Young in the Temple at Nauvoo. We sat opposite each other, with our feet in a clear, lively pool of water, and we conversed together.
>
> He asked, "Brother Franklin, would you accept it if I should appoint you one of the Quorum?"
>
> I replied, "Brother Brigham, I always have accepted, and as far as I could, have obeyed every appointment that has been given to me, and I always intend to."
>
> [President Young] showed me several books containing peculiar drawings and diagrams, many of which were lightly colored and in the Prophet Joseph's own hand writing. While I was examining the books I awoke, and felt as happy as if I had really been in the company of President Young, and the holy influence seemed to rest upon my whole person.[20]

Elder Richard's dream was fulfilled two years later when he was called to be a member of the Quorum of the Twelve Apostles.

George F. Richards

George F. Richards, the father of LeGrand Richards, was born on 23 February 1861 in Farmington, Utah. He was counselor in a stake presidency before becoming a stake patriarch. He was a ordained an apostle on 9 April 1906 and later became president of the Quorum of the Twelve.

During general conference, President Spencer W. Kimball related a personal experience of Elder Richards. President Kimball began his remarks by saying:

> The Lord has revealed to men by dreams something more than I ever understood or felt before. I heard this more than once in quorum meetings of the Council of the Twelve when George F. Richards was president. . . .
>
> [Elder Richards would say] "It is not out of place for us to have important dreams. . . . More than 40 years ago I had a dream which I am sure was from the Lord. In this dream I was in the presence of my Savior as he stood in mid-air. He spoke no word to me, but my love for him was such that I have not

words to explain. I know that no mortal man can love the Lord as I experienced that love for the Savior unless God reveals it to him. I would have remained in his presence, but there was a power drawing me away from him.

"As a result of that dream, I had this feeling that no matter what might be required of my hands, what the gospel might entail unto me, I would do what I should be asked to do even to the laying down of my life. And so when we read in the scriptures what the Savior said to his disciples, 'In my Father's house are many mansions: . . . I go to prepare a place for you . . . that where I am, there ye may be also,' (John 14: 2–3) I think that is where I want to be. If only I can be with my Savior and have that same sense of love that I had in that dream, it will be the goal of my existence, the desire of my life."[21]

David W. Patten

David W. Patten was born 14 November 1799 in Theresa, New York. He was one of the original members of the Quorum of the Twelve Apostles and the first apostle to be martyred in this dispensation. He was shot and killed during the Battle of Crooked River, which occurred in October 1838.

In the early days of The Church of Jesus Christ of Latter-day Saints, missionaries and Church leaders were frequently threatened and often suffered beatings and other physical mistreatment from enemies of the Church. However, in this particular incident, Elder Patten escaped from a mob after being warned in a dream.

On 28 May 1836, representatives from all the branches in the Southern States gathered for a region-wide conference. Unfortunately, during the conference, Church members faced intense persecution from the local people. This persecution increased when a new convert was baptized. Then, a short time later, Elder Patten baptized two more men, causing an irate minister to go to the local sheriff. The minister obtained warrants against Elder Patten, Elder Parrish, and Elder Woodruff. The warrant accused the missionaries of the "crime" of testifying that Christ would come in this generation and complained that the elders had promised that the Holy Ghost would come to anyone they baptized.

Elders Patten and Parrish were arrested on 19 June 1836. Elder Woodruff escaped arrest because he was in another area at the time.

When the two elders were brought before the judge, witnesses were brought in to testify in their defense. New converts testified before the judge that they *did* receive the Holy Ghost after being baptized and confirmed. Despite these testimonies, the two missionaries were found guilty. However, the judge said he would release them if they would pay the expenses of the court.

After consulting with each other, the elders agreed to pay the fees. After announcing their decision, Elder Patten was allowed to address the judge. In a strongly worded speech, he told members of the court that they were guilty of great wickedness for arresting two harmless men for preaching the gospel of Jesus Christ. Indeed, Elder Patten spoke so fearlessly that the judge accused him of having concealed weapons.

Elder Patten replied, "I have weapons that you know not of, and they are given me of God, for He gives me all the power I have."[22]

The missionaries paid their fine and left the building. However, many who had watched the proceedings were unhappy with the results. As these men gathered outside the court building to angrily discuss the trial, they decided the two missionaries had been let off too easily. Soon, the crowd decided to go after them and administer their own brand of justice.

Fortunately, a member of the Church heard the mob's intentions. Quickly mounting his horse, he rode after the missionaries. He was able to catch up with Elder Patten and Elder Parrish and warn them about the mob. The missionaries hid in the woods, staying there for some time.

Then, when the elders felt they were safe, "they traveled along about three miles to Brother Albert Petty's, and went to bed. The night was dark, and they fell asleep, but Brother Patten was warned in a dream to get up and flee, as the mob soon would be there. They both arose, saddled their animals, and rode into the adjoining county. The house they had just left was soon surrounded by the mob, but the brethren escaped through the mercy of God."[23]

Mark E. Petersen

Mark E. Petersen was born on 7 November 1900 in Salt Lake City, Utah. He served a mission to Nova Scotia and after returning home became a productive writer. In addition to writing many missionary pamphlets and thousands of editorials in the Church News, *Elder Petersen authored more than forty books. He was called to serve in two stake presidencies, was on the board of directors for the Genealogical Society, and was also on the board of the Deseret Sunday School Union. Elder Petersen was ordained a member of the Quorum of the Twelve Apostles in April 1944.*

Shortly before being called as an apostle and while still working for the *Deseret News,* Elder Petersen received a prophetic dream. The following account of his dream is related by Elder Boyd K. Packer, who spoke at Elder Petersen's funeral. Elder Packer said:

"In the dream, he [Elder Petersen] saw a headline announcing his call to the Council of the Twelve and also the name of a man whom he was to replace. He sent a reporter, Henry Smith, to the Church offices to inquire discreetly as to the health and well-being of that member of the Twelve. Brother Smith returned with the report that all was well, but Mark Petersen knew otherwise. . . .

"For three weeks came the testing, the struggle known only to those men called to the apostleship. Then events unfolded, a vacancy occurred and the venerable President [Heber J.] Grant called Mark E. Petersen to the quorum of the Twelve Apostles. . . .

"Thus began the ministry of Mark, the apostle. A ministry that would span 40 years and end, significantly enough, with an assignment to the Holy Land from which he returned 11 weeks ago; a journey in which he followed the steps of the Christ, whose devoted servant he was."[24]

William W. Phelps

William W. Phelps was one of the early leaders of the Church, serving as a counselor in the first stake in Missouri and as a clerk and scribe to Joseph Smith. He assisted Emma Smith in compiling the Church's first hymnbook. Elder Phelps was born 17 February 1792 in Hanover, New Jersey. Although he was later excommunicated for misusing Church funds, he repented and was reinstated as a member of the Church. William Phelps then remained a faithful member until his death in 1872.

Elder Phelps wrote about an unusual spiritual experience he had three years after he was baptized. He records:

> I am not often in the habit of telling dreams and visions,

and rarely write them, but on the 6th of last November [1834], after I retired to rest, it appeared that I was standing in the door of a house, werein were a number of brethren and sisters lamenting the situation of the church, when, of a sudden, I saw a whitish cloud in the clear sky of the south east, gently coming towards me; and something, which, at first sight, resembled the portrait of a man's head; but, in a moment, as it came nearer, it looked like the full image of a man. When nearest it made a graceful bow to me, then receded till out of sight.—I cried with a loud voice, The Lord preserve us for an angel is here! The Lord is with us, for his angel has come!! His appearance and countenance were beautiful; and his robe was white. His skin was a touch nicer than virgin snow, tinged with a crimson glimmer of sun-set.[25]

Brigham Henry (B. H.) Roberts

Brigham Henry Roberts was a prominent historian for the Church. He was born in Warrington, Lancashire, England, on 13 March 1857. One of Elder Roberts's most significant contributions was the writing of the six volume treatise A Comprehensive History of The Church of Jesus Christ of Latter-day Saints. *Besides his exhaustive work as a historian, Elder Roberts wrote more than one thousand books and was a member of the First Council of the Seventy. He was also president of the Eastern States Mission for four years.*

B.H. Roberts had a difficult life as a child, yet things could have been worse. Because he was warned in a dream, young Brigham escaped unscrupulous guardians who were planning to force him to join the army as a drummer boy.

When Brigham was a little boy, his mother, Ann Everington Roberts, became converted to the gospel. Her husband, Ben, was interested enough in the Church to be baptized, but his interest soon waned. Eventually, he refused to take part in any activities. When Ann asked if the family could go to America and join the Saints in Zion, Ben refused to consider it.

Ben's job took him away from home quite often, and he only sent money home infrequently. One time he was gone for several months without sending any support for his family. When Ben finally did send money, Ann decided to use it to pay for passage to America. However, Ann didn't have enough money to take all of her children. She decided to leave behind her oldest daughter, Mary, who was twelve, and Brigham. Ann took her youngest daughter, Annie, and her baby, Thomas, with her across the ocean and across the plains to Salt Lake City. The journey was difficult, and Thomas died before reaching the Salt Lake Valley.

Ann left Brigham in the care of a Mr. and Mrs. Tovey, recent converts to the Church who seemed trustworthy. However, shortly after Ann left for the United States, the Toveys grew tired of the Church. They began drinking again and lost their jobs. Their situation worsened, and they were forced to move many times, taking whatever odd jobs they could find. The couple taught Brigham to sing and had him pass his hat on the street to collect pennies from bystanders. One day some soldiers noticed that the boy had good rhythm as he sang and told Mr. and Mrs. Tovey that Brigham would make a good drummer boy for the army.

After some time, the couple had a bitter quarrel and decided to separate. While trying to decide what to do with Brigham, the Toveys remembered the soldier's comment. They took the boy to the recruiting office of the British Army. He was accepted as a drummer and measured for a uniform. The Toveys were told to bring Brigham back the following day, when the army would take charge of him. That night Brigham had a dream that altered his life. The account relates:

"That night as Henry slept his Mother's face appeared before him. She was weeping and the promise she had made at their parting flashed into his mind—'Promise me,' she had said, 'that if I am unable to send for you, that you will, when you grow to be a man go to Utah.'

"The dream awakened him and something within him said, 'If you serve in the army you will never get to Utah.' He got up quietly and taking his clothing in his arms crept down the stairs and out into the dark street. He stopped to dress, and then started on his pilgrimage back to Thorplton where he thought he could find the Elders who had known his mother."[26]

Brigham wandered about, living on the streets for weeks. He continued to inquire about the whereabouts of the Mormon elders, but no one had heard of them. In time, however, the missionaries found *him*. They helped him locate his sister, Mary, and made travel arrangements for the two youngsters to go to America.

Late in April 1866, Henry and Mary left England. After a long and difficult voyage and journey across the plains, brother and sister arrived in the Salt Lake Valley in October. Their mother had been contacted about their arrival and was waiting for them.

Robert L. Simpson

Robert L. Simpson served in many different capacities before he was called as an assistant to the Quorum of the Twelve Apostles in 1972. Elder Simpson served as president of the New Zealand Mission from 1958–1961 before being called to the Presiding Bishopric. In April 1972, he was asked to be the Managing Director of Church Social Services, and in 1974, he was called to be the Associate Managing Director of the Melchizedek Priesthood MIA.

When Elder Simpson was serving his mission in the South Pacific, he had a dream that proved to be a major turning point in his life. Before he left the United States, Rulon S. Wells, then a member of the First Council of the Seventy, set him apart for his mission. In the blessing, Elder Wells blessed the young man with a knowledge of the language of the people among whom he would labor. Elder Simpson felt sure that this meant that he would easily learn Maori.

However, once he arrived in the South Pacific, Elder Simpson did not put a lot of effort into learning the language. In addition, his companion, an elder on the verge of going home, provided no encouragement for the new missionary to study the Maori language. Elder Simpson recalls:

> After about three or four weeks had gone by with not much activity on the Maori language, I had a dream. I would like to tell you about this dream. To me it is very real. And to me it is one of the significant events of my life. In this dream I had returned home from my mission. I was getting off the boat down in Los Angeles harbor from whence I had left, and there was my bishop, my stake president, my mother and dad, all of my friends.
>
> As I came down the gangplank of the boat they all started talking to me in Maori, every one of them—my mother,

my father, my bishop—all talking in Maori, and I could not understand a word they were saying. I was so embarrassed. I was humiliated. I thought to myself, "This is terrible. How am I going to get out of it?" And I started making excuses.

Right then I woke up and I sat straight up in bed and the thought came to my mind so forcefully, "You will *have* to do something about learning this language. The Lord has given you a blessing but you are going to have to do something about it yourself. You are going to need this language when you get through with your mission. You are going to need it."

This thought kept ringing through my ears all through that day, so arrangements were made and we had study time allotted each day to learn the Maori language. The Lord blessed me and we were able to bear testimony in the language after a short time. Then, to make a long story short, the mission was finished. I came home and came into Los Angeles harbor. They were all there to meet me, but they all spoke English. Not one of them spoke Maori to me.

World War II had broken out. All of the missionaries had been called home. I thought "Now if I am called into the Army, I am just sure that I will be sent right back down to New Zealand where I can also help President Cowley. Maybe the Lord will send me down there to help him with the mission activity between military assignments."

I went into the Air Force, and sure enough when it came time for overseas processing after a few months, I was sent to San Francisco. All the Pacific processing was done here. I thought to myself, "Here I go right back to New Zealand." About two days before the ship was to sail with all of our groups of several hundred men they took out about five of us. That is all—just five—and sent us all the way back to the Atlantic seacoast for shipment over to Europe.

I thought to myself, "Well, I guess I can always preach to the Maori spirits in prison when I get on the other side!"

We joined a convoy and went across the Atlantic Oceans. I saw the Rock of Gibraltar go by, and finally the ship stopped in Egypt. We got off the ship in Egypt and we were taken to our American air base. . . . Well, if you know anything about New Zealand, here is Cairo, Egypt, and here is New Zealand. You can not get further away from New Zealand than Cairo, Egypt. . . .

Not more than forty-eight hours had gone by when I found that right there within the very shadows of this American air base was the entire Maori battalion—the entire Maori battalion were stationed there! This was *their* overseas base for processing, for all of their fighting in North Africa and Italy. For nearly two years I had the privilege of being there and meeting each Sunday with these Maori boys, bearing testimony with them in their own tongue, organizing them into small groups as they went up into the front lines in order that they might have their sacrament meetings and do the things that they needed to do . . . I just want to tell you that the Lord is mindful of his own.[27]

Joseph Smith Jr.

Joseph Smith Jr. was the first prophet, seer, and revelator of the Church in this dispensation. He was born in Sharon, Vermont, on 23 December 1805. After praying to know which church was true, Joseph received a heavenly vision. He saw the Father and the Son and was told that none of the churches were correct. Later, Joseph was directed to unearth a buried record, which told the history of the people who had lived in ancient America. Joseph Smith translated the record, which is now called The Book of Mormon, Another Testament of Jesus Christ, *and helped found The Church of Jesus Christ of Latter-day Saints.*

In 1844, shortly before his martyrdom, Joseph Smith received a dream showing him the coming persecutions. Wilford Woodruff wrote about those dark days in his journal, saying, "There was a strange commingling of spirits in Nauvoo at that time. Spirits of life and death were at war, and the Prophet's approaching end was made manifest to him in a dream which he related in his office to Willard Richards, and W. W. Phelps. The Prophet clearly saw the coming storm of persecution which awaited him."[28]

In June 1844, during a meeting held in the Seventies Hall in Nauvoo, the Prophet Joseph related a dream he'd had. Recalling that evening, the Prophet wrote:

> George J. Adams preached and I made some observations afterwards, and related a dream which I had a short time since. I thought I was riding out in my carriage, and my guardian angel

was along with me. We went past the Temple, and had not gone much further before we espied two large snakes so fast locked together that neither of them had any power. I inquired of my guide what I was to understand by that.

He answered, "Those snakes represent Dr. Foster and Chauncey L. Higbee. They are your enemies and desire to destroy you; but you see they are so fast locked together that they had no power of themselves to hurt you."

I then thought I was riding up Mulholland street, but my guardian angel was not along with me. On arriving at the prairie, I was overtaken and seized by William and Wilson Law and others, saying, "Ah! Ah! We have got you at last! We will secure you and put you in a safe place!" and, without any ceremony dragged me out of my carriage, tied my hands behind me, and threw me into a deep, dry pit, where I remained in a perfectly helpless condition, and they went away.

While struggling to get out, I heard Wilson Law screaming for help hard by. I managed to unloose myself so as to make a spring, when I caught hold of some grass which grew at the edge of the pit. I looked out of the pit and saw Wilson Law at a little distances attacked by ferocious wild beasts, and heard him cry out, "Oh! Brother Joseph, come and save me!"

I replied, "I cannot, for you have put me into this deep pit." On looking another way, I saw William Law with outstretched tongue, blue in the face, and the green poison forced out of his mouth, caused by the coiling of a large snake around his body. It had also grabbed him by the arm, a little above the elbow, ready to devour him.

He cried out in the intensity of his agony, "Oh Brother Joseph, Brother Joseph, come and save me, or I die!"

I also replied to him, "I cannot, William; I would willingly, but you have tied me and put me in this pit, and I am powerless to help you or liberate myself."

In a short time after my guide came and said aloud, "Joseph, Joseph, what are you doing there?"

I replied, "My enemies fell upon me, bound me and threw me in." He then took me by the hand, drew me out of the pit, set me free, and we went away rejoicing.[29]

Elder Joseph G. Romney remembered reading about the Prophet's dream in his father's journal. "This dream would seem to have had its fulfillment in the actions of those two men," Elder Romney noted later, "for all who are acquainted with their proceedings know that they plotted against the Prophet, and did all they could to overthrow his authority; and, finally, by apostatizing, they put themselves where it was no longer possible for him to help them to their salvation."[30]

A few days before the Prophet Joseph Smith was killed, he had a dream, which he shared with his brother Hyrum and W. W. Phelps. W. W. Phelps relates the dream as follows:

> In June 1844, when Joseph Smith went to Carthage and delivered himself up to Governor Ford, I (W. W. Phelps) accompanied him, and while on the way thither, he related to me and his brother Hyrum the following dream.
>
> He (Joseph) said: "While I was at Jordan's in Iowa the other night, I dreamed that myself and my brother Hyrum went on board a steamboat lying in a small bay, near the great ocean. Shortly after we went on board there was an alarm of fire, and I discovered that the boat had been anchored some distance from the shore, out in the bay, and that an escape from the fire, in the confusion, appeared hazardous: but, as delay was folly, Hyrum and I jumped overboard. . . .
>
> "On looking towards the burning boat in the east, we saw that it was drifting towards the wharf and the town, with a great flame and clouds of smoke; and, as if by whirlwind, the town was taking fire, too, so that the scene of destruction and horror of the frightened inhabitants were terrible.
>
> "We proceeded on the bosom of the mighty deep and were soon out of sight of land. The ocean was still; the rays of the sun were bright and we forgot all the troubles of our mother earth. Just at that moment I heard the sound of a human voice, and turning around, saw my brother Samuel H. approaching towards us from the east. We stopped and he came up. After a moment's conversation he informed me that he had been lonesome back there, and he had made up his mind to go with me across the mighty deep.
>
> "We all started again, and in a short time were blest with the first sight of a city, whose gold and silver steeples and towers were more beautiful than any I had ever seen or heard of on earth. It stood, as it were, upon the western shore of the mighty deep we were walking on, and its order and glory seemed far beyond the wisdom of man. While we were gazing upon the

> perfection of the city a small boat launched off from the port, and, almost as quick as thought, came to us. In an instant they took us on board and saluted us with a welcome, and with music such as is not on earth.
>
> "The next scene, on landing, was more than I can describe; the greeting of old friends, the music from a thousand towers, and the light of God Himself at the return of three of His sons, soothed my soul into a quiet and a joy that I felt as if I was truly I heaven. I gazed upon the splendor; I greeted my friends. I awoke, and lo, it was a dream.
>
> [Elder Phelps added] "I will say that Joseph never told this dream again, as he was martyred about two days after. I relate from recollection as nearly as I can."[31]

As Joseph had seen in his dream, Samuel did join his two brothers. One month after Joseph and Hyrum were killed at Carthage Jail, Samuel H. Smith died as well.

Joseph F. Smith

Joseph F. Smith, the son of Hyrum and Mary Fielding Smith, was born in Far West, Missouri, on 13 November 1838. When he was fifteen years old, young Joseph was called to serve a mission. At the age of twenty-seven, he was called to be an apostle by President Brigham Young. In October 1901, Joseph F. Smith became the sixth president of The Church of Jesus Christ of Latter-day Saints.

When Joseph F. Smith was only fifteen years of age, he was sent to serve a mission in Hawaii. Being only a boy, he was timid and afraid and became very discouraged. However, the Lord was mindful of him, and young Joseph was comforted by a dream that changed his life and helped him overcome his fears. President Smith records:

> I did have a dream one time. To me it was a literal thing; it was a reality. I was very much oppressed, once, on a mission. I was almost naked and entirely friendless, except the friendship of a poor . . . people. I felt as if I was so debased in my condition of poverty, lack of intelligence and knowledge, just a boy, that I hardly dared look a . . . man in the face. While in that condition I dreamed that I was on a journey, and I was impressed that I ought to hurry—hurry with all my might, for fear I might be

too late. I rushed on my way as fast as I possibly could, and I was only conscious of having just a little bundle, a handkerchief with a small bundle wrapped in it. I did not realize just what this was, when I was hurrying as fast as I could; but finally I came to a wonderful mansion, if it could be called a mansion.

It seemed too large, too great to have been made by hand, but I thought I knew that this was my destination. As I turned aside quickly and went into the bath and washed myself clean, I opened up this little bundle that I had, and there was a pair of white, clean garments, things I had not seen for a long time, because the people I was with did not think very much of making things exceedingly clean. But my garments were clean and I put them on. Then I rushed to what appeared to be a great opening, or door. I knocked, and the door opened, and the man who stood there was the Prophet Joseph Smith. He looked at me a little reprovingly, and the first words he said: 'Joseph, you are late.'

Yet I took confidence and said: "Yes, but I am clean—I am clean!" He clasped my hand and drew me in, then closed the great door. I felt his hand just as tangible as I ever felt the hand of man. I knew him, and when I entered, I saw my father, and Brigham, and Heber, and Willard, and other good men that I had known, standing in a row. I looked as if it were across this valley, and it seemed to be filled with a vast multitude of people, but on the stage were all the people that I had known. My mother was there, and she sat with a child in her lap; and I could name as many as I remember of their names, who sat there, who seemed to be among the chosen, among the exalted.

The Prophet said to me, "Joseph," then pointing to my mother, he said: "Bring me that child." I went to my mother and picked up the child, and thought it was a fine baby boy. I carried it to the Prophet, and as I handed it to him I purposely thrust my hands against his breast. I felt the warmth—I was alone on a mat, away up in the mountains of Hawaii—no one was with me. But in this vision I pressed my hand up against the Prophet, and I saw a smile cross his countenance. I handed him the child and stepped back.

"President Young stepped around two steps, my father one step, and they formed a triangle. Then Joseph blessed that baby, and when he finished blessing it, they stepped back in line; that is, Brigham and Father stepped back in line. Joseph handed me the baby, wanted me to come, and take the baby again; and this time I was determined to test whether this was a dream or a reality. I wanted to know what it meant. So I purposely thrust myself up against the Prophet. I felt the warmth of his stomach. He smiled at me, as if he comprehended my purpose. He delivered the child to me, and I returned it to my mother, laid it on her lap.

When I awoke that morning, I was a man, although only a boy. There was not anything in the world that I feared. I could meet any man or woman or child and look him in the face, feeling in my soul that I was a man every whit. That vision, that manifestation and witness that I enjoyed at that time has made me what I am, if I am anything that is good, or clean, or upright before the Lord, if there is anything good in me. That has helped me out in every trial and through every difficulty.

Now, I suppose that is only a dream? To me it is a reality. There never could be anything more real to me. I felt the hand of Joseph Smith. I felt the warmth of his stomach, when I put my hand against him. I saw the smile upon his face. I did my duty as he required me to do it and when I woke up, I felt as if I had been lifted out of a slum, out of a despair, out of the wretched condition that I was in; and naked as I was, or as nearly as I was, I was not afraid . . . and I have not been very much afraid of anybody else since that time. I know that this was a reality, to show me my duty, to teach me something, and to impress upon me something that I cannot forget. I hope it never can be banished from my mind.[32]

Lorenzo Snow

Lorenzo Snow was born 3 April 1814 in Mantua, Ohio. He was widely known for his emphasis on tithing. After his baptism, Elder Snow served missions to various areas of the United States and to Great Britain. He was called to the Quorum of the Twelve Apostles in 1849 and in April 1873 was called to be a counselor to President Brigham Young. He became the fifth prophet of The Church of Jesus Christ of Latter-day Saints in 1898.

When Elder Lorenzo Snow was serving a mission in Ohio, he dreamed that a mob was planning to attack him. The following day, when he was asked to speak to a group, Elder Snow suddenly remembered the dream, which could have become a frightening reality if he had not heeded its warning. Elder Snow writes:

> When at the house of Brother Smith, in Stark County, Ohio, I dreamed one night that arrangements were in progress to mob me. The following evening after I had the dream, as I sat conversing with friends who had called on me, a loud rap at the door preceded the entrance of two well-dressed young men, who politely invited me to accompany them to a schoolhouse about one mile distant and to address an audience already assembled.
>
> After a little hesitation on my part, they began to urgently request my acceptance of their invitation, when the dream of the preceding night instantaneously flashed across my mind, and I told them I could not comply with their wishes. They still persisted to urge and insist on my accompanying them. When they were convinced that I was immovable in my determination of noncompliance, they not only manifested disappointment, but were exceedingly angry.
>
> The next day I leaned that they told the truth so far as a congregated audience wanting my appearance at the schoolhouse was concerned, but the object was entirely different from that reported by the young men—it corresponded precisely with my dream.[33]

John Taylor

John Taylor was born in Milnthorpe, England, on 1 November 1808. His future wife, Leonora Cannon, was persuaded to accept his proposal of marriage after she had a vivid dream reassuring her that she was doing the right thing. In December 1838, Elder Taylor was ordained one of the Twelve Apostles. He later served a mission in England. When Elder Taylor returned, he was active in Church and civic affairs and worked as an editor for various Church periodicals. He was with Joseph and Hyrum Smith in Carthage Jail when the two brothers were killed. When President Brigham Young died, John Taylor became the third president of The Church of Jesus Christ of Latter-day Saints.

When President Taylor spoke at the funeral of Elizabeth H. Cannon, a friend whom he had known since she was a little girl, he recalled a disturbing dream that he'd had when serving a mission many years before. In the dream, his wife was close to death. President Taylor relates:

> When I was in Paris, France, about thirty years ago, I had a dream that troubled me very much, in which I saw my first wife . . . lying sick at the point of death. And it so affected me that I awoke, being troubled in my feelings. I fell asleep again, and again the same scene presented itself to me when I again awoke and experienced the same feelings of sorrow, and after some time slept again, and it was repeated a third time. I knew then that my wife was very sick, lying at the point of death.
>
> I got up and fervently prayed the Lord to spare her life until, at least, I should have another opportunity of meeting her in the flesh. He heard my prayer. I took a note of the circumstance at the time, and learned afterwards that such had been the case exactly as it had been shown to me.
>
> On the following morning I remember meeting a gentleman who was a Protestant minister, and he observed that my countenance looked sorrowful, and he enquired the cause. I told him that my wife was lying at the point of death, and he asked me if I had received a letter? I told him no; but related to him how it had been shown to me. But, I said, I got up and prayed the Lord to spare her life, and I feel consoled in knowing that she will be healed.[34]

Elder Taylor began writing in a journal a few months after the Prophet Joseph Smith was killed. One of his entries relates a dream he had about the temple. On Wednesday, 18 June 1845, Elder Taylor wrote:

> I dreamt that I stood by the temple and looked up and saw that it was finished. I admired the elegance and symmetry of the building, and felt animated in my spirits and rejoiced to see the building finished. I remarked to a person standing by, what a beautiful structure this is, how elegant the design and how well it is executed. I then said it is only a very short time since we laid the topstone, and now it is finished. I knew that a great deal of the wood work was prepared, but did not anticipate that the building would be so soon completed. I felt at the same time filled with the spirit of God, and my heart rejoiced before the Lord.

While I stood gazing with pleasure at the temple, I saw another tower rising like unto the one that is on the west end of the temple, and immediately exclaimed to the person that I had before conversed with, why there is another tower. And said I, pointing my finger, still further there is another, and yet another. We have not yet begun to see the whole.

The scenery gradually changed, and a temple very much large in dimensions than the one which we are building stood before me. There were a number of towers, placed apparently at equal distances on the outside, each of which were supported by buildings as large as this temple, and yet were united with, and were a part of the great temple. They were of as large dimensions as that which is on the temple. For the midst of these towers and in the center of the building arose in majestic grandeur an immense large dome that seemed to tower as high above the towers as the towers were from the earth. It was not quite finished at the top and there were some workmen employed near the top of the dome, who, in consequence of the extreme height of the building, appeared very small.

I was much delighted with the scenery that presented itself to my view, and soon after awoke retaining for some time afterward the same pleasing sensation that I had enjoyed during my dream.[35]

Orson F. Whitney

Orson F. Whitney, an early Church leader, was an able speaker and accomplished writer who wrote hundreds of books and articles. He was born 1 July 1855 in Salt Lake City, Utah. Elder Whitney's grandfather was Heber C. Kimball. When he returned from his mission, Elder Whitney began serving as a bishop, a position he held for twenty-eight years. He was called to be one of the Twelve Apostles in 1906.

Elder Whitney always enjoyed writing. While he was on a mission in Pennsylvania, Elder Whitney wrote to officials of a Salt Lake newspaper, asking if they would be interested in publishing his missionary experiences. They replied favorably, and his first piece was published in March 1877.

After that publication, Elder Whitney began writing in earnest. He spent so much time on his literary efforts that his companion, Elder

Musser, chided him, saying, "You ought to be studying the books of the Church. You were sent out to preach the Gospel, not to write for the newspapers."[36]

Although Elder Whitney admitted that his companion was right, he was so caught up in the excitement of having his work published that he could not stop. At least, not until he had a remarkable dream. He later spoke of this dream as a turning point in his life and said he owed all his future accomplishments to it. Elder Whitney records:

Then came a marvelous manifestation, an admonition from a higher Source, one impossible to ignore. It was a dream, or a vision in a dream, as I lay upon my bed in the little town of Columbia, Lancaster County, Pennsylvania. I seemed to be in the Garden of Gethsemane, a witness of the Savior's agony. I saw Him as plainly as ever I have seen anyone. Standing behind a tree in the foreground, I beheld Jesus, with Peter, James and John, as they came through a little wicket gate at my right. Leaving the three apostles there, after telling them to kneel and pray, the Son of God passed over to the other side, where He also knelt and prayed. It was the same prayer with which all Bible readers are familiar: "Oh my Father, if it be possible, let this cup pass from me; nevertheless not as I will, but as thou wilt."

As He prayed the tears streamed down his face, which was toward me. I was so moved at the sight that I also wept, out of pure sympathy. My whole heart went out to him; I loved him with all my soul, and longed to be with him as I longed for nothing else.

Presently He arose and walked to where those apostles were kneeling—fast asleep! He shook them gently, awoke them, and in a tone of tender reproach, untinctured by the least show of anger or impatience, asked them plaintively if they could not watch with him one hour. There He was, with the awful weight of the world's sin upon his shoulders, with the pangs of every man, woman and child shooting through his sensitive soul—and they could not watch with him one poor hour!

Returning to his place, He offered up the same prayer as before; then went back and again found them sleeping. Again He awoke them, readmonished them, and once more returned and prayed. Three times this occurred, until I was perfectly familiar with his appearance—face, form and movements. He was of noble stature and majestic mien—not at all the weak, effeminate being that some painters have portrayed; but the very God that he was and is, as meek and humble as a little child.

All at once the circumstance seemed to change, the scene remaining just the same. Instead of before, it was after the crucifixion, and the Savior, with the three apostles, now stood together in a group at my left. They were about to depart and ascend into Heaven. I could endure it no longer. I ran from behind the tree, fell at his feet, clasped Him around the knees, and begged him to take me with him.

I shall never forget the kind and gentle manner in which He stooped, raised me up, and embraced me. It was so vivid, so real. I felt the very warmth of his body, as He held me in his arms and said in tenderest tones: 'No, my son; these have finished their work; they can go with me; but you must stay and finish yours.' Still I clung to Him. Gazing up into his face—for he was taller than I—I besought him fervently: 'Well, promise me that I will come to you at the last.'

Smiling sweetly, He said: "That will depend entirely upon yourself." I awoke with a sob in my throat, and it was morning.[37]

When Elder Whitney related the experience to his companion, Elder Musser said solemnly, "That's from God."

In his account, Elder Whitney stated that he saw the moral clearly and, although he had never thought of being an apostle, he knew that the sleeping apostles represented him. He continued:

> I was asleep at my post—as any man is who, having been divinely appointed to do one thing, does another. But from that hour all was changed. I was never the same man again. I did not give up writing; for President Young, having noticed some of my contributions to the home papers, advised me to continue using writing "for the establishment of truth and righteousness." I therefore continued to write, but not to the neglect of the Lord's Work. I held that first and foremost; all else was secondary.[38]

Wilford Woodruff

Wilford Woodruff was born in Farmington, Connecticut, on 1 March 1807. After he was baptized, he served a series of missions and had immense success. In the United Kingdom alone, he baptized hundreds of people. He was called to be an apostle by the Prophet Joseph Smith in 1838. Elder Woodruff served as president of the mission in Great Britain. After the Saints moved west, he served as Church historian, presided over the St. George Temple, and played a central role in the leadership of the Church. Wilford Woodruff became president of the Church in April 1889.

In the early part of 1835, Elder Woodruff was serving one of his many missions to the Southern States when he experienced an unusual dream. Although it was symbolic, he came to understand that the snakes in it represented enemies of the Church. Elder Woodruff recorded the following in his journal:

> We arrived that night within five miles of Mr. Akeman's and were kindly entertained by a stranger. During the night I had the following dream: I thought an angel came to us, and told us we were commanded of the Lord to follow a certain straight path, which was pointed out to us, let it lead us wherever it might. After we had walked in it awhile, we came to the door of a house, which was in the line of a high wall running north and south, so that we could not go around.
>
> I opened the door and saw the room was filled with large serpents, and I shuddered at the sight. My companion said he would not go into the room for fear of the serpents. I told him I would try to go through the room though they killed me, for the Lord commanded it. As I stepped into the room the serpents coiled themselves up, and raised their heads some two feet from the floor, to spring at me. There was one much larger than the rest, in the center of the room, which raised his head nearly as high as mine and made a spring at me. At that instant I felt as though nothing but the power of God could save me, and I stood still. Just before the serpent reached me he dropped dead at my feet; all the rest dropped dead, swelled up, turned black, bust open, took fire and were consumed before my eyes, and we went though the room unharmed, thanking God for our deliverance.
>
> I woke in the morning and pondered upon the dream. We took breakfast, and started on our journey on Sunday morning to visit Mr. Akeman. I related to my companion my dream, and told him we should see something strange. We had great anticipation of meeting Mr. Akeman, supposing him to be a member of the Church. When we arrived at his house, he received us very coldly, and we soon found that he had apostatized. He brought railing accusations against the Book of Mormon and the authorities of the Church. Word was sent through all the

> settlements on the river for twenty miles that two Mormon preachers were in the place. A mob was soon raised, and warning sent to us to leave immediately or we would be tarred and feathered, ridden on a rail, and hanged. I soon saw who the serpents were. My companion wanted to leave; I told him, no. I would stay and see my dream fulfilled.[39]

The Hubbel family invited Elder Woodruff and his companion, Elder Brown, to stay with them, and the missionaries gladly accepted. During the next three weeks, the elders helped the family clear the land to pay for their board and room and preached as they were able.

Then, in the middle of February, Elder Woodruff said, "The spirit of the Lord came upon me like a rushing of mighty wind. The voice of the spirit said, 'Go up again and visit Mr. Akeman and again bear testimony to him of the truth of the Book of Mormon and of the work of God.'"[40]

When Elder Woodruff told Elder Brown what the Spirit wanted them to do, his companion replied that Elder Woodruff could do it by himself. So, Elder Woodruff set off to walk the mile and a half through the woods alone. Elder Woodruff states: "As I approached the house I saw the door open and Mr. Akeman walking the floor. I felt particularly impressed to ask if he was well. He said he never felt better in health. I told him I had come to bear testimony again to him of the truth of the Book of Mormon and of the work of God."[41]

At this, Mr. Akeman became angry and began raging against the Church. Elder Woodruff said he was unable to speak any further to the man because the house was filled with an awful darkness.

"I did not understand why the Lord should send me into the midst of such spirits to bear testimony of his work. I felt very strange," Elder Woodruff observed. "I could not speak. I arose to my feet to leave the house. I felt as though the floor moved under my feet. . . . I had a desire to flee as Lot did when he went out of Sodom, without looking behind me."[42]

A short time later, Mr. Akeman suffered a sudden attack and died. Oddly enough, Elder Woodruff was asked to speak at the funeral. He accepted and preached an inspired message to the congregation.

On another occasion, Elder Woodruff noted that he and many other members of the Church were prepared in advance for the death of the Prophet Joseph Smith. The record states that "on the night of their arrival in Cincinnati, Elder Woodruff dreamed that Joseph would again be arrested and tried in Illinois, and the same night Brigham Young dreamed that the Twelve were called home. These dreams were the preparation for coming events which cast their shadows before. The hearts of those brave men and devoted missionaries were receiving a preparation for the troubled times that were to come."[43]

While on a visit to Maine in October 1844, Elder Wilford Woodruff received two dreams. In both of them, he saw the Prophet Joseph Smith, who had been killed earlier that year. Elder Woodruff wrote the following in his journal:

> While I was at the home of my father-in-law I had a peculiar dream. Much of it was unutterable and cannot be written; indeed, I do not comprehend it myself. Among other things I was called with the Twelve to hold the keys of the Kingdom in all the world. I traveled with them over much of the earth and I also traveled through many countries alone. When I finished my journey I saw many things which I cannot write, but in the end, Joseph, the Prophet, assisted me to come where he was and pointed out to me my place and work. I immediately entered into the duties of the new calling to which I was appointed.
>
> The same night I had another dream. I was in the presence of the Prophet, and was conversing with him about his death. I told him I felt bad over it, and that had I known he would have been taken so soon I should have conversed with him more while he lived. I would have asked him many questions. In reply he said that it was not his fault that I did not.[44]

After Joseph Smith was killed in 1844, Wilford Woodruff felt it was important to build upon the foundation that the Prophet had already laid. He was pleased that Brigham Young worked steadily to follow the plans that Joseph Smith had already set in motion. However, Elder Woodruff felt that in order to proceed in a satisfactory manner, the Church needed to cut off those men who had secretly worked against Joseph Smith at the end of his life, while maintaining relationships with those who had proved faithful. Elder Woodruff had a symbolic dream that concurred with his feelings. Elder Woodruff recorded:

I had a dream which I will relate here. I saw a fruit tree and went to it in search of fruit. I soon discovered that some of the main branches at the top of the tree growing from the body were dead. It seemed necessary to cut off the dead branches in order to save the tree. I asked someone to help me cut them off. He (His helper) stepped on a large green limb. He was afraid it would break, so I put my shoulder under it and held it up while he cut off the dead branches. The green limb was cracked but it did not break. After we cut off the dead branches the wounds healed up and the tree grew nicely.[45]

Even as a child, Wilford Woodruff had received revealing dreams. While speaking to an audience in the Tabernacle in Salt Lake City, he shared this experience he'd had as a young boy. He said:

> When I was a boy eleven years old, I had a very interesting dream, part of which was fulfilled to the very letter. In this dream I saw a great gulf, a place where all the world had to enter at death, before doing which they had to drop their worldly goods. I saw an aged man with a beaver hat and a broadcloth suit. The man looked very sorrowful. I saw him come with something on his back, which he had to drop among the general pile before he could enter the gulf. I was then but a boy.
>
> A few years after this my father and mother removed to Farmington, and there I saw that man. I knew him the moment I saw him. His name was Chauncy Deming. In a few years afterwards he was taken sick and died. I attended his funeral. He was what you may call a miser, worth hundreds of thousands of dollars. When the coffin was being lowered into the grave my dream came to me, and that night his son-in-law found one hundred thousand dollars in a cellar belonging to the old man. I name this merely to show that in this dream I had manifested to me certain things that were true.[46]

The same night Elder Woodruff had this dream, he had another one about his own family. President Woodruff stated:

> After this scene [the above dream] had passed before me I was placed in a great temple. It was called the kingdom of God. The first man who came to me was Uncle Ozem Woodruff and his wife I helped into the temple. In process of time, after embracing the Gospel, and while on my first mission to Tennessee, I told Brother Patten of my dream, who told me that in a few years I would meet that man and baptize him. That was fulfilled to the very letter, for I afterwards baptized my uncle and his wife and some of the children; also my own father and

step-mother and step-sister, and a Methodist priest or class-leader;—in fact I baptized everybody in my father's house. I merely mention this to show that dreams sometimes do come to pass in life.[47]

Elder Woodruff received other dreams. On one of his many missions, he had a dream that prepared him for sad news. He states:

> When I was in the City of London on one occasion, with Brother George A. Smith, I dreamt that my wife came to me and told me that our first child had died. I believed my dream, and in the morning while at breakfast, I felt somewhat sad. Brother George A. Smith noticed this and I told him my dream.
>
> Next morning's post brought me a letter from my wife, conveying the intelligence of the death of my child. It may be asked what use there was in such a thing. I don't know that there was much use in it except to prepare my mind for the news of the death of my child. . . . My dream gave me a strong testimony of the resurrection. I am satisfied, always have been, in regard to the resurrection. I rejoice in it."[48]

Before he ever laid eyes on the Salt Lake Valley, Wilford Woodruff had a dream in which he saw the Salt Lake Temple. He related this experience during a talk he gave at general conference. In that talk, he said:

> Many years ago, before we came to the Rocky Mountains, I had a dream. I dreamed of being in these mountains, and of seeing a large fine looking temple erected in one of these valleys, which was built of cut granite stone, I saw that temple dedicated, and I attended the dedicatory services, and I saw a good many men that are living to-day in the midst of this people. And I saw them called of God and sent forth unto the United States and to Babylon, or what is called the Christian world, to bind up the law and seal up the testimony against the nations of the earth, because they had rejected the testimony of Jesus, and of the establishment of the kingdom of God upon the earth.
>
> When the foundation of that temple was laid, I thought of my dream and a great many times since. And whenever President Young held a council of the brethren of the Twelve and talked of building the temple of adobe or brick, which was done I would say to myself, 'No, you will never do it;' because I had

> seen it in my dream built of some other material. I mention these things to show you that things are manifested to Latter-day Saints sometimes which we do not know anything about, only as they are given by the Spirit of God.[49]

President Woodruff dedicated the Salt Lake Temple and later wrote in his journal: "Near[ly] fifty years ago while in the city of Boston I had a vision of going with the Saints to the Rocky Mountains building a temple and I dedicated it. Two nights in succession before John Taylor's death [1887] President Brigham Young [who had died ten years earlier] gave me the keys of the temple and told me to go and dedicate it, which I did."[50]

And on yet another occasion, Wilford Woodruff received another dream. It was a cold, November day in 1879 as he trudged through the mountains with his companion, Elder Smith. The snow was a foot deep, and the wind was piercingly cold. At night, the two men cut pine boughs to shield their beds from the wind. It was so cold that Elder Smith worried that the horses might freeze, so they brought them closer to the fire, which they piled high with wood and kept blazing through most of the night. It was during this difficult trip that President Brigham Young and Elder Orson Hyde appeared to Elder Woodruff in a dream.

Elder Woodruff "asked President Young if he would not address the Saints. . . . President Young replied, 'Tell the people to get the spirit of the Lord and keep it with them.'"[51]

President Woodruff saw President Young in another dream as well; this time the deceased prophet was accompanied by Heber C. Kimball. President Woodruff relates:

> And on one occasion, I saw Brother Brigham and Brother Heber ride in (a) carriage ahead of the carriage in which I rode when I was on my way to attend conference. . . . When we arrived at our destination I asked Prest. Young if he would preach to us.
>
> He said, "No, I have finished my testimony in the flesh, I shall not talk to this people any more. But (said he) I have come to see you; I have come to watch over you, and to see what the people are doing. Then (said he) I want you to teach the people—and I want you to follow this counsel yourself—that they must labor and so live as to obtain the Holy Spirit, for

> without this you cannot build up the kingdom; without the spirit of God you are in danger of walking in the dark, and in danger of failing to accomplish your calling as apostles and as elders in the church and kingdom of God."[52]

President Wilford Woodruff dreamed that the Church leadership and elders needed to warn people about the calamities that would one day be unleashed upon the earth. About this dream, he wrote, "On January 28th I was again given a vision. It concerned the destiny of our nation and of Zion. My pillow was again wet by a fountain of tears as I beheld the judgments of God upon the wicked. I was strongly impressed that the apostles and elders should warn the inhabitants of the earth."[53]

Wilford Woodruff was blessed to be able to see not only the Prophet Joseph but other departed leaders many times in his dreams. President Woodruff related the following experience while speaking at general conference in 1880. He said:

> I will here make a remark concerning my own feelings. After the death of Joseph Smith I saw and conversed with him many times in my dreams in the night season. On one occasion he and his brother Hyrum met me when on the sea going on a mission to England. I had Dan Jones with me. He received his mission from Joseph Smith before his death; and the prophet talked freely to me about the mission I was then going to perform. And he also talked to me with regard to the mission of the Twelve Apostles in the flesh, and he laid before me the work they had to perform; and he also spoke of the reward they would receive after death. And there were many other things he laid before me in his interview on that occasion.
>
> And when I awoke many of the things he had told me were taken from me, I could not comprehend them. I have had many interviews with Brother Joseph until the last 15 or 20 years of my life; I have not seen him for that length of time. . . . The thought came to me that Brother Joseph had left the work of watching over this church and kingdom to others, and that he had gone ahead and that he had left this work to men who have lived and labored with us since he left us. This idea manifested itself to me that such men advance in the spirit world. And I believe myself that these men who have died and gone into the spirit world had this mission left with them, that is, a certain

portion of them, to watch over the Latter Day Saints."[54]

On 5 December 1878, Elder Woodruff attended the funeral of Elder Orson Hyde, one of the original Twelve Apostles. During remarks given at the funeral, Elder Woodruff related yet another dream. He said:

> I saw a short distance from the Missouri River, where I stood, twelve men dressed in the robes of the Temple. They stood in a square near by and I was given to understand that they represented the twelve gates of the new Jerusalem. Their hands were uplifted while they were consecrating the ground; and later they laid the corner-stones of the house of God. I saw myriads of angels hovering over them, and above their heads there was a pillar-like cloud. I heard the most beautiful singing in the words: "Now is established the Kingdom of our God and His Christ, and He shall reign forever and forever, and the Kingdom shall never be thrown down, for the Saints have overcome."
>
> I saw people coming from the river and from distant places to help build the Temple. It seemed as though there were hosts of angels helping to bring material for the construction of that building. Some were in Temple robes, and the pillar-like cloud continued to hover over the spot. Later I found myself in the Ogden Tabernacle, where I was calling upon the people to listen to the beautiful strains of music there. I rolled over in my bed and heard the clock of the City Hall strike twelve." This was December 16, 1877."[55]

Brigham Young

Brigham Young was born in Whitingham, Vermont, on 1 June 1801. He was called to be one of the Twelve Apostles in February 1835. After Joseph Smith's martyrdom, President Young became the leader of The Church of Jesus Christ of Latter-day Saints in August 1844. (He officially became the second president on 27 December 1847). He led the Saints to the Salt Lake Valley and supervised the establishment of hundreds of colonies throughout the Great Basin. President Young was influential in the economic, political, and spiritual development of the state of Utah.

On 23 February 1847, Brigham Young met with the Twelve Apostles to discuss moving the Saints across the plains. During the meeting, President Young told the brethren about a dream he had in which the Prophet Joseph Smith had visited him. President Young related:

> While sick and asleep about noonday of the 17th inst., I dreamed that I went to St. (see) Joseph. He looked perfectly natural, sitting with his feet on the lower round of his chair. I took hold of his right hand and kissed him many times, and said to him: "Why is it that we cannot be together as we used to be. You have been from us a long time, and we want your society and I do not like to be separated from you."
>
> Joseph rising from his chair and looking at me with his usual, earnest, expressive and pleasing countenance replied, "It is all right."
>
> I said, "I do not like to be away from you."
>
> Joseph said, "It is all right; we cannot be together yet; we shall be by and by; but you will have to do without me a while, and then we shall be together again."
>
> I then discovered there was a hand rail between us, Joseph stood by a window and to the southwest of him it was very light. I was in the twilight and to the north of me it was very dark; I said, "Brother Joseph, the brethren you know well, better than I do; you raised them up, and brought the Priesthood to us. The brethren have a great anxiety to understand the law of adoption or sealing principles; and if you have a word of counsel for me I should be glad to receive it."
>
> Joseph stepped toward me, and looking very earnestly, yet pleasantly said, "Tell the people to be humble and faithful, and be sure to keep the spirit of the Lord and it will lead them right. Be careful and not turn away the small still voice; it will teach you what to do and where to go; it will yield the fruits of the kingdom. Tell the brethren to keep their hearts open to conviction, so that when the Holy Ghost comes to them, their hearts will be ready to receive it.
>
> "They can tell the Spirit of the Lord from all other spirits; it will whisper peace and joy to their souls; it will take malice, hatred, strife and all evil from their hearts; and their whole desire will be to do good, bring forth righteousness and build up the kingdom of God. Tell the brethren if they will follow the spirit of the Lord they will go right. Be sure to tell the people

to keep the Spirit of the Lord; and if they will, they will find themselves just as they were organized by our Father in Heaven before they came into the world. Our Father in Heaven organized the human family, but they are all disorganized and in great confusion."

Joseph then showed me the pattern, how they were in the beginning. This I cannot describe, but I saw it, and saw where the Priesthood had been taken from the earth and how it must be joined together, so that there would be a perfect chain from Father Adam to his latest posterity. Joseph again said, "Tell the people to be sure to keep the Spirit of the Lord and follow it, and it will lead them just right."[56]

Chapter 3

Angelic Visits that Guided and Directed

In 1889, Elder H. Ricks wrote in *The Millennial Star,* "It is the belief of the Latter-day Saints that every person who keeps the commandments of God is entitled to inspiration or counsel from heaven for his individual guidance, not only when engaged in the work of the ministry, but also in ordinary occupations. Among other agencies employed, at times, by the Lord to communicate His directing counsel to His people, visions and dreams have been somewhat prominent. They do not belong to any particular age, but have characterized every dispensation which the Lord has established in the earth."[1]

Certainly, individuals have received incredible dreams and visions that have been critical to the establishment of the Church. One that comes to mind is a vision received by President Woodruff directing him to issue the Manifesto and save the Saints from devastation. In this vision, the Lord showed President Woodruff what would happen if members of the Church continued to practice polygamy. "I saw by the inspiration of Almighty God what lay before this people," President Woodruff observed, "and I knew that something had to be done to ward off the blow that I saw impending. . . . I should have seen all this [destruction happen] had not Almighty God commanded me to do what I did [issue the Manifesto]."[2]

President Harold B. Lee reinforced the principle that the Lord directs His Church at least partially through dreams and visions when he noted, "We know that the Lord gives revelation today. . . . The Lord is in His heavens; He is closer to us than you have any idea. . . . The Lord is giving revelations day by day."[3]

Every person who prays with sincerity can receive inspiration in his or her life. In Job, we read that people can indeed enjoy dreams given them for personal guidance and instruction. "For God speaketh once, yea twice, yet man perceiveth it not. In a dream, in a vision of the night, when deep sleep falleth upon men, in slumberings upon the bed; then he openeth the ears of men, and sealeth their instruction" (Job 33:14–16).

President Harold B. Lee was speaking to women in the Church when he counseled them to walk by the spirit of revelation. "Let the Holy Spirit's promptings guide you night and day," he said. "If you'll learn to give heed to those promptings of the Holy Spirit and then follow them, you'll find those things that are presented to your mind [will come] true very shortly thereafter. If you'll learn to follow your impressions, you'll be amazed to see how you'll walk daily by the spirit of revelation. Now, every one of you is blessed to receive that."[4]

John Morgan was not a member of any religion, nor was he interested in becoming a member of any religion. Those two facts made a dream he received particularly surprising—not only to himself but to the Heywood family, with whom he was staying.

One morning at breakfast, John told the Heywoods about an unusual dream he'd had. John dreamed that he was back in North Georgia near the battlefield of Chickamauga, where he had fought in the Civil War. He was traveling south on a road that led to Rome, Georgia. John knew the road well, having traveled it many times. However, in his dream when he came to a fork in the road, he was unsure which turnoff to take. Looking off the side of the road, he saw Brigham Young standing in front of a large tree. President Young told him that the right-hand road led to Rome, but that if he took the left-hand road, "he would have an experience that would give him a strong and abiding testimony of the divinity of the Book of Mormon."[5]

John Morgan laughed aloud as he recalled this part of his dream and assured the Heywoods, "I am not interested in the Book of Mormon or its divinity." John then asked Sister Heywood what she thought of his dream.

Sister Heywood responded by saying prophetically, "It is my conviction that the time is not far distant when you will become a member of our Church and that in due time you will be called to do missionary work in the Southern States. It is my thought that in your missionary work you will one day be following the road and will arrive at the fork you saw in your dream—but President Young will not be there. However, I counsel you to remember his instructions and take the road that will lead to the left."[6]

After John Morgan returned to his home, he forgot about his dream.

Sometime later, however, he began investigating the Church. And eventually, he developed a testimony and was baptized. Ten years later, John was called to be a missionary and sent to the Southern States Mission.

One day Elder Morgan was traveling along the road leading to Rome, Georgia, when he came to a fork in the road that he did not remember. He stopped, unsure which fork would take him to Rome. Suddenly, the memory of his long ago-dream came flooding back. He looked off to the side of the road. There was the large tree. Although Brigham Young was not standing there, Elder Morgan remembered the counsel he had been given: taking the left fork would allow him to gain a strong and abiding testimony of the divinity of the Book of Mormon.

He set off down the left-hand road. After walking for about an hour, Elder Morgan came to a beautiful valley that had been settled by twenty-three prosperous families. He called at the first house and, while there, spent the evening talking about the first principles of the gospel. Afterwards, the father brought out the family Bible and began turning to many of the scriptures that Elder Morgan had used in explaining the principles of the gospel. All of the scriptures had been underlined.

When Elder Morgan asked who had underlined the passages, the family told him that ten days earlier a man who seemed very intelligent had come to their home and asked their permission to mark certain passages in their Bible. Furthermore, the stranger had said that another man would be coming by in a few days to teach them the meaning of the marked passages and explain the plan of salvation. John asked the family if they knew the name of the man who had visited them, but they did not.

Elder Morgan spent the next six weeks in that valley. He discovered the stranger had called on nearly every house in the valley. In every home where he stopped, the stranger had marked the family Bible and told the family members that another man would soon visit them and explain the scriptures in their fullness.

Elder Morgan baptized twenty of the twenty-three families in the valley. One of the men he baptized was a Methodist pastor. In time, the pastor was ordained the presiding elder of the branch, and his church building became a meetinghouse for The Church of Jesus Christ of Latter-day Saints.

"John Morgan's dream had come true," the account of his dream states, "and in his heart he felt he had gained a missionary companion in none other than one of the Three Nephites."[7]

Others have known what lies in their futures. Castle Murphy received a vivid dream that informed him ahead of time that he and his wife would be called to new positions in the Church; the dream did not, however, specify exactly what those positions would be. When Elder Murphy woke from his dream, he told his wife that they would soon be receiving a phone call from President Grant. Elder Murphy stated:

> In the dream which I remember very vividly, President Grant came to our home, together with his secretary, Joseph Anderson. As he began to talk with me, people who evidently had learned of his arrival, began to crowd into our living room. As they chatted with the President, Brother Anderson called out that if the president did not leave soon that he would be late for another appointment in the city. President Grant, being a man who respected appointments and promptness, turned to me and said, "Brother Murphy, I am sorry that we must leave you now, but you will be hearing from me very soon."[8]

Elder Murphy then woke up. Within a week, the expected call came. Elder and Sister Murphy were asked to go to Salt Lake City to see the president of the Church. After they were seated, President Grant asked them, "How would you like to return to Hawaii and take charge of the Hawaiian Temple?"

"Although we had fully expected the phone call because of the vividness of the dream," Elder Murphy noted, "we were certainly surprised with such a call."[9]

Visions and dreams often provide direction and guidance during critical times. While on his mission, Elder Oscar W. McConkie Jr. had many companions, one of whom was a recent convert. After this companion returned home, he wrote a letter to Elder McConkie, saying that he wanted to share a sacred experience with him—one that had renewed his testimony and given him great peace of mind.

His former companion said that after he returned home, he began to struggle with many heavy responsibilities that were suddenly placed on him. He had a large family and was working many long hours trying to develop a new business. Then, he was called to serve as a member of the bishopric. He felt so burdened that he began to wonder if the time he spent in the service of the Church was worth the time it took away from his family. Doubts began to arise.

Finally, he decided to fast and pray about the matter.

One night, after pouring out his heart in prayer, this man received a vision. Elder McConkie Jr. tells about his friend's dream, saying, "He saw himself in a great struggle, in the midst of a huge battle, fighting with every ounce of his strength. But the terrible doubt was [still] there. He didn't know whether he was fighting on the right side or not. Just as he was about to abandon himself to destruction, a shaft of light appeared over his head. It rested upon one of the troopers leading the battle in the section in which he was engaged. He recognized the man."[10]

The man was none other than Elder Oscar W. McConkie, his former missionary companion.

In his account of the vision, Elder McConkie concluded, "Then he heard the voice of the Spirit: 'When you are on his side, you are on the right side.' Calmness and certainty were his once again. The scene closed. He knew, and was given tranquility."[11]

Occasionally, William Vestal Coffin had dreams that foretold future events. One time he had a dream that informed him that his granddaughter Margaret Martindale would one day do an important work that would benefit the family. At the time of his dream, William had no knowledge of The Church of Jesus Christ of Latter-day Saints and knew nothing about temple work.

Margaret later recalled that on a summer afternoon when she was ten, her grandfather told her about his dream. "Grandfather reached over and took my hand," Margaret recalls, "saying in a very solemn voice: 'Margaret, I have had a dream. One day you will be called upon to do a great religious work for our family. It will be an important work. You must do it.'"[12]

Years passed. Margaret grew up, graduated from college, and began to teach school. Then, her grandfather fell ill, and she went to help care for him for a month. While there, Margaret spent a lot of time sitting by her grandfather's bed. Her grandfather often reminded her about the dream he had that she would do an important work for the family.

"Do you remember?" he asked many times.

Margaret assured him she would do whatever she needed to do. Four months later, her grandfather passed away.

Sometime later, Margaret heard about the restored gospel and agreed to listen to the missionaries. She was baptized two years after her grandfather passed away. Shortly after this, she discovered a box that contained six typewritten volumes about her grandfather's family. The last volume was entitled *Genealogy*. When she picked it up, Margaret wondered if it might have something to do with her grandfather's dream.

During the following years, Margaret read and learned more about her ancestors. She also studied the plan of salvation. After learning about the sealing power, which allowed families to be sealed together forever, Margaret made plans to do this work for her grandparents.

"When it came time to do the sealing for Grandfather and Grandmother," Margaret states, "I was aware of Grandfather's presence as I participated in the ordinance. A peaceful feeling came over me, and with great joy I knew that I was doing what Grandfather had said I should. The 'great religious work' for my family was under way."[13]

While crossing the Atlantic to fill a mission in Great Britain, Elder William J. Facer had a dream that served as a warning. The account states:

> One night he [Elder Facer] dreamed that he was standing on the deck of the vessel with one of the other passengers, Elder Joseph Nelson. There was a very heavy sea, and the ship was rolling dangerously. Suddenly his companion lost his footing and shot across the deck to the edge of the vessel, but seemed to catch one of the upright bars of the railing and this saved his falling into the sea. The writer [Elder Facer] rushed to him, drew him up and helped him back. A peculiarity about the dream was that when the writer bent over his companion, one of those strange transformations, so common in dreams occurred; the prostrate figure seemed to be some one else.
>
> The dream was so impressive that on rising the writer went to the door of Elder Nelson's cabin and related it, with a warning that he should be careful. The young man was just ready to go on deck, and as the sea was very rough, he promised to take care. He had been gone only a few minutes when he returned to the cabin, pale as death, saying that the dream had not needed to wait long for an interpretation.
>
> On reaching the deck he had taken pains not to expose himself to any danger. A young lady, less watchful, however, had lost her footing on the wet deck, slipped partly under the railing at the vessel's edge, but had caught herself exactly as had been seen in the dream. Elder Nelson quickly rescued her from the dangerous position, and brought her back to safety.
>
> What would have happened had the warning not been observed, no one, of course can tell. It was a testimony, however, that the Lord foresees all things, though we have of ourselves such limited knowledge, and that He is willing to impart to us what is necessary for us to know.[14]

William Palmer was serving a mission in Michigan in 1876 when he had a dream showing him a glimpse of the next life. At the time of his experience, Elder Palmer was temporarily without a companion.

Although he continued to work hard, preaching the gospel without a missionary companion was hard. It would be difficult for anyone, but it was doubly so for Elder Palmer, because he was illiterate. As a young boy, his eyesight had been so poor that he had never learned how to read. Because he lacked an education, Elder Palmer's knowledge of the gospel was somewhat limited, but he declared, "I always had, however, great faith in prayer."[15]

At this time, Elder Palmer was working among a group of people who believed in what they called "the sleep of the dead," or the concept that people had no immortal soul and at death they ceased to exist until they were renewed by the resurrection. This group also believed that people's spirits did not exist prior to this life.

As Elder Palmer met with the local populace and discussed doctrine regarding the premortal life and what happens to people after this life, he felt a desire to know more. One evening, after spending a full day preaching, he laid down, exhausted. "My mind was trying to comprehend the spirit world," he noted. "All at once I was lost in sleep. I seemed to be standing by the bedside; my body lay on the bed upon the right side just as I had laid down. . . . I thought I was dead. I moved about at my will, went back to the bed and looked at my body again."[16]

Elder Palmer said he felt affection for his body and was reassured that he would obtain it again in the Resurrection. His only regret at leaving his body was that it was not among the Saints in Zion.

He continued, "Just then a personage came in the room dressed in a white robe, and said: 'You are wanted to meet some of the brethren in the woods north of Greenville [about fifteen miles away] in Maple Valley, to preach to the spirits who know not the Gospel.'

"I inquired, 'What will become of my body?'

"The answer was: 'They will send it to your family.'"[17]

Elder Palmer felt a deep pang at this news, thinking of how his family would mourn, but the messenger reassured him that the Saints would look after his family and all would be well. He then says:

"I know not how I got into the street, but I was there and everything looked natural. It was broad daylight. I started for Greenville. . . and came to two men who were sawing a log with a crosscut saw, and talking on the doctrine of 'The sleep of the dead.' I went close to them and I was so anxious to correct them that I spoke and said: 'Don't believe that foolish doctrine any longer. I tell you man has a spirit.'

"They stopped sawing and looked straight at me. One answered: 'I hear you; but where are you?'

"I went within three or four feet of him and said: 'You are looking right at me.' It seemed so strange they could not see me, and I could see them and myself so plainly. I said, 'I am a spirit. You have seen the Mormon preacher who has been around here?'

"'Yes,' was the answer.

"'I died a little while ago, and my body is at John Harrington's.'

"'What shall we do?' was asked.

"I have not time to tell you; but go to Henry Thompson (who was President of the branch), and he will tell you.'

"Everything looked natural and very beautiful. I came to the hill that enclosed Maple Valley, and climbed it easily, with the thought of what a task it would be if I had my body. When I got on top I looked into the valley, and saw hundreds of men and women gathering from all directions. . . and when I came to the congregation they seemed to know I was an Elder, for they parted. I walked to the center. There, standing upon a fallen tree, was President Heber C. Kimball and my father, who died a faithful Elder. They motioned me to come to them, and as I arose without any effort, I awoke."[18]

Thomas A. Shreeve was serving a mission when he had a dream and saw two angelic visitors—one of them his long-dead brother. Elder Shreeve's experience occurred while he was traveling to a new area in New Zealand. One evening during his journey, the missionary found himself among a small group of friendly people. One of the men was relating his experiences in the Crimean War when Elder Shreeve fell asleep. Elder Shreeve writes:

> I dreamed that I was back in Sydney, sick in bed. Brother May was at a table in the room, and we were conversing. Across the room, to the right of my bed, was an open door, which I could see without lifting my head from the pillow. While I lay there listening to the words of Brother May, a personage clothed in a white robe entered the room. He appeared to be a young man, and had a very pleasing countenance. This personage passed around the bed and stood near the table. Brother May

rose and offered the visitant a chair, and then withdrew. The young man seated himself at the table and opened a book.

"He said, 'Are you ready to report the Sydney Branch?'

"'Yes, sir,' I responded.

"Then proceed.

"I gave him an account of all our doings in Sydney, beginning with our first effort of reorganizing, and closing with my last act previous to sailing—for all these things seemed plain to my mind. The recital seemed to occupy me several minutes and I continued to speak freely. He wrote in the book rapidly, and never once interrupted me. I felt that he was taking every word I uttered. When I stopped, he asked:

"Have you anything more to say?

"'No sir,' I answered. Then he turned the leaves back, and seemed to read from the beginning.

"He said, 'Very well. Now where are you going?'

"To New Zealand.

"He recorded my answer in the book, and then signed his name—I could not see the words of his name, but I felt that he was writing his own signature. He closed the book and walked around to the right side of the bed, shook hands with me, and said:

"Good-by; I will be there before you.

"He passed from the room and then I saw the figure of a little child standing at the foot of the bed. I looked closely and recognized my little brother Teddy, who had been drowned nearly twenty years before. I seemed to know that he had come from the spirit world. . . . I gazed intently at him. He stepped near me. . . .

"'I think you are my little brother Teddy; but it is so long since I saw you that I had almost forgotten how you looked.' Then the thought came into my mind that I must ask him some question. I said, 'Teddy, have you seen our Heavenly Father yet?'

"He answered in the sweet voice of a child: 'No, but I shall see Him.'

"Have you brought any message to me?

"To this question he answered, 'Yes.' . . .

"His eyes looked straight into mine, and he came nestling into my arms. He lifted the forefinger of his right hand toward my face and said: 'Only be true!'"[19]

When Mary Briggs lost her husband, she was left with three children to raise. Years later, her brother-in-law Will Harston lost his wife, Clara. Will was left alone with five children. Mary felt she could understand Will's feelings of sadness at losing his spouse and wrote him a letter expressing her sympathy.

Sometime after the funeral, Will wrote Mary, thanking her for the sympathetic letter regarding his wife's death. When Mary received his letter, she hesitated to respond. She was afraid a reply might encourage an idea some of her friends had already promoted, which was that she ought to marry Will and help him raise his children. Mary did not agree with her friends. She felt that her primary responsibility was to raise her own three children.

One night Mary had a dream, which alarmed her. She had a second dream that caused nearly as much anxiety as the first. After some time, Mary had a third dream. When she finally sorted the three dreams out, she realized that all three were from God. The account of her dreams states:

"In [the first dream] her deceased sister-in-law, Clara, was standing beside her husband, Will, and as she watched, Clara beckoned her to come and stand on the other side of Will. Mary immediately knew what Clara had in mind—that she should marry Will—and she said to her, 'No, I won't,' and she seemed to turn as the dream faded. When she awoke she thought about the dream. She was sure that her answer was still, 'No, I won't.' After all, he was her brother-in-law, or more correctly, her sister-in-law's husband, and that was always the way she thought of him." She tried to push the dream out of her mind.

Mary had a second dream. In this one, she was holding her hand out and when she looked into her palm, she saw her children's faces pictured there. As she looked, Mary had the thought, "Why, there's room for more children there." This second dream alarmed her as much as the first. Mary could not and did not want to think of Will in a romantic way.

One day Will came to visit her. They enjoyed each other's company, and Will began to stop by occasionally. As time went on, Mary's feelings about Will underwent a gradual change. Eventually, they fell in love. When Will asked her to marry him, Mary said yes. As the years passed, they had four children, making a total of twelve children in their home.

Then came the third and last dream.

The account states, "Mary had still another dream in which Clara returned, radiantly happy, and told Mary, 'I want to thank you so much. Now I can do my work without worrying about my family.' She left with a beautiful sweet smile."[20]

Like Mary Briggs, Jayne Redd had a dream that helped her to know who she should marry. Jayne was dating a young man, Marty Kearl, when Marty decided that he wanted to go on a mission. Although Jayne and Marty had much in common and enjoyed each other's company, they had not talked seriously about marriage, and they made no commitment to each other before he left.

After Marty had been gone a year and a half, Jayne met Rick, a returned missionary. They also enjoyed each other's company and began dating. As Jayne continued to see Rick, he began talking about their future together. She was unsure whether to continue dating him so steadily or to stop and wait for Marty to return and then decide which man she wanted to marry. When Rick began to talk openly about marriage, Jayne didn't feel it was right to keep putting him off as she had been doing. Confused and unsure, she asked the Lord for help.

In an answer to her prayers, Jayne dreamed she and Rick were married in a wonderful temple ceremony. She was very happy. When Marty returned home from his mission, she attended his homecoming. When Jayne saw Marty, she was surprised at the strength of her feelings for him and thought, "Oh, how could this be? I have married the wrong man!" When she woke, Jayne was so upset that she was nearly crying.

Jayne decided to wait until Marty came home before making any commitment to Rick. When Marty finished his mission and returned home, he and Jayne both knew they wanted to spend eternity together. Marty and Jayne were married in the Salt Lake Temple.[21]

A recent convert, Brother Beard was feeling unsure and confused about whether he had done the right thing in being baptized. He received a dream, which providing comforting guidance.

Prior to his conversion to The Church of Jesus Christ of Latter-day Saints, Brother Beard had been a Campbellite preacher and had strong ties to that religion. Shortly after his conversion and baptism, a close friend lectured him at length about the flaws and shortcomings of the LDS Church, trying with all his power to convince Brother Beard that he had joined a false religion. The visitor was extremely persuasive, and his arguments caused Brother Beard to have doubts about the restored gospel. He began to wonder if he was on the wrong track.

Then, Brother Beard had an angelic visitor. An account of his experience states:

> One day soon after, while reading the Book of Mormon, a drowsy feeling seemed to come over him and the book dropped into his lap. At the same time he saw himself walking along a railroad track and looking at another track which seemed to parallel the one on which he was traveling. He was bothered in his mind as to whether he was on the right road, and wondered if he had better get on the other track. Just then a woman, dressed in white, came and placed her hand on his shoulder, saying, "You are on the right track," and, pointing back, she commanded him to look, which he did, and beheld that the other line was simply a switch that had come off of the main track.[22]

Brother Beard then awoke. After pondering the dream and the peaceful feelings he felt, he concluded that when he joined the Church, he had been on the right track after all. Brother Beard related this experience during a conference in Xenia, Ohio, in the late 1800s. The account concludes by saying, "Brother Beard spoke of the satisfaction this [incident] was to him, and bore an earnest and sincere testimony to the truthfulness of the Gospel as advocated by the Latter Day Saints."[23]

Prior to his conversion, Brother Rex had a significant experience that stayed with him the rest of his life. One bright, spring, Sabbath morning Brother Rex was sitting in his chair, wishing he could attend church services. Although he longed to walk outside in the sunshine, Brother Rex was recovering from a severe illness and was unable to leave his house. As the bells in London began to toll their chimes, Brother Rex closed his eyes, picturing the church he longed to be in. Then he fell asleep.

Brother Rex dreamed that people were passing him on their way to church. Suddenly, an angel appeared and told him that before entering God's house again, he ought to consider his previous inattention while attending, lest, when he was well, he should repeat his guilty inattentiveness. The angel then took him inside, where he could hear aloud the prayers of the people who were worshiping. Brother Rex discerned that many of the people only *seemed* to be praying—actually their minds were elsewhere.

His attention was then captured by a young child's prayer. Brother Rex said the child's voice was "distinct and clear above all other sounds, a sweet childish voice softly and reverently repeating the Lord's prayer. . . . I turned in the direction of the sound, and distinguished among one of the children of the poor people, a very little boy. His hands were clasped together as he knelt, his eyes were closed, his gentle face composed in reverence, and as the angel wrote on his tablets the words that fell from those young lips, his smile, like a sunbeam, illuminated the church for a moment."[24]

Brother Rex noted that few people were as attentive as this small child. He could hear the wandering thoughts of the crowd as they reflected upon their work, homes, neighbors, activities, and friends. The angel told Brother Rex that he should make a sincere effort to keep his thoughts upon the Savior during church services and recall his thoughts when they wandered.

The angel concluded his visit by saying, "Remember the solemn warning."

Brother Rex then awoke. "May the lessons I learned in those few minutes never be effaced from my heart," he related later, "and if this account of them should recall one wandering thought in the house of prayer, or teach any to value more highly, and cultivate more carefully the privilege of joining in the public worship of our god and Father, it will not have been written in vain."[25]

In 1885, Elder William Daybell left his home to serve a mission in Tennessee. He and his companion, Elder Jesse N. Perkins, were assigned to work in the Cumberland Mountains but did not have much success. The people would not listen to their message, and the elders were consistently denied food and shelter. Finally, they decided to leave the area and prayed that God would inspire them to know where they could go to share the gospel. On their final night in the area, the elders were allowed to stay in a home. That evening Elder Daybell had a dream. He recalled later:

> I thought we arose in the morning, and directed our way from the head of the Stones River in a northerly direction, up a certain ridge, in the vicinity. Arriving at the top of the mountain, we passed a school house in which school was in session. As we passed, the children came to the door and evinced surprise at seeing us, but remained very quiet while we went on our way. Going a half mile further on, we came to a house near which, as we approached, we could see two women peeling apples, while two men stood by a well busy in getting the women a drink. On nearing the place, I thought we were asked to come in. They brought us two chairs, and asked us to be seated, we accepting the invitation. . . . They wished to know who we were, and upon being told by me seemed much surprised.
>
> One of the men said he would like to hear us preach our doctrine, and I told him we would be pleased to speak if they would secure their school house for our service, whereupon the other man said that he was a trustee of the district and furthermore owned an interest in the house and the land upon which it stood, and declared that we could preach there as long as we desired. I then thought we gave out an appointment for a meeting at ten o'clock the following Sunday morning, and we were invited to stay with them.[26]

Elder Daybell then awoke. After telling his companion about his dream, the two missionaries set out in a northerly direction. As they walked, they came upon the various scenes Elder Daybell had seen in his dream. The account continues:

> During that day's travel everything came to pass as I had seen it in my dream: the school house, the children, the people at the well—every detail was fulfilled to the letter. The school house was offered, the appointment made, the people at the house entertained us, and became our friends. Further than this, we opened up a prosperous field of labor, and it was only a day's journey from where every avenue seemed closed and we could do nothing. . . .
>
> During our further labors, we received many additional

testimonies proving to us that the prayer of faith is answered by God, and that in the hour of trial and need, the Lord opens the way and comes to the rescue of his servants."[27]

Carry Frisbey was asleep in his home in Braidwood, Illinois, in the late 1800s when he dreamed he saw the Prophet Joseph Smith. Joseph told Brother Frisbey to go to Denver, Colorado, to meet a man who would be waiting for him. From there, Joseph instructed, the two men were to go to Richmond, Missouri, to see David Whitmer.

At the time, Brother Frisbey's wife was just recovering from the measles, and two of his sons were ill with the same disease. He did not want to leave his family when they were so sick, but after hearing about his dream, Sister Frisbey insisted that her husband obey the Prophet's instructions. The account states:

"Arriving at the Denver station, he stepped out onto the depot platform and a man came up to him and asked what was wanted of him. They had never met before. The man introduced himself as John Jacob Snyder." Brother Snyder explained that he had been told by the Spirit to meet the train and that a man with a full, bushy beard would meet him and tell him what to do.

Unfortunately, Brother Frisbey did not have enough money to pay for his train fare. In order to fulfill his obligation, he asked a friend to take his place and accompany Mr. Snyder to David Whitmer's home in Missouri.

The account states "They met with David Whitmer, who told them that he had promised the Lord that he would make a statement of his beliefs and his testimony. He called it his 'living testimony' of the Book of Mormon and asked John J. Snyder to write it for him, which he did."[28]

Because of Brother Frisbey's dream, David Whitmer was able to leave a statement of his testimony for the entire world to read. After being introduced to each other in such an unusual way, Brother Frisbey and Brother Snyder remained friends for the rest of their lives.

James Ward was disturbed by his dream, a reoccurring one in which he saw a shoebox full of his "dreams" on fire. James felt sure the dream was some kind of warning, but he had no idea what it could mean.

Early one spring morning, James was sitting in the kitchen when his wife, Charlene, walked in. She knew by the look on his face that he'd had the dream again.

James told his wife that he'd had the dream three nights in a row then added, "I sure would be relieved if I could figure out what it means. I know its some kind of a warning because I keep dreaming it every night. I see myself down at the dump burning trash and when I throw this big old shoebox in the fire, I see all my dreams burning up too. It sure bothers me, that dream."[29]

The dream was not the only thing bothering James. He had decided to go into the hauling business for himself and was trying to get a second mortgage on his house so he could buy a truck. He worried about giving up his steady job, one which he'd had for ten years. Although James thought he could do well in his new business, doubts plaged him because the stakes were high. If he were unable to pay the loan, he might fail in his venture, and he and his wife could lose their home.

That morning when James went to work, his boss sent him to clean up an abandoned warehouse. The owner wanted to lease the building immediately and needed it cleaned up quickly. The owner told James that if he was able to do the job in one day that James could have anything of value he might find in the building. "Just get that place in shape today," he promised, "and anything that isn't nailed down is yours."[30]

James was sure that everything of value had already been carted off. The floors were strewn with rubbish, and huge piles of trash and empty cardboard boxes were piled up everywhere. James worked hard, clearing away the debris. Then he began carrying boxes and papers to the backyard where he lit a fire to burn them. The account states:

> He was about to throw a big pasteboard box containing a number of empty smaller boxes inside it into the fire when he stopped abruptly, recalling his dream. He had an eerie feeling that everything which he had pictured in the dream was suddenly coming true, happening just as he had known it would.
>
> He put the big carton down and poked around inside it, examining with curiosity a shoebox that looked oddly familiar. Of course, James thought, it was the shoebox full of dreams! He

> opened it and blinked in amazement. Now he understood the "warning" of his recurrent dreams. Inside that box was a large bundle of banknotes, $8,700. Had it not been for his inexplicably recurring dream he would not have looked inside that box and the money would have been burned.[31]

James finished cleaning the warehouse and then went to see the owner. Although the owner was astonished at the large sum, he remained true to his word and allowed James to keep the money. James Ward was able to buy his truck without getting a second mortgage. He went into business for himself and became a prosperous businessman.

Winona Hammond had always planned to have her first baby at her mother's home. Arrangements for the home birth had been made with the doctor, and he assured Winona that he would be able to come when called. Everyone in the family was eagerly looking forward to the birth. Suddenly, however, Winona's mother told Winona that she ought to have the baby at the hospital instead of at home as they had planned.

Winona was confused and wondered why her mother had changed her mind. Winona also felt disappointed; she had been looking forward to having her mother present when the baby was born. She decided to talk to her mother about the matter. When pressed for a reason, her mother revealed why she felt her daughter ought to go to the hospital. "I didn't want to tell you," she said, "for fear you'd become alarmed, but I had a dream last night and in it was a warning. The dream was so vivid that I knew you should not try to have the baby at home, but that you should go to the hospital instead."[32]

Winona agreed to have her baby at the hospital. When she went into labor, Winona promptly headed to the hospital. All went well during labor and delivery. But after the baby was born, Winona began hemorrhaging. She lost so much blood that a call went out for blood donors. Her mother could not donate because she had pernicious anemia. However, Winona's father gave blood—not once, but twice—to try and save his daughter's life.

Despite the transfusions, Winona went into shock because of loss of blood. Finally, the doctors managed to control the bleeding. Then the baby began having trouble breathing. The doctors tried artificial respiration and then placed the infant in a resuscitator. The baby's condition slowly improved, as did Winona's. In time, mother and child recovered enough to go home.

Later, Winona found out that her mother had not told her the entire dream. In Sister Hammond's dream, Winona and the baby had both died. However, because the family heeded the dream's warning, the lives of the both mother and infant were preserved.[33]

In the fall of 1861, Claudius Spencer was asked to provide an oxen team outfit, which was to be sent to Dixie in the southern part of Utah, to help the Saints who were homesteading there. He had part of the outfit but had to take out a loan for the rest of it. However, after sending the team off with a driver, Claudius was alerted in a dream that his outfit had been stolen. "One night, after retiring," he wrote, "I saw in my sleep the oxen and wagon coming down the Bingham canyon with a load of wood as plainly as I ever had seen them when awake."[34]

Sure that his dream was true, Claudius took one of his ranch hands and the two men started to hunt for the outfit. They had no luck locating the team. After returning home and eating lunch, the ranch hand starting hitching the mules to a wagon, intending to go plow in the fields, the original plan for the day. "I thought you had chased a dream long enough, and I would go and plow," he told Claudius.

Stung, Claudius told the man he had other plans for the afternoon. Claudius reported:

> I told him to take off the harness and I would prove to him that the dreams of the Saints amounted to something. We started out again on our search. About half past three, P.M. I noticed a sloping-roofed shed with the front shut up close with new boards. And on stopping our mules I saw the end of a wagon-tongue sticking out from under the bottom board. I alighted and went around to the back part of the shed, got in and found my wagon that I had sent to "Dixie." I took it home and the next day had the man, in whose charge the outfit was placed, before Bishop E. D. Woolley.[35]

While Elder J. D. C. was serving a mission to Wisconsin in 1899, his father passed away. Elder C. did not receive word of his father's death until the day of the funeral. Then, one week later, his father appeared to him, giving the young missionary advice and instruction. Elder C. said he took great comfort in seeing his father and was happy to receive his counsel.

After his father left, Elder C. was visited and instructed by other angels, one of whom was a young woman he knew from his childhood. Speaking of this visit, Elder C. said:

> She, like my father, told me I should not be able to record all the instruction she gave me, but that I would be convinced upon certain matters that had been rather obscure in my mind.
>
> She then told me of a number of our old playmates of our childhood days, who had gone from this sphere of action, and stated that some of them had not yet quite overcome some of their little habits of expression, which they had possessed in mortality: that in one instance in particular, a certain girl whom she called by name, sometimes felt that her associates were somewhat unkind to her, because of their neglecting to give her as much recognition in their games as she felt she should receive.[36]

Elder C. noticed how the angel dressed. He said:

> On one occasion while we were standing facing each other in conversation, I said: "You do not wear shoes do you?"—meaning leather shoes—although her beautiful white skirt hid her feet from view so that I could not see whether they were clad or not. . . .
>
> She raised her skirt sufficiently for me to see that she had on black leather slippers. She then lowered herself to the carpet and shuffled her slippers so that I could hear the sound distinctly, after which she arose to her former position and left the slippers on the carpet, side by side. She then told me that when it became necessary for heavenly beings to assume mortal appearance they could do so at pleasure, putting on or laying off the mortal clothing at will."[37]

After speaking with his visitor, Elder C. fell asleep. He later wrote:

> When I awoke to my natural surroundings in the room where I had slept, it was daylight, but I could still feel the heavenly influence of my visitor, and that feeling remained with me until about 4 P.M. of that day. There was one very peculiar feature of the visit which impressed me very much, and still seems to be very vivid in my recollection of that occasion, and it was the very pleasant feeling which passed through my whole body from head to foot whenever my heavenly attendant smiled on me. It was an indescribable feeling which was perfectly satisfying in its effects."[38]

Mary Dunster was not sure she wanted to marry William Chittenden. However, Mary decided to accept his proposal if he agreed to one condition: at some time in the future, he would take her to America. William promised to do so, and they were married in England. Years passed, but because of their financial situation, no plans were formulated to immigrate to America.

Then William and Mary moved to Goulburn, Australia. More years passed. Mary's hope of moving to America became fainter and fainter. When the couple had been married forty-two years, Mary had a dream.

The story states, "A personage came to her (Mary) and began talking to her of her affairs. This personage said to her among other things: 'You shall take a farm, on the opposite side of the road to where you now live. And, after, you shall prosper exceedingly. Then you shall take money, constantly, from this side of the road, and you shall be blessed, insomuch that you shall soon go to Zion thereafter.'"[39]

When Mary woke, she told her husband about her dream. Shortly afterwards, they learned that a near neighbor, by the name of Grimson, was about to move away and his property was available to rent. Mary was very excited, sure that this was the property of her dream. However, her husband refused to take on the farm, saying he had neither the tools to take care of it nor the animals to stock it.

Eventually, the farm was rented to someone else. A month or so later, Mary had the same dream, but this time she did not mention it to her husband. Asking around, Mary discovered that the new renters had left abruptly and the farm was once again available. She went to

William and told him about her second dream, begging him to rent the property.

Again, William refused, saying he did not have the means to run it.

Disappointed, Mary left to go to work. She was a housekeeper for Mrs. Day, who lived nearby. Mary mentioned the vacant farm to Mrs. Day, saying that she longed to rent the property but that her husband had no teams, machines, or animals.

She was overjoyed when Mrs. Day offered to lend William her horses, plows, and other farm machines without charge. Furthermore, Mrs. Day said she would provide seed grain for the first year's planting if William would pay her back after he got a good start on the farm. Mary hurried home and eagerly told her husband all the details. William then went to talk with Mrs. Day to confirm and accept her offer.

Just as her dream had foretold, the property across the road allowed William and Mary to make enough money to emigrate. William and Mary Chittenden left Sydney on 7 April 1877 with their children and made their way to Utah, where they made their home in Provo.

Henry Savage and his wife were living in England when they heard the gospel. They were both baptized. Shortly after, Henry was called to go on a mission. During his mission, Henry often felt discouraged because as a new convert he only had a superficial knowledge of the gospel.

Then, Henry had a dream where a stranger appeared and taught him various principles of the gospel. This unusual learning experience helped Henry immensely. For years Henry wondered about the man in his dream, but his identity remained a mystery—until a missionary from the United States brought a portrait of one of the Church leaders with him. When Henry saw the picture, he recognized the man in it as the one who had taught him the gospel in his dream. Elder Savage's experience is recorded by his son as follows:

> In 1844 my parents heard their first sermon on Mormonism and on June 2, 1844, were baptized by Elder John Banks of the London Conference. . . . It was customary not to ordain new converts to the priesthood until they had manifested their integrity to the faith by a godly attitude of life, but my father

[Henry Savage] had been a member but a short time when the president suggested that he be ordained an Elder. Some of the members of the Priesthood thought it was not well to be in a hurry about the matter.

Then the president of the branch said, "We will try the Spirit," which meant the Priesthood members would sit in silence for a short time and await the promptings of the Spirit. After a brief interval the president announced that it was the mind and will of the Lord that Henry Savage be ordained an Elder and sent out to preach the Gospel; whereupon the congregation consented.

Soon after entering the ministry he had the following divine dream or vision. In this dream he sat weaving at his loom which was in a room upstairs over the apartment where the family lived. As he thus sat weaving, a knock came on an outside door. As was the custom he called out, "Come In" without arising from the loom; whereupon a tall, fair, blue-eyed man of noble, majestic bearing entered the room. After cordially greeting the latter, the stranger accepted a seat and opened the scriptures and began instructing my father through the entire night until the Plan of Salvation was made clear to his understanding.

The stranger then bade my father goodnight and took his departure. When my father arose the next morning, he pondered much over the teachings he had received and who this strange personage might be. He was sure it was not any Elder either local or from Zion that he had met up with. He questioned a number from Zion . . . but it still remained a mystery for some time. Finally an Elder brought over to England a portrait of the Prophet Joseph Smith; and my father instantly recognized the face as the man of his dream.[40]

Elder John Van Wagoner had a dream where he saw a stranger as well. When he awoke, he was sure that the old woman he'd seen sitting in a rocking chair in his dream was waiting to hear the restored gospel. The dream had been so real that he could recall the hardwood floors of her home and that she lived in a circle-like neighborhood. Elder Van Wagoner only had one problem. He didn't know where the neighborhood was.

After praying, Elder Van Wagoner looked carefully at a map of Keene, New Hampshire, and picked out a neighborhood that had a circular layout. Later, during breakfast, the word *green* came into his mind. After eating, Elder Van Wagoner checked the map again and saw that right in the center of the neighborhood he had picked out earlier was a Green Street.

He and his companion, Elder David Israel, set off for Green Street. They began knocking on doors. After visiting ten homes with no success, Elder Wagoner wondered if he had made a mistake. But at the next house, an older woman came to the door. Although she was not as old as the woman he had pictured in his dream, Elder Van Wagoner felt a new wave of confidence, which diminished rapidly when he saw that there were no hardwood floors and no rocking chair.

Although the woman agreed to listen to the elders, she refused to set a return appointment. Elder Van Wagoner wondered if he had truly been inspired or if his dream meant nothing. Elder Israel reassured him that his dream was surely sent from God, and the two men continued their efforts. At the next home, there was no response to their initial knock, but Elder Van Wagoner felt impressed to knock again.

"An older lady came to the door," the story goes. "Marian Davis, recently widowed, said she was a member of another church. Elder Van Wagoner asked her to let them share an important message with her. On the condition that they be brief, she let them in."[41]

The missionaries followed the elderly woman over the hardwood floors to the sitting room where she sat down in a rocking chair. She listened to their message and invited them to return. Three weeks later, Sister Davis was baptized.

A critically ill woman had a dream that instructed her what to do in order to survive. An account of her experience was published in the *Juvenile Instructor*:

"A sister belonging to one of the branches of the Church in Europe was taken suddenly very ill while in a settlement at some little distance from where the Saints were located. She was taken to the hospital where both physicians and nurses pronounced her beyond recovery."

The woman knew that if something did not happen soon, she would die. "While reflecting on her condition she fell asleep, and dreamed that she was taken on her bed to the place where the branch to which she belonged was located, and there, through the administration of the Elders, was restored to health. The impression left on her mind by this dream was so vivid that on awakening she requested her attendants to take her to the cars and place her therein that she might return to her home."

Everyone was appalled at her request. "Her physicians and nurses protested, but to no purposes, and she was accordingly sent to her home. Here the Elders were called in and she was anointed and blessed: her recovery was almost instantaneous and an affliction, from which she had suffered more or less for years, was removed as if by magic."[42]

Elder Milton R. Hunter was attending stake conference one Sunday when the stake president related an interesting story about a woman who had a dream that convinced her to follow the teachings of the Church more closely. Elder Hunter recorded the following story:

> He [the stake president] reported that there was a certain lady living in his ward who had joined the Church over in Europe when she was a girl; and like many of the European people she had formed the habit of drinking tea. After she joined the Church of Jesus Christ, like quite a few Mormons (I am sorry to say) she continued the habit of drinking tea. She reared a large family. Her children married. Her husband died, and she became a widow. And then she became a temple worker. Day after day she went to the temple, and no doubt the consciousness of the tea-drinking habit she had bore rather heavily on her mind or on her conscience. One night she had a dream.
>
> She dreamed that she died and that she passed on into the other world. There she came into the presence of the Savior, the Prophet Joseph Smith, and many other great and good people who had lived on this earth and whose lives had been such that they were now worthy to become celestial beings. Very sweet, serene, and happy were the feelings that she experienced there. In fact, there were no words to describe how beautiful the conditions were there, until she looked down into her hand and saw her old dirty, black teapot. Then her happiness turned to sorrow and shame.
>
> She immediately looked all around in the heavenly realm for

> some place to hide that teapot, but she couldn't find any place. She had to hang on to it. Then she awoke. Cold drops of perspiration were running down her face. She got out of bed, turned the light on, dressed, and went in the other room. There on her stove sat her old dirty teapot. She picked it up, went down to the back of the lot and threw it into the Jordan River, and she said, "There! I am not going to take you to heaven with me."[43]

Marilyn S. Bateman had a dream reassuring her that she and her family were making the right decision when they decided to move. At the time, her husband, Merrill J., had been offered a position at Brigham Young University but had turned it down. Undaunted, President Dallin H. Oaks contacted her husband a number of times, hoping that Merrill would change his mind. Marilyn and Merrill finally decided to accept the job, although Marilyn remained uneasy about the move—being concerned about her children. Because of her uneasiness, Marilyn continued to pray but received no comforting assurance that she and her husband were doing the right thing.

Then, she had a dream. She states:

> One night a few weeks before we were to leave for Provo, I had a dream that awakened me in the middle of the night. In the dream I was terribly upset because my father was dying and I was unable to return home. I woke up my husband and related the dream to him. After some discussion we felt that it was the Lord's way of assuring me that the decision to move was right.
>
> A few weeks later we arrived in Provo, where we were glad to be with our parents again. We enjoyed spending time with them and renewing family relationships. One month after our arrival we were visiting my parents when my dad began having chest pains. Mother hurriedly took him to the hospital. By evening he was gone.
>
> The experience of losing a parent is traumatic. I will never forget the sadness I felt, but I remembered the dream and now more fully understood its meaning and purpose. The month prior to my father's death was an important time for our children to become reacquainted with their grandfather and for President Bateman and me to express our love and support for both Dad and Mom. It was also important that we were there

to support my mother in a time of great need. In the months that followed, our appreciation for the Lord deepened as we knew He was aware of us and had prompted us to change our course.[44]

When Mary Elizabeth Rollins Lightner fell critically ill and the doctors were unable to help her, she received lifesaving guidance when an angel spoke to her in a dream.

Mary first became ill while living near Nauvoo, and doctors tried various remedies without much success. She continued to grow weaker and weaker, until everyone was convinced she would soon die. But Mary held onto life and even managed to rally slightly. Unfortunately, because her husband had used every penny they had on doctors and medicines, they could no longer afford to stay in their home. After being forced out of their house, all of the children came down with chills and fever—most likely caused from malaria. Brother Lightner was left to do all the cooking and nursing by himself. Mary states:

> My case proved to be biliousness, with a fever, in a bad form. I was again given up to die. We got a little girl to stay a day, then Mr. Lightner took the baby on a pillow and rode horseback to Nauvoo for mother to take care of it. I never expected to see it again, the thoughts of leaving my little children in the condition we were in, seemed more than I could bear.
>
> I thought of all that the Prophet Joseph had told me, and felt in my heart that it was all true. I prayed for help to get well, but the doctor coming in, said there was no hope for me.
>
> But I dreamed that an angel came to me and said if I would go to Nauvoo and call for a Brother Cutler, that worked on the temple, to administer to me, I should be healed. But we could get no team to go. I was in despair; however, my brother was impressed to send for me, he felt that something was wrong, so he sent a boy with an ox team after me. I was so glad, that for a few moments I felt new life. But the people said I would not get a mile from town when he would have to bring back my dead body. But I said I wanted to be buried in Nauvoo, and pleaded with them to take me there, dead or alive.
>
> So after fixing a bed in the wagon, they placed me on it; the neighbors bid me goodbye as they supposed for the last

time. . . . We went a few miles further, stopped at a house and asked to stay all night. The woman was willing until she saw me. She said I would die before morning and she did not want me to die in her house.

Mr. Lightner told her that I would certainly die if I was left in the open wagon all night. She finally let us in. She made us as comfortable as she could and fixed me some light food; after drinking some tea, I felt better and had a good night's rest. But she was glad when we left, for she thought I would never see Nauvoo. After traveling a few miles further, we finally reached Nauvoo. They still thought me dying.

Mr. Lightner asked Brother Burt if there was an old man by the name of Cutler working on the temple. He said, "yes." Mr. Lightner told him my dream; soon they brought him, he administered to me and I got up and walked to the fire alone. In two weeks I was able to take care of my children.[45]

When Elder M. F. Cowley went into the mission field in 1878, he was told by Elder John Morgan, who presided over the Southern States Mission, about "the absolute necessity of traveling without 'purse or scrip.'" Elder Morgan cautioned all new missionaries to avoid sending home for money, explaining that many elders who depended upon support from home had "made total failures of their missions."[46]

Wanting to be successful as a missionary, Elder Cowley decided that he would follow Elder Morgan's advice to the letter. He and his companion, Elder Barnett, began tracting in Kentucky and from there went to Virginia. A few months later, the missionaries started out for a new area but ran out of money before reaching their destination. As they had been advised to do, the elders wrote members of the Church in the area, asking for help in the way of loans. Unfortunately, they did not receive any assistance. After a few days, Elder Cowley and Elder Barnett managed to find a landlord willing to extend them credit for their lodging, but they had little money left over for meals.

Elder Cowley said that for food, he and Elder Barnett "expended sometimes five cents, sometimes ten cents a day each for a few crackers and a little cheese or a bowl of bread and milk."[47]

While in these dire circumstances, Elder Cowley had a dream. He wrote that "I dreamed that I was housed up in a room where there was no air, and in struggling for breath I would turn to the North, then to the East, then to the South, but in vain, until I turned my face to the West, when it seemed that an opening was made in the enclosure and I breathed with freedom. Upon awakening I felt very depressed, for it seemed to me that the dream meant while we had friends North of us in Kentucky, East in Virginia, and South in Georgia, the only hope was to write home for money and this I fought against with a strong resolution."[48]

Then, Elder Cowley had a second dream. He continues:

> Again, I slept and dreamed that I received two letters from home in the same mail, one was in a pale, cream-colored envelope, the other, the old-fashioned deep yellow, and addressed to me in my mother's hand-writing. When I awoke in the morning I was still depressed, for while the dreams were clear to my mind as having a decided importance, it was against my inclination to write home for money, so I held out for several days, and did not tell my companion the dream.
>
> In a few days, however, Elder Barnett made a remark to me, which impressed me that it was my duty to write for means, which I did, and when the answer came, there were two letters instead of one. One was contained in a pale, cream-colored envelope, the other a deep yellow, addressed to me in my mother' s handwriting, in all particulars just as I had seen it in my dream, and containing means for our assistance. . . .
>
> The lessons I learned by my experience of trial and dreams in Chattanooga were very useful. The experience taught me that while a doctrine is true . . . no man can carry it out by his own strength, it must be done by the help of the Lord, or it can not be done at all.[49]

David L. Hardy had a dream that guided him to protect his young son. The story begins in early spring when David got a call from an old friend, Bill Olsen, who wanted David to rebuild the roof on his cabin, which had collapsed during the winter from heavy snow. The mountain cabin was above Sundance, Utah, in a beautiful area, nestled in the midst of tall pine trees with a picturesque stream nearby. As the weather became warmer, David began taking his little son, Kenny, with him. Kenny was three years old and loved being with his father. Every day he would wake up, eager to dress just like his dad in a flannel shirt, Levis, and little work boots. He proudly wore a little pouch around his waist to carry his own miniature tools.

While at the cabin, Kenny loved to explore and was fascinated by the birds, squirrels, and other wildlife. David was careful to keep a close watch on Kenny and taught him to stay well away from the stream, which was swollen from melting snow. David's brother, Rusty, came to work with David every day and also helped keep an eye on his nephew.

As the weeks passed, Kenny began to feel more confident about his surroundings and began exploring further, widening his range. He especially liked to sit on a stack of logs piled a short distance from the stream, where he could throw rocks and sticks into the water.

Then David had a dream.

"One night," he recalled, "after taking Kenny with me for four or five weeks, I had a terrible dream. It was not a normal dream, it was much more intense. I woke up literally in a cold sweat after dreaming that he had fallen into the rushing water and drowned. It was so real and scared me so badly that I sat up in bed and found myself shaking. I couldn't go back to sleep. . . . I had the distinct feeling that this dream was a warning not to be disregarded. I woke (my wife) Georgia up and told her the experience."[50]

Georgia declared, "We knew right then that it was indeed a real warning." She agreed with her husband that it would be best not to take their son to the cabin again.

David continues, "Then I started worrying about disappointing Kenny and wondered how I could tell him that he wouldn't be able to go with me to work on the cabin again."[51] Georgia also was concerned about how her son would react, knowing how much Kenny loved playing around the cabin.

The next morning, Kenny got up and went into his parents' bedroom. David began helping him put on his shoes and socks, trying to think how he could tell his son that he had to stay home.

But little Kenny spoke up first. He had something important he wanted to tell his father.

Kenny said, "Dad, I can't go to work with you today."

"Why not, Kenny?" David asked, surprised.

"'Cause I will drown in the river."

Tears came to David's eyes as he realized that his son had received the same warning dream that he had received.

Although David and his wife had been anxious that Kenny would be upset about not being able to go to the cabin as he had been doing, Georgia said, "He never showed an interest in going again during the reconstruction process. We thought he'd cry, but he never raised a fuss."[52]

Receiving this dream filled David and Georgia with joy and peace because they knew that Heavenly Father was watching over them and had given them a warning that helped preserve the life of their young son.

In 1832, John Tanner saw an advertisement for a meeting that would be presented by missionaries from The Church of Jesus Christ of Latter-day Saints. He decided to go. On the appointed evening, John started out, limping as he went because his leg had never healed from being bitten by a dog six months earlier.

As he listened to the message of the restored gospel, John was impressed. Afterwards, he went up and asked the missionaries if they would give him a blessing. They agreed to do so. Laying their hands on his head, the elders pronounced a blessing upon him. When John stood up to shake their hands, he discovered that his leg had been instantly healed. Because of this miraculous healing, John was immediately converted and asked Elder Simeon Carter to baptize him.

Sometime later, John heard that Joseph Smith was asking for volunteers to join Zion's Camp. He talked with his family, and together they decided that two of his sons would go. Unlike most Church members, John Tanner was wealthy and was able to provide his two sons, John and Nathan, with a team, wagon, and first-class outfits.

Later in the year, in December, John dreamed that the leaders of the Church needed him. When he woke up, John felt impressed to leave immediately. As he began making preparations, his neighbors tried to persuade him to stay, citing the snow and the cold weather. However, John pressed on, sure that the dream meant there was some unknown crisis the Church was facing that he alone could help with.

John Tanner left his home on Christmas day, accompanied by another son. In the dead of winter, they traveled five hundred miles and reached Kirtland on 20 January 1835. The record states:

> On his arrival in Kirtland, he learned that at the same time he received the impression that he must move immediately to the Church (in Kirtland), the Prophet Joseph and some of the brethren had met in prayer-meeting and asked the Lord to send them a brother or some brethren with means to assist them to lift the mortgage on the farm upon which the temple was being built.
>
> The day after his (John's) arrival in Kirtland, by invitation from the prophet, he and his son, Sidney, met with the High Council, and were informed that the mortgage of the before mentioned farm was about to be foreclosed. Whereupon he loaned the prophet two thousand dollars and took his note on interest for which amount the farm was redeemed. He loaned to the Temple Committee, Hyrum Smith, Reynolds Cahoon and Jared Carter, thirteen thousand dollars in merchandize at cost prices in New York, and took their note for the same. This amount, and that loaned to the prophet, were not included in his liberal donations to the building of the temple, from time to time.[53]

Elder Tom Shreeve was serving a mission in South Wales when his companion, Elder May, was called away. Although Elder Shreeve continued to labor diligently, he felt somewhat lonely and dispirited.

"Not long after I was left alone I had a strange dream concerning my labors," Elder Shreeve relates. "I thought that I was called to take a mission to the East. The idea was very vivid in my mind, though no steps or time seemed to have been made clear to me. When I awoke, I thought upon the matter, and interpreted it as meaning that, after my return to Zion, I should have another mission—probably to Europe."[54] Elder Shreeve tried to dismiss the dream from his mind but found that it continued to pop up from time to time.

He recalls, "The idea remained persistently with me for three or four days; and then one afternoon when I took up a book and sought to read, suddenly the printed lines were blurred from me, and these words started out from the page:

"'You must go to New Zealand.'

"I rubbed my eyes, astonished, and looked again. The words had disappeared, and for a few moments I was able to read the book. But again these words came upon the page, shutting out the printed lines from my sight:

"'You are wanted in New Zealand.'"[55]

Despite these manifestations, Elder Shreeve never felt that he should go *immediately,* since he and Elder May already planned to travel there together in December.

Elder Shreeve explained, "Not understanding that this was a command to me which I ought to obey; and feeling in a measure bound by my agreement with my companion, I could not, despite all these repeated instructions, bring myself to a compliance with it."[56]

However, during the next few days, several strange and terrible incidents occurred. The first happened one night when Elder Shreeve went to bed. When he laid down, the missionary said he felt as if he were being crushed by some invisible force. "It seemed to me that I was losing myself and must soon die, if I could not obtain relief."[57] In fear and anguish, he called out to the Lord for help. Instantly, the terrible, overpowering feeling went away, leaving him grateful for God's protecting hand.

But it happened again. Later that night, the same horrible feeling came over him. He was convinced that he was about to be overpowered by the forces of darkness. The missionary stated, "The sensation which I experienced at the time I was in the grasp of this power was as distinctly painful as any physical suffering I ever endured, and more intense than any ordinary physical pain can be."[58]

Elder Shreeve thought the feeling might be somewhat similar to the torment Joseph Smith experienced just before seeing the Father and the Son.

"After this, the feeling that I must go to New Zealand was borne irresistibly," Elder Shreeve stated. "The last emphatic warning had shown me that Sydney was no place for me at this hour, and that I must heed the commandments which were given to me."[59]

The next day, he obtained passage on a ship. After his arrival, the missionary was hauling his luggage across the gangway when a man suddenly rushed up to him and asked, "Do you know of anyone by the name of Shreeve on board this vessel?"

Although he had never seen the man before, Elder Shreeve exclaimed, "You are Brother Nordstrand!"

"Yes; and you are Brother Shreeve! Allow me to welcome you to New Zealand."[60]

The man clasped the missionary's hand as if they were old acquaintances. Later, Elder Nordstrand told the missionary how he had happened to arrive at the ship in time to meet him. Elder Shreeve noted:

> [Elder Nordstrand explained,] "I live at Styx. This morning in a dream, a personage—a young man of pleasing appearance, clothed in a white robe—visited me and instructed me to go to Port Littleton this morning and meet the steamer Wakatipu and find among her passengers a man named Shreeve, who was a 'Mormon Elder coming to visit the Saints in New Zealand.'
>
> "The vision was so vivid that I was roused from my sleep; and, when it was ended, I sprang out of bed and looked at the clock. I found the hour to be 4 A.M. Two hours later I saddled my horse and rode to Christchurch, a distance of six or seven miles. There I took train for Port Littleton, nine miles away, and arrived here to meet you."
>
> The sole information and instruction upon which Brother Nordstrand acted was that conveyed to him in this dream. In a later conversation I learned that in the same vision he had been shown all the consequences which would attend upon my ministration in New Zealand. The event proved that this dream to Brother Nordstrand was one of the greatest blessings of my life. I encountered much tribulation in New Zealand; no more from the bigotry of the world than from the perfidy of my own brethren. But through all the trouble Brother Nordstrand was my devoted friend. He had never a moment of doubt, because all which happened had been by him foreseen.[61]

Shortly after his arrival, Elder Shreeve held his first meeting at Prebbleton. He told the audience about the strange circumstances that had led him to arrive in New Zealand much sooner than he had intended.

When Elder Shreeve finished speaking, he said, "When I sat down a good sister named Mortensen arose and said: 'Brother Shreeve, I can tell you why you received the command to come to New Zealand immediately. It was in answer to our fervent prayer. For more than three months previous to your arrival here we had been anxiously supplicating the Lord to send us an Elder from Utah."[62]

In one instance, a doctor, who isn't identified by a complete name, was guided by a dream, which proved later to be a provident warning that protected him from danger.

The account states, "A few years ago, Dr. W., now residing in Glasgow, dreamt that he received a summons to attend a patient at a place some miles from where he was living; that he started on horseback; and that, as he was crossing a moor, he saw a bull making furiously at him, whose horns he only escaped by taking refuge on a spot inaccessible to the animal, where he waited a long time, till some people, observing his situation, came to his assistance and released him."[63]

When Dr. W. woke, he puzzled over the vivid but curious dream and then went about his usual morning routine. The account continues:

> While at breakfast on the following morning, the summons came; and, smiling at the odd coincidence, he started on horseback. He was quite ignorant of the road he had to go; but by and by he arrived at the moor, which he recognized, and presently the bull appeared, coming full tilt towards him. But his dream had shown him the place of refuge, for which he instantly made; and there he spent three or four hours, besieged by the animal, till the country people set him free. Dr. W. declares that, but for the dream, he should not have known in what direction to run for safety.[64]

A tired father, weary from long, late night hours spent watching over his seriously ill baby had a dream that reminded him about the power the priesthood has to heal the sick. The dream prompted him to call the elders and ask them to give his infant son a life-preserving blessing.

Lewis Stewart was one of the elders asked to administer to the sick infant. Elder Stewart noted that when he arrived at the house, "my heart first throbbed with fear and then it seemed almost to stop beating, for there I saw, lying on its mother's lap, the little child; disease had blanched its little cheek, and oh! its eyes were sunken and glazed. Surely that was death.

"But rousing myself . . . we blessed the baby, and the great Physician heard our prayers. It seemed to me that even while our hands were on the little head sickness left and life and health, taking its place, flowed like a fountain through all the little veins carrying to the limbs strength and to the features beauty."[65]

The baby made an amazing recovery. After the blessing, the father told the elders why he had called them to come and administer to his baby.

He said, "You know the baby had been sick for some time and we had doctor's help; we gave it the medicine prescribed, and watched and nursed it day and night. I would tend the baby from evening until three or four o'clock in the morning, then waking my wife from her too short sleep, would lie down to get a nap before going to work. In this way we worked until we were nearly worn out, as you know. One morning I laid down, with my clothes on as I always did, and while sleeping had an interesting dream.

"I thought that going to Z.C.M.I. drug store to get medicine for the baby, I got a bottle, wrapped in white paper and tied with a red string (the way drug store goods are usually fixed up) and returning home untied the string, and removing the paper found a bottle of what seemed to be *olive oil.*"

The father explained that seeing the oil reminded him of the consecrated oil the elders used to administer to those who were ill or afflicted. Recalling the power of the priesthood in healing, the father said, "I awoke, and thanking God for the lesson, asked you brethren to call, with the happy result we witnessed."[66]

Dreams truly can be remarkable experiences with life-altering consequences. Jane Elizabeth Manning, an early convert to the Church, saw the Prophet Joseph Smith in a dream long before she met him in person.

Jane Manning was a Presbyterian when a missionary, Elder Charles Wandell, came to Connecticut to preach. Jane listened to his message and wanted to know more. The elders taught the Manning family, eventually baptizing Jane and eight members of her family. The Mannings then decided to join the Saints at the headquarters of the Church, which at that time was in Illinois.

In October 1843, Jane and her family joined a large group of Saints who had also decided to move to Illinois. However, they became separated from the rest of the group when boat authorities refused to let the Manning family members, who were black, on a steamer taking the Saints the eight hundred miles to Nauvoo.

The Mannings began walking but were briefly imprisoned in Illinois when they could not show their "free papers." They explained to the local authorities that they were not slaves and had always been free, so they were not required to have free papers.

When Jane and her family finally arrived in Nauvoo, they asked Orson Spencer to direct them to the home of Joseph and Emma Smith. At their knock, Emma opened the door and invited them in. Joseph was in another room talking with a friend when Emma called him to come to the front parlor and meet their guests.

When the Prophet walked into the room, Jane said, "I knew it was Brother Joseph because I had seen him in a dream." Later, she reiterated that experience, noting that "when he came in with Dr. Bernhisel I knew him. Did not have to tell me because I knew him. I knew him when I saw him in Old Connecticut in a vision, saw him plain and knew he was a prophet."[67]

John H. Thorpe dreamed that a departed neighbor returned to inform him that he was going to be called to go on a mission. John recalls:

> In the fall of 1885 I had a visit or a dream from Brother Leatham who was dead. I dreamed that I went to Brother Leatham's home to do some house cleaning . . . and when I went outside to the gate, who should I meet but Brother Leatham himself.
>
> I knew he was dead and he held out his hand and shook hands with me, and I felt his hands, I said, "Why, Brother Leatham, you have got your resurrected body," and he said, "Yes, I have got it." . . .
>
> Then he shook me by the arm and started to walk off with me up a path, and he said to me, "John, how would you like to go on a mission?"
>
> And I said, "If I am worthy I would like to go on one."
>
> And he said, "I have come to tell you that you are going to

be called on a home mission right away, and then after you have finished that mission, you are going to be called on a mission a long, long ways from home."

And I said, "Then if I am called I will go."

And he said, "Yes, I know you will, and you will fill a faithful mission."

So then he talked to me and wanted to know how all my folks was getting along, and I told him.

So when we came to the end of the road he said, "Then I will have to be going," and he turned his back to me and started off and I started the other way, and then I thought I would like to have another look at him as that is the first resurrected being that I ever saw, but when I turned around he had disappeared.[68]

Not many months passed before John Thorpe's dream was realized. John continues his story:

> While at a Cache Stake Conference on the 7th of February, 1886, I was called on a home mission with Aaron D. Thatcher, brother of Apostle Moses Thatcher, to travel for twelve months, visiting all the settlements in Cache Valley from Avon to Clarkston.
>
> "Then came May 17th, 1889, then came my call to New Zealand. I just had a contract and was plastering the Thatcher Bank and Opera House, so I turned it all over to my brother Thomas, and he and the boys finished up the building. When I got in Salt Lake City, Thomas Morgan, the main boss of the Salt Lake Temple wanted me to stay and plaster there. I told him, no. I had a more important job than that. I was going to New Zealand on a mission. And they gave me a companion, Monroe Hexon, from Southern Utah. And Apostle Heber J. Grant set us both apart and gave us some valuable instruction for our mission and said that we would be protected against dangers, both seen and unseen, and fulfill faithful missions and return in safety.[69]

Many people receive valuable guidance and direction through dreams. When Thomas Durham was very young, his parents discovered that he was talented musically. They encouraged Thomas to develop his musical abilities, and when he turned twelve, they sent him away to a special academy so he could study music.

Thomas was a teenager when he and his parents were introduced to The Church of Jesus Christ of Latter-day Saints. He and his parents began attending a local branch while they were being taught by the missionaries and naturally, Thomas was very interested in the choir. When the choir leader decided to immigrate to the United States, the branch president asked young Thomas to be the new choir leader, even though he was not yet a member of the Church. He happily accepted.

Thomas was baptized in 1849 and three years later received a remarkable blessing from Elder Cyrus H. Wheelock.

The account records, "[Thomas] was told that he should be blessed with the visitation of heavenly beings who should reveal music to him in his dreams, and that he should remember that music and write it and sing it in the congregations of the Saints and in the temples of the Most High."

In 1856, Thomas sailed to America and then traveled across the plains with the Martin Handcart Company. After arriving in Salt Lake City, he set out for Parowan, arriving in mid-December. Thomas was immediately asked to take charge of the choir in his new ward.

In May 1870, President Brigham Young was passing through the area when he stopped and listened to the choir. Impressed by the lovely music, President Young asked Thomas if he would take his choir to Salt Lake to sing during the October general conference. Thomas and his choir returned several times to Salt Lake in the coming years. Over the years, he directed several choirs and led several bands and orchestras.

Elder Wheelock's prophetic blessing did come to pass. Over the years, Thomas had at least seven tunes revealed to him in his dreams. He wrote the following account of how he received one of those tunes:

> I dreamed I was standing at the head of a large river which ran due west. There was a neck of land about eight rods long and about two rods wide. . . . The sun was nearly down and I was alone. The country was heavily timbered behind me. All at once I heard a rustling in the underbrush; I turned and saw an Indian coming toward me. He resembled a Navajo Indian. . . .
>
> At this time I heard another rustling behind me. I looked and saw about thirty more Indians coming toward me. They came to where I was standing and formed a circle. The old chief stood on the east side, and on his left was a young man with a

rifle in his hand, and on the west of the circle was a young man with a brass horn in his hand. When the circle was formed the chief pointed his finger at the one with the horn, who stepped out and walked down to the edge of the water to the west end of the neck of land and played a tune, which I heard. He missed the two high notes in the latter part of the tune, but I seemed to know what he was trying to get. Then he came back and took his place in the circle. . . .

I awoke and lay thinking whether to get out of bed and go to the organ and play it, for I knew then that I should not forget it, but as I lay I fell asleep again and I heard the same tune repeated on a horn. And I again awoke. It was then just breaking day, so I arose and went immediately to the organ and played it over. My family wondered what was the matter, until I explained the circumstance to them. I afterwards wrote it and arranged it for the choir, and it is quite a favorite here—we sing it to (the tune of) the hymn "O My Father."[70]

Although Jesse Knight was a member of The Church of Jesus Christ of Latter-day Saints, he was not active and was troubled because he did not have a testimony. However, all that changed when he had a dream. Not only did Jesse's dream give him a testimony that Joseph Smith was a true prophet of God, (and that the Church was true as well), it also revealed the location of a mine. While the location of a mine might seem out of place in a dream sent from God, this bit of information turned out to have tremendous consequences—not only for Jesse but for the entire Church.

After the dream, Jesse meticulously followed the instructions he had been given. By doing so, he was able to find—on a mountain in Eureka, Utah—the place that had been shown to him in his dream. Just as the dream had foretold—Jesse found a rich vein. He hired workers, gathered the necessary mechanical equipment, and began to dig.

At this time, the Church was in a desperate financial condition. The country was in a depression, and money was very scarce. President Woodruff was increasingly worried about the Church's finances. He did not know how he could save the Church's credit, for he did not have the resources needed to pay even the interest on the loans the Church had taken out. Meanwhile, Jesse was optimistic about the future.

In 1896, Jesse told his son, J. William Knight, "We (the family) are going to have all the money we want as soon as we are able to handle it properly. We will someday save the credit of the Church." When his son argued that such a thing was not possible, Jesse replied, "I don't want to quarrel with you about it, but I never had anything come to me with greater force than the impression that came to me at this time."[71]

In a short time, the mine began to yield as the workers worked the vast mineral body. When the first large batch of ore came out, it was worth much more than had been initially projected. After paying the miners and the cost of production, Jesse found that he had a profit of ten thousand dollars.

Following October's general conference in 1930, Jesse Knight's bishop, Joseph B. Keeler, was at a special priesthood meeting. At this meeting, President Woodruff had a special request to make. President Woodruff asked all the bishops that were present to visit any members of their ward who were "possessed of means and who might be able to lend money to the Church for a short period."

Bishop Joseph B. Keeler said, "This particular request went entirely out of my mind until . . . I was returned home from our Tabernacle services and . . . a voice said to me . . . 'Jesse Knight will lend the Church $10,000.' . . .

"[I] immediately changed my clothes and went to the home of 'uncle Jesse' and found him in his parlor reading. After a few preliminary greetings, I rehearsed to him what President Woodruff has said about the Church being financially embarrassed. But before I could ask him whether he would make the loan, he said instantly, 'Yes, I'll lend the Church $10,000.'"[72]

Jesse gave the money to President Woodruff, who then used it to pay the interest on the Church's loans, saving the Church's credit.

The mine kept producing, and Jesse continued his philanthropic inclinations. He blessed the lives of many and was known as the patron saint of Brigham Young University. Jesse continued to give generously until his death in 1921. His contributions to Brigham Young University amounted to over $500,000. One of Jesse's sons said that his father "tried to impress his children that any money we should get should be used wisely, for he thought it was being shown to him for the purpose of doing good. . . . He regarded the money as a trusted stewardship."[73]

Alexandre Mourra was a man of faith. He was also the only member of the Church in Haiti when J. F. Templeman, a diplomat for the Canadian Embassy, arrived there. The two men quickly became good friends. One day, J. F. confided to Alexandre his deep desire to go to medical school but acknowledged there were so many obstacles that it seemed very unlikely.

Then Alexandre had a dream.

Since J. F. knew his friend was in close contact with God, he listened intently when Alexandre told him about the dream—and then he acted. J. F. said of Alexandre:

> He had visions. When it was time for me to go to medical school, I was 36 years of age. You just didn't get into medical school. There were 800 applicants for 40 places or something like that.
>
> So he (Alexandre) came to me and he said, "I had a dream. I saw you in a room with four people. They were congratulating you and shaking your hand, so you're in. You'll get in." He told me that it was a big room with funny floors, like they were marble only they really weren't. It was terrazzo. So he saw the interview. And, at the end, they all shook my hand. I didn't find out then, that I was accepted, but he said, "You can go. You'll be all right."
>
> I had so much faith in what he said, that I quit my job in advance of getting into medical school, and I got into medical school. And there were four people that interviewed me, but he saw them. So when I applied I had to quit my job as a diplomat before I knew I was accepted or not.[74]

Ogden Kraut had a warning dream that protected him from serious harm, perhaps even death. He states:

> I dreamed that I was alone driving my car down a road at night. The lights of the car showed the road to be clear and in good condition. Strangely, the car seemed to be gaining speed.
>
> Suddenly a voice spoke to me and said, "Slow down."
>
> I could see no danger in the road; but the voice repeated the

same word twice more as though it was a serious warning to me. In an instant everything seemed to vanish into blackness and I awoke in terror. There didn't seem to be any interpretation so I soon dismissed it and went back to sleep.

The next evening I was visiting some friends who lived in the country. It was quite late in the evening when I left. They lived on a high hill; and as I was driving down the hill, the car began to gain in speed. Suddenly I recognized everything exactly as I saw it in my dream—alone in my car, driving at night, the lights on the clear road and my car gaining speed.

Immediately I slowed down not waiting for the strange voice to tell me to do so. At the bottom of the hill there was a little rise in the road. As I went over this rise, there was a herd of black cows in the middle of the road. I would have crashed into them if I had not been warned of that danger in that dream.[75]

Emelius Berg had a dream that came in two parts. In the first, Emelius found himself preaching the gospel in the next life, and in the second, he learned more about temple ordinances and the Resurrection. Emelius records his experience as follows:

About the latter part of February of this year I had the following dream: I found myself in the spirit world, and I saw a great multitude of people, in fact, millions upon millions of them. I thought I had come there to preach the gospel. There appeared to be several persons preaching the gospel, and hearing and seeing those persons thus engaged brought to my mind the object of my visit there.

I then started in to preach the gospel of Jesus Christ as it was given to me. I taught them that those present should believe in Jesus Christ, as the Son of God, who had been there and introduced Himself as the Son of God, and who had been slain in the flesh. I promised them that inasmuch as they would receive His doctrine, work should be done for them upon the earth in the temples of our God.

I awoke, and meditated for a time upon the dream, and then fell asleep again, when I had a continuation of the dream. I thought I saw persons being resurrected from the dead, which caused me to wonder. All at once through the Spirit, or some person, was shown to me the manner of the resurrection, and I thought I had the power given me to bring forth the dead. It was as simple in performance as baptism for the remission of sins. The dead were called forth in the name and by the authority of the Lord Jesus Christ, and I saw them come forth. Those that I saw arise were arrayed in white robes.

I now awoke, and cannot describe joy and satisfaction that the Spirit gave me. I rejoiced before the Lord. I saw in my dream no other preachers than Latter-day Saint Elders.[76]

A woman whose name is not known had the following experience in the fall of 1884. "It was in September when the following dream was given to me, after I had retired to rest," she relates. "I dreamed I was sitting in a room, when Sister Abigail Abbott (who had been dead for many years) appeared to me. She was dressed in white and looked most beautiful, although in my dream I realized that she was dead. She gazed at me most intently for a moment and then asked me if I fully understood the parable of the 'wise and foolish virgins.' That there was still something else required of us besides striving to keep the 'laws of God.'"[77]

Abigail went on to explain that everything people did to prepare to meet Christ would be futile to some extent unless they had certain items of clothing prepared. She did not elaborate on exactly what type of clothing this was, other than to explain that there were various pieces that should be worn in order to be prepared to meet the "bridegroom."

"Abigail asked how many people in Israel would be ready if they heard the following cry; 'Lo, the Bridegroom cometh, go ye out to meet him?'"

Abigail then answered her own question by stating very solemnly, "'Few indeed.'"

The woman said that Abigail "looked me full in the face and said very earnestly, 'I want you to get yours ready, and tell *all* your sisters to do the same.'" Abigail cautioned her to not put them in a drawer with other clothing but to put them in a little box all by themselves and added once more, "'Be sure and get them ready.'"

Then, as if worried that she might not fully understand the importance of being ready, Abigail allowed her friend to see a vision of the Savior coming to earth during His second coming. The woman said that people were running back and forth in all directions. Some were dressed in their best clothes, while others were only half dressed.

She said, "Among all this confusion I saw the Saints of God who had prepared their wedding garments going quietly along, for they made no noise excepting the rustling of their apparel, to meet their Savior."

After this vision, Abigail turned to her friend and said earnestly, "You see how few are prepared."

Although she wanted to be prepared, the woman wondered how she could obtain those articles of clothing, for she had no money. Abigail discerned her thoughts and said that she knew that the woman was a poor widow and didn't know where the money would come from.

Abigail promised, "Before the week is out you will have five dollars in gold put in your hand." Then she disappeared.

The woman relates, "Before the week ended my son came and stayed over night and started away the next morning; he had even got in his wagon to go, but got out and came back into the house, and in shaking hands again with me he put five dollars in gold in my hand. The whole dream flashed before my eyes in a moment, for here was the gold placed in my hands to convince me it was not a dream but a reality, which filled me with such joy and delight that I trembled from head to foot, but I never spoke to my son, I was so overjoyed at receiving the money.

"I treasured it for some time, keeping it for some time . . . then I was tempted to use it, being so destitute of food and clothing and being almost entirely barefoot, but after using it I was very unhappy and miserable, I could not rest day or night, I felt a reproof because I had used it for another purpose than the one it was intended for. I prayed most earnestly for the Lord to forgive me for what I had done and open the way that I might get the money."

She said that the Lord "did not trust me with the money again." However, a lady asked her if she could do some sewing. In exchange for the sewing, the lady would give her the articles of clothing that she wanted.

The woman said, "I thanked the Lord with joyful feelings, more than I can express. . . . Since that time the Lord has blessed me abundantly, both spiritually and temporally, so that I may be ready when the cry shall go forth, 'Lo the Bridegroom cometh, go ye out to meet Him.[78]

Because Brother Goff heeded a dream that warned him of danger, his life and the life of his friend were spared. The following account was published in *The Millennial Star* in 1866.

"There is a saw-mill a few miles from Scipio, or Round Valley, Millard county, Utah," the paper states. "Two men were working at that mill by themselves. One of them—brother Goff—dreamed one night that he must go away from there . . . or else he would be in mortal danger.

"The dream made a deep impression upon him. In the morning, being thus warned, he persuaded the brother who was working with him to leave there too. They both started for Deseret City—their place of residence—upwards of forty miles distant. They took the road which led directly to their home, and did not call at Scipio."[79]

The next morning, a band of marauders swept down on the small town of Scipio, stealing horses and cattle and killing a man and a young boy. After the attack, the townspeople worried about Brother Goff and his friend, knowing the mill would be an easy place for the marauders to attack since it was some distance from town. When men rode to the mill to investigate, they could not find Brother Goff or his friend and concluded the two had been killed. Everyone was relieved when they were later discovered alive and well. "Brother Goff's dream had saved himself and companion."[80]

When Leslie Bushell had a dream about her deceased brother, she felt it was to remind her about the importance of doing temple work and to inspire her to begin working for her ancestors. Leslie was living in England when she became converted to the Church. As she studied the gospel, Leslie learned about the importance of baptism and other ordinances. She was grateful that the Lord had prepared a way for these ordinances to be done vicariously for those who did not have the opportunity to do the work themselves while they lived on earth.

Leslie began researching her family lineage. One evening, she did not go to bed but spent almost the entire night going over old records. When Leslie finally fell asleep at 3:00 A.M., she had a dream. She writes:

In my sleep I was visited by my younger brother Keith, who had been killed during World War II while flying on a mercy mission over the sea. He took me by the hand and we moved upward, passing before our ancestors. We passed my grandparents, who were dead, my great-grandparents, great-great-grandparents, and so on until there were literally thousands who stood before us. So vividly did they appear that I could assess and distinguish the peculiarities of their features and easily recognize the paternal and maternal families.

When I awoke after five hours I was humbly aware of my obligations to my ancestors, who had made it possible for me to be here in this dispensation of time. I began my search for their records right away.[81]

Elizabeth Stoecker had a difficult time paying her tithing—until she had a revealing dream. For many years, Elizabeth, who had been raised in a part-member home and had married out of the Church, felt confused about the principle of tithing. Finally, Elizabeth prayed and had a dream that convinced her that paying tithing was the right thing to do.

In her dream, Elizabeth's branch president announced in a meeting that the Saints were going to the promised land. Elizabeth hurried home and packed bags for herself and her two children. When Elizabeth and her children arrived at the meeting place, the branch president began reading the names of those who were worthy to go to Zion. He read from a large book titled *The Book of Life.* However, he called only a few names, leaving the rest of the branch to murmur among themselves. Surprised that her name had not been called, Elizabeth wondered what she had done wrong.

Elizabeth approached the branch president and asked if he felt that she had been a faithful member. He assured Elizabeth that she had. Out loud, he wondered if he might have overlooked her name. The branch president looked in the book carefully, going over the list of names three times. Finally, he looked up at Elizabeth and asked: "'Sister, have you paid your tithing?'"[82]

Elizabeth awoke with a burning in her chest. She knelt to thank God for His guidance and committed from that time on to pay her tithing.

In another instance, a mother determined to do anything that might possibly save the life of her young daughter—no matter how peculiar and unbelievable it seemed. This woman, unfamiliar with the Church and its teachings, obeyed the instruction she had been given in a dream and sent for missionaries. Edward J. Wood, who later became president of the Alberta Temple, was one of the elders summoned by the anxious mother.

Elder Wood said that just prior to the beginning of the Samoan civil war, a native approached him and his companion, Elder Dean. The native told the missionaries that a lady on another island wanted the missionaries to come and heal her sick child. He said this woman had seen Elder Dean and Elder Wood in a dream and urged them to come quickly.

However, because of the impending war, the missionaries had been told to stay where they were. When other natives heard about the request, they told the elders that it could be a trap and advised the missionaries not to go.

The elders hesitated for another reason. What would happen if they were not able to heal the child? Would that cause doubt and unbelief among the people and set back the missionary work? On the other hand, they knew that if they were able to heal the child, they could use that experience as a wonderful missionary tool.

The missionaries decided to take their dilemma to the Lord. Going to a quiet spot under a banyan tree to pray, they inquired whether they should go. In response, Elder Wood heard a voice saying it was all right to go.

The elders made their preparations and were soon on their way. When they arrived, the mother was waiting for them on the beach and led them quickly to her home.

She said, "I am glad that you have come. It is alright. Here is my child." She then lifted a white sheet off the floor, uncovering her daughter, who appeared dead.

When the mother saw how startled the missionaries were, she assured them that the child was not dead. The woman encouraged them, saying, "You do what I saw you do last night in my dream, and she will be well."[83]

The elders, however, were still dumbfounded. They had expected an ill child, not one that appeared to be dead. Doubts flooded their minds. They remembered how superstitious the natives were and, once again, worried about the consequences if they were not able to heal the child.

The mother was exasperated at their hesitation and exclaimed, "Have you the authority to do what I saw you do in my dream? You anointed that child with oil; you laid your hands upon her head."[84]

The elders hesitated no longer. They gathered around the child, anointed her, and blessed her. When there was no immediate change, they covered the girl gently with the cloth and returned to their island. There was no word as to whether their efforts had been successful or not.

Two years passed, and Elder Wood was called to preach on another island. When he arrived, he was met on the beach by natives swinging long knives. He didn't know what to think as they surrounded him, but he offered no resistance. Then a woman stepped up and called him by name. Surprised, Elder Wood returned her greeting but said that he did not recognize her. The woman replied that he *did* know her. She then called to her daughter, asking her to come and stand beside her.

The woman turned to the crowd and, holding out a hand toward her daughter said, "This is a living testimony of the great power of the gospel, and the power and authority held by Mr. Wood and his associates. They administered to this child over two years ago. I have never seen them since, but I know they have the power of God with them, and all of you must listen to their message."[85]

The woman told Elder Wood that she was the daughter of the high chief of that island and that Elder Wood could stay at her home. The people followed Elder Wood as he went with the child and her mother to her father's house. Elder Wood spent most of the night preaching to them, and his message was warmly received. The woman told Elder Wood that "she had been praying earnestly for Mormon missionaries to be sent to her home, where, she felt, there would be great good accomplished in the spreading of the gospel."[86]

Chapter 4

Angelic Visits that Provided Comfort

Dreams can bring divine comfort to those who suffer trials or face hardships; they can also warn of impending danger. Warning dreams can be comforting because they let us know that Heavenly Father is aware of us, loves us, and is watching over us. Dreams that contain messages of inspiration or reassurance can also give us comfort.

As children of Heavenly Father, we can all receive comfort and guidance from God. From the earliest days of the Church down to the present time, countless people have had their lives touched for good by manifestations of the Spirit. Spencer W. Kimball said, "If all the spectacular manifestations and visions and pertinent dreams and healings and other miracles were written in books, it would take a great library to hold them."[1]

We can receive many blessings if we strive to live the commandments. President Heber C. Kimball reminded us that we need to keep the covenants we make with God in order to receive comforting personal revelation. "Are you faithful to your vows?" he asked. "If you are, you will have dreams, and visions, and revelations from the world of light, and you will be comforted by night and by day. But if you do not fulfill your covenants you cannot enjoy these blessings."[2]

If we follow Heavenly Father and are obedient to His commands,

He will give us personal revelation that will help us feel happier than we ever thought possible. Inspiration illuminates our paths with the divine light and power that comes from God. In *The Millennial Star,* Elder Joseph G. Romney wrote, "It is by dreams that God often makes known his mind and will to mankind. In the holy scriptures we find many notable instances of this power, or of this gift, in which man, visited in his slumbers by the angels of God's presence, has partaken of that Spirit of light and intelligence that surrounds Him."[3]

How comforting it is to know that God is leading His people and that if we follow Him, He will bless us with inspiration that will lighten our days, give us peace during times of trouble, console us when we have cause to mourn, and testify to the truth of His holy gospel. If we will only trust the Lord, He and His angels will watch over us during our lifetime. President John Taylor reiterated this truth when he said:

> God went with his Elders, and they have gathered together his people as they are here today. They have been seeking to carry out the desire of the Lord and the wish of the Almighty in regard to the human family. They were told to go trusting in the name of the Lord, and he would take care of them and go before them, and that his Spirit should go with them and his angels accompany them. This is all true; and these Elders have preached to you in your various homes and tongues, those principles which God revealed from heaven, and you were influenced by dreams and visions and by the Spirit of the Lord to give heed to their words."[4]

Although Samuel Harris Hurst Jr. had many concerns when he was called to go on a mission, he faithfully accepted the call to serve the Lord. Samuel was blessed for his obedience, for when he arrived at his destination, he witnessed the fulfillment of a dream that he'd had two years earlier.

Samuel had recently lost his wife when he was unexpectedly called to serve a mission to Hawaii. Although his patriarchal blessing had told him that one day he would go to the land of his forefathers, such a thing did not seem possible. For one thing, at thirty-six years old, Samuel thought he was too old to learn Hawaiian fluently. He felt anxious about his ability to speak well in front of people who grew up knowing the language. His second concern about serving a mission centered around his ten-year-old daughter, Inez.

Despite his worries, Samuel made preparations to leave. One of the first things he did was sell his farm in Cache Valley, Utah, so he had money to pay for his missionary expenses. He also began writing in a journal. In it, he confessed that being called to Hawaii was "quite a test to my faith."[5]

During the voyage to Hawaii, Samuel began to wonder if his call had actually been inspired. He did his best to cling to his faith but fretted about his abilities—or rather lack of abilities—during the entire trip.

However, all of Samuel's worries disappeared once the boat docked and he stepped off the ship to see Wesley Smith, the mission president. As Samuel walked toward the mission president, he was more than a just a little shaken. The two had never met, yet Samuel knew Elder Smith's face because he had seen him two years before in a dream.

In his dream, Samuel worked as a missionary alongside Elder Smith, the man who was now standing before him. What made the dream especially impressive to Samuel is that he had experienced this dream one year *before* Elder Wesley Smith was even called to be the mission president in Hawaii.

Seeing the fulfillment of his dream reminded Samuel that his mission call *was* inspired and had truly come from God. Samuel wrote in his journal, "With this, I knew that some power other than that of man was having something to do with it."[6]

Sister Rebecca Rosetta Peterson Bean and her husband, Elder Willard Bean, served a mission to Palmyra, New York, from 1915 to 1940—a remarkable twenty-five years. At that time, there was no visitors' center in Palmyra, but many people still traveled to see the Hill Cumorah and the Joseph Smith home. When visitors came to stay, whether it was for a few days or several weeks, they often boarded with Sister and Brother Bean. The constant influx of visitors was a significant burden for Sister Bean, who also had her own family to care for. Sometimes she couldn't help but feel a little overworked. Then Sister Bean had the following dream, which had a surprising ending. This dream infused her with strength so she was able to continue her labors with a heart full of love. Sister Bean writes:

> It was a hot summer day and we had a lot of visitors that day. It had been a hard day for me. I had a baby just a year old, and I had carried my baby around on my arm most of the day to get my work done. It was too warm. Everything had gone against us. We had had lunch for our visitors, and we had had supper at night, and I had put my children to bed. Dr. [James E.] Talmage was there and some missionaries and we had really had a wonderful evening talking together. They all seemed tired and I took them upstairs and showed them where they could sleep, and I came down and thought, "Well, I'll pick up a few things and make things easier for in the morning."
>
> But I was so weary and so tired that I was crying as I went straightening things around a little. Everybody was in bed and asleep but me. I looked at the clock and it was eleven o'clock. I said, "I'd better call it a day." I went into my room and. . . . It was peaceful and quiet. I got ready for bed, and I was crying a little. I said my prayers and I got into bed and I was crying on my pillow. And then this dream or vision came to me.
>
> I thought it was another day. It had been a wonderful morning. I had prepared breakfast for my visitors, and my children were happily playing around, and I had done my work and cared for the baby, and he was contented and happy. I prepared lunch, and I called my visitors in to lunch and we were all seated around the table, my little baby in the high chair. Everything was peaceful and wonderfully sweet. There was a knock at the front door, and there was a very handsome young man standing there. I just took it for granted that she was another new missionary come to see us, and I said, "You're here just in time for lunch. Come with me."
>
> As I walked through the little hall into the dining room, I noticed he laid some pamphlets down on the table there. I introduced him around, and then I said, "Now you sit right here by Dr. Talmage, and I'll set a place for you." I thought he was strange to all of us, and yet he and Dr. Talmage seemed so happy to see each other, and they talked about such wonderful things while we were eating. Some of them we could hardly understand. But the spirit that was there in the meal was so peaceful and nice, and everyone seemed so happy to be together. After the meal was over, Dr. Talmage said to the missionaries,

"Now let's go outside and just linger here and enjoy the spirit of this wonderful place, because we'll soon have to leave."

I put my baby to bed, and the other little ones went out to play, and then I was alone with this young man. He thanked me for having him to dinner, and told me how much it meant for him to be there, and he told me he thought that the children were so sweet and well trained, and I felt happy about that, and then we walked in the hall together. He said, "I have far to go, so I must be on my way."

Then I turned from him just a moment to pick up these little pamphlets that he had laid on the table, and when I turned back to him it was the Savior who stood before me, and he was in his glory. And I could not tell you the love and sweetness that he had in his face and in his eyes. Lovingly, he laid his hands on my shoulders, and he looked down into my face with the kindest face that I have ever seen, and this is what he said to me: "Sister Bean, this day hasn't been too hard for you has it?"

And I said, "Oh no, I have been so happy in my work and everything has gone on so well."

Then he said, "I promise you if you will go about your work as you have done it this day you will be equal to it. Oh, remember these missionaries represent me on this earth, and all that you do unto them you do unto me." And then I remember I was crying as we walked through the hall onto the porch, and he repeated the same thing: "These missionaries represent me on earth, and all that you do unto them you do unto me." And then he started upwards. The roof of the porch was no obstruction for him to go through, nor for me to see through. He went upward and upward and upward, and I wondered and wondered how I could see him so far away. And then all at once he disappeared, and I was crying on my pillow like I was when I went to bed.[7]

This experience had a profound effect upon Sister Bean, and she was never again frustrated at her work. She always made room for the missionaries, no matter how many wanted to stay, and she always felt great love for them.

Anson Call was present when Joseph Smith spoke to a congregation, prophesying that the Saints would be driven out of their homes and suffer much affliction while traveling to their new home in the Rocky Mountains. When Joseph Smith was killed at Carthage Jail, Anson was shocked, since he believed that Joseph Smith would be the one to guide the Saints to their new home in the West.

A few days after Joseph died, Anson had a dream. He said:

> The third night I had a dream, or a vision. . . . I was traveling by myself in a lonely place till I came to a new field about three acres in size. I discovered in the center of the field a nice block house. I went to the door of the house. I discovered Joseph standing in the middle of the floor. I sprang and clinched him by the hand.
>
> I threw my arms around him, and kissed him, and said, "Joseph, I thought you was dead!"
>
> He said "I am."
>
> I said, "This is certainly Joseph."
>
> He said, "Yes, this is Joseph; take your seat and I will tell you all about it." I seated myself and then discovered I was in a congregation of Saints whom I was acquainted with.
>
> Joseph then said, "Brethren, I have been killed in Carthage Jail, and it will not make any difference with you, if you will do as you are told. I shall continue to govern and control this kingdom as I have hitherto done. The keys of this kingdom were committed to me. I hold them and shall continue to hold them, worlds without end. I am dead, and I am out of the power of my enemies. I am now where I can do you good. Be no longer troubled. Be faithful, be diligent, do as you are told, and you shall see the salvation of God."[8]

Lucinda Taylor Hamblin was shocked when her husband, Jacob, was instantly converted the first time he listened to a missionary preach about the restored gospel. For a time, her husband's split-second conversion caused problems in their marriage. However, because of an angelic visitation during a dream, Lucinda was reassured that The Church of Jesus Christ of Latter-day Saints was truly the Lord's Church.

After the dream, Lucinda supported her husband completely, and when they moved to Utah, Jacob became an extraordinary influence for good while serving as a missionary to the Indians.

However, before Lucinda had the dream, she was extremely upset about her husband's rash decision to be baptized. She was sure that Jacob was being overly hasty when he heard about the gospel one evening and was baptized the following morning.

When Jacob came home from the meeting where Elder Stoddard had preached about the gospel, he could talk of nothing else. Lucinda was horrified when Jacob told her that he wanted to be baptized the next day. She knew nothing about this strange, new religion and tried everything she could think of to get Jacob to wait. Finally, Lucinda told him that he shouldn't expect her to live with him if he went ahead and was baptized.

When Jacob's family learned about his decision, they were upset as well. Jacob's father refused to see him after his baptism. All of Jacob's relatives, except for one brother, would have nothing to do with him. Although Lucinda's father did not refuse to see Jacob, he only consented to see his son-in-law so he could insult him to his face.

One day Jacob had had enough. Without knowing how prophetic his statement was, he told his father-in-law, "You will not have the privilege of abusing me much more."[9]

A few days later, his father-in-law suddenly became sick and died.

Then Lucinda had a dream. Jacob recorded the following account of the angelic visit that changed his wife's feelings: "Soon after the death of her father, my wife asked me, good-naturedly, why I did not pray in the house or with her. I replied that I felt better to pray by myself than I did before unbelievers. She said that she was a believer; that her father had appeared to her in a dream, and told her not to oppose me any more as she had done; and that he was in trouble on account of the way he had used me. Soon after this she was baptized, which was a great comfort to me."[10]

Niels Eskildz suffered a serious injury when he was a young boy, and when he became an adult, his body was short and bent from a curved and deformed spine. When Niels was a boy, recuperating from his accident, he spent many long hours lying in bed. To pass the time, his mother taught him to sew. This knowledge proved invaluable, for when Niels grew up, he depended upon his stitching skills, along with assistance from others, to provide a living for himself. Though he tried to stay busy and happy, Niels was often discouraged and downcast when he saw how repelled people were by his deformities.

Over time Niels became more and more depressed. He had not yet been converted to The Church of Jesus Christ of Latter-day Saints, and it was hard for Niels to see any good in life. Then Niels had a glorious vision, one which he never forgot and which had a tremendous impact on the rest of his life. It occurred one evening while Niels was preparing his dinner. The account states:

> During the summer preceding his baptism, after a day of extreme melancholy, an incident occurred that produced an entire change in his feelings. While engaged preparing his evening meal a glorious vision burst upon his view. It was not a single scene that he beheld, but a series of them. He compares them to the modern moving pictures, for want of a better illustration. He beheld as with his natural sight, but he realized afterwards that it was with the eye of the spirit that he saw what he did. His understanding was appealed to as well as his sight.
>
> What was shown him related to his existence in the spirit world, mortal experience and future reward. He comprehended, as if by intuition, that he had witnessed a somewhat similar scene in his pre-mortal state, and been given the opportunity of choosing the class of reward he would like to attain to. He knew that he had deliberately made his choice. He realized which of the rewards he had selected, and understood that such a reward was only to be gained by mortal suffering—that, in fact, he must be a cripple and endure severe physical pain, privation and ignominy. He was conscious too that he still insisted upon having that reward, and accepted and agreed to the conditions.
>
> He emerged from the vision with a settled conviction that to rebel against or even to repine at his fate, was not only a reproach to an Alwise Father whose care had been over him notwithstanding his seeming abandonment, but a base violation of the deliberate promise and agreement he had entered into, and upon the observance of which is future reward depended."[11]

Niels realized that others might ridicule the vision and think it was merely a product of his imagination, but he knew without a doubt that it came as a gift from a loving, compassionate Father in Heaven.

The account adds that Neils "has unshaken faith in it [the vision, and] has derived comfort, satisfaction, resolution and fortitude from it. He has ever since been resigned to his affliction, and, though never mirthful, is serene and composed and uncomplaining. He has always felt that the vision was granted to him by the Lord for a wise and merciful purpose—that he might, through a better understanding of his duty, be able to remain steadfast thereto."[12]

Approximately a year after this vision, Niels was baptized a member of The Church of Jesus Christ of Latter-day Saints. Through a series of extraordinary blessings, Niels gathered enough money to immigrate to the United States, cross the plains, and settle in Salt Lake City.

Lucille Clark was worried and frightened. Her eldest son, who was nineteen, lay near death in the intensive care unit at a San Francisco hospital, suffering from acute pylo-nephritis. One night Lucille had a dream about her son. In the dream, Lucille was given a choice. She could keep her son or let him return back to heaven. However, if her son lived, he would never be able to work again but would be bedridden the rest of his life. Then Lucille saw her son lying in a casket. When she awoke, the dream was still fresh in her mind, and she heard a voice that told her the choice was hers to make.

"Rather than see him unhappy as an invalid," Lucille wrote, "and unable to do any work, I would rather that he be taken home. I know that he would be very miserable if he could not work, and he would be so unhappy if I had to work to support him. I knew I must give him up."[13]

After Lucille made her choice, she cried but felt resigned to what she believed was inevitable. Two days later, her son passed away. Lucille felt that the dream prepared her for his death. Although her heart was heavy, she was comforted and knew it was better for her son to be in heaven than bedridden on earth. Lucille was grateful to Heavenly Father for blessing her with this dream, which helped her cope with her loss.

Addison Everett was so critically ill that everyone thought he would die. Then Brother Everett had a remarkable dream. In the dream, a man told Brother Everett that the Prophet Joseph Smith was at the temple and wanted to see him. "He (Bro. Everett) went immediately and found there Joseph and Hyrum," the account states. "Joseph shook hands with him remarking at the same time: 'You have got a great many friends behind the veil.' He awoke, and got well quickly."[14]

Dreams change people's lives. Lucy Mack Smith became deeply interested in religion some time between 1800 and 1804. At the time, Lucy and her husband, Joseph Smith Sr., were living in Tunbridge, Vermont. After investigating various religions, Lucy decided to join the Methodists. For a time, Joseph went with her to their meetings—until his brother Jesse found out. Because Jesse was bitterly opposed to his brother and sister-in-law attending the Methodist church, Joseph stopped going.

In her history, Lucy wrote that Joseph told her that "he considered it hardly worth our while to attend the meetings any longer as it would prove of but little advantage to us; besides this, it gave our friends such disagreeable feelings."[15]

One evening Lucy was so downcast by her husband's lack of support and interest that she went out into a grove to pray so that "the true gospel might be presented to him and that his heart might be softened so as to receive it, or, that he might become more religiously inclined."[16] After praying, Lucy returned to the house and went to bed.

That night she had a dream.

In the dream, she was standing in a large meadow. Lucy wrote:

> The first thing that attracted my special attention in this magnificent meadow, was a very pure and clear stream of water, which ran through the midst of it; and as I traced this stream, I discovered two trees standing upon its margin, both of which were on the same side of the stream. These trees were very beautiful, they were well proportioned, and towered with majestic beauty to a great height. . . . I saw one of them was surrounded with a bright belt, that shone like burnished gold, but far more brilliantly. Presently, a gentle breeze passed by, and the tree encircled with this golden zone, bent gracefully before the wind, and waved its beautiful branches in the light air. . . . I turned my eyes upon its fellow, [the other tree] which stood opposite; but it was not surrounded with the belt of light as the former, and it stood erect and fixed as a pillar of marble. No matter how strong the

wind blew over it, not a leaf was stirred, not a bough was bent.

I wondered at what I saw . . . and the interpretation given me was, that these personated my husband and his oldest brother, Jesse Smith; that the stubborn and unyielding tree was like Jesse; that the other, more pliant and flexible, was like Joseph, my husband; that the breath of heaven, which passed over them, was the pure and undefiled gospel of the Son of God, which gospel Jesse would always resist, but which Joseph, when he was more advanced in life, would hear and receive with his whole heart, and rejoice therein; and unto him would be added intelligence, happiness, glory, and everlasting life.[17]

Dreams can play critical roles in our lives as we strive to do what the Lord wants us to do. While being taught the gospel, Antonia Flores was touched by the Spirit and developed a testimony. She was soon baptized. A few years after her conversion, the branch president asked Antonia if she would accept a calling to be the Relief Society president. Antonia felt inadequate and worried about accepting such a demanding calling. Then she had a reassuring dream. Antonia states:

I was very afraid to be Relief Society president. I just didn't see how I could handle such a job and was afraid to tell him (branch president) yes. Later that day, I remembered the principle of fasting and prayer. I fasted and prayed about accepting this position that I was so afraid of.

In the night, I had a revelation. I dreamed that I was walking, carrying a great weight in my hands. I had been walking a long time and was tired from carrying such a heavy weight. Then I saw our Lord Jesus Christ, and he took the weight out of my hands and invited me, saying, "Come, follow me." The next morning I felt wonderful; the fear had left me. I hurried to the branch president to tell what had happened, that I was no longer afraid and was sure it was right, and so, I have been able to continue working in the Relief Society several years as president with two wonderful counselors.[18]

Antonia then relates another wonderful incident:

I have also had another great experience. I work as a seamstress, and every time someone pays me for my work, I set aside one-tenth as my tithing. One time there was no money in the house; I didn't have even one cent other than the money I had set aside for tithing. It was Sunday, and time to pay my tithing at church.

My son, who was very small at the time, said to me, "But, Mama, if you pay your tithing today, what are we going to eat tomorrow?"

I told him to have confidence in the Lord and He wouldn't let us go without food. So I went to church, paid my tithing, and came home with peace of mind, but still not knowing what we would do for our next meal, for we had absolutely no money. However, very early the next morning, a lady knocked on my door, bringing me material to make her a dress and paying me in advance for the work, and so we had money to live on the next day.[19]

Elder George W. Larkin was a friend of the Stevens family. One night Elder Larkin had a dream about Briant, who was one of the younger boys in the family. The dream was so disturbing that Elder Larkin told his family, "I had a strange and sad dream about little Briant Stevens last night. I wonder if the boy is sick."[20]

A short time later, Briant's father stopped at Elder Larkin's home. Brother Stevens mentioned that Briant had recently broken his arm, and it had been an extremely bad break; the bone actually protruded from the young boy's arm. The doctors had set the bone, but lockjaw had set in. Brother Stevens was so worried about his son that Elder Larkin did not have the heart to tell him about his dream.

Brother Stevens asked Elder Larkin if he would be willing to come and take a turn watching over his son during the night, giving him a blessing if needed. Elder Larkin was happy to oblige and along with several other elders took a turn sitting with Briant that night.

Briant was a precocious boy for his age. One of his greatest hopes was to help build the temple in Jackson County. He confided that desire to a friend, saying, "I want to go back to Jackson County to help to build the temple there for Him. And I know that I *will* aid in this work."[21]

One night Briant restated this desire to a group of elders who were sitting with him. One of the men was so moved at this heartfelt declaration that he gave Briant a blessing and declared that he would be with the Saints in Jackson County when they built the temple.

Each night a group of elders took turns sitting with Briant, who grew weaker and weaker. One night one of the elders fell asleep by the young boy's bedside and had a dream. The account states:

> "He dreamed that himself and three of his companion Elders, who had also waited on Briant, went upon a journey into a distant and a beautiful country. . . . When they reached the fair land of their destination they saw a superb building, which they at once divined to be a temple of the living God. . . . It was constructed of white, shining stone, seemingly as hard as granite. Many workmen appeared to be engaged in the building; and one of them, clothed in a white robe, with his head and hands and feet bare, stood upon the ground near the entrance to the structure. In the white outer wall, at one side of the mighty arched doorway, and at the height of a man's head, a monogram seemed to be newly set into the stone. It was composed of three letters; the top one being B, clearly distinguishable; and the other two being fainter. The Elder who dreamed, thought that he reached forward and attempted to take it from its place. But the white robed workman stayed his hand, saying: "You cannot take it. It has been set here by order of the Master, as an ornament to this temple."[22]

Three different times the elders tried to pluck the monogram from its place in the glittering wall, but each time the guardian workman stopped them.

"On their last try, the workman said, 'Brother [calling him by name] you must go back; your wish cannot be granted.' Then they withdrew. Soon the Elder awoke, and he felt certain that the prayers which had been offered concerning Briant Stevens—though they had reached the throne of the eternal Father—were powerless to change the decree that had been made in heaven concerning the boy and that Briant must speedily pass from earth."[23]

During the next few days, Briant's condition continued to deteriorate. Elder Larkin was in the room when Briant passed away. He was asked to help prepare the body for burial. When Elder Larkin had finished that sad task, he burst into tears and told Brother Stevens, "Now my dream is fulfilled. The night before you called for me, a vision came in my slumber. I saw Briant lying dead in this room, and mine was the dread duty to wash and dress his deserted tabernacle and place it in the coffin. And so it has come to pass, exactly according to my dream."[24]

After young Briant Stevens passed away, his father and one of Briant's good friends, Fred Bluth, were comforted when—in two separate dreams—they saw Briant.

Briant died of tetanus on 3 February 1887. The following night, his father had a dream. The account states, "At length he [the father] saw a light and in this light was little Briant, standing in the air, robed in snowy whiteness, with a face transfigured in its light and beauty. The boy smiled at him and moved his hands as if in loving recognition. This ethereal form of Briant moved about in the room without effort. A single inclination of the shining head seemed to project the body in any directed direction."[25]

Fred J. Bluth also saw Briant in a dream. Fred and Briant had gone to school together, and each day when classes let out, they walked home together. Two nights after Briant died, Fred had a dream. He states:

> I thought that Briant was waiting for me at the (school) gate as usual—only he was dressed in white raiment, like that in which he lay in the coffin. When I came near him, he sprang to my side and threw his arms around my neck. He took my hand, and said: "Come, Fred, with me."
>
> Hand in hand, we ran up town together. . . . We came out, and a large wagon stood before the door. The driver came down from his seat, and we got in and drove to a building like a granary. Briant opened the doors. And then I heard a voice saying: "You must fill the wagon with corn."
>
> Briant and I began to shovel corn into the wagon; but soon he stopped. I asked: "Is it enough?" And he answered: "Not yet."
>
> I worked a little longer, and again I called to him: "Is it enough, Briant?" And once more he replied: "Not yet, Fred."
>
> After a still longer time, during which I worked diligently, I asked him for the third time: "Is it enough?" And Briant replied: "Yes, it is enough. Now you must come with me, Fred." I climbed into the wagon with him; and then we drove away together. At once I awoke.[26]

At first, Fred was disturbed by the dream and unsure what it meant. He told the dream to an older man, Edgar Peterson. Edgar asked Fred if he knew what the dream meant. When Fred replied he did not, Elder Peterson replied, "Then I will give you the interpretation. It means that your earthly work is not yet finished and that when it is done, Briant will call for you."[27]

Of course, dreams don't always foretell death. A woman dreamed that John Powell—who was a stranger to her at the time—would come to her home and teach her the gospel.

This experience occurred in 1855, when Elder John Powell was sent by the leaders of his St. Louis stake to Clarkston, Missouri, to collect money for the Church. Elder Powell started off on his journey, but when he arrived at the broad Missouri River, he didn't know how to cross it. He watched and waited until he finally saw a man in a small canoe paddling along. Elder Powell waved the man over and explained his predicament.

When the man offered to take him to the other side of the river, the missionary gladly accepted. Since the boat had been made out of a hollow log and was very small, Elder Powell sat very quietly so the vessel would not capsize. After the man let him off on the other side of the river, Elder Powell asked for directions to Clarkston and was directed over the prairie.

Elder Powell walked all day without seeing a single person. As dusk began to fall, he realized he was lost. Not wanting to spend the night alone on the prairie, Elder Powell decided to pray for help. The account states:

> The answer to his prayer came in an impression to go in a particular direction. He walked rapidly for some time and seeing no one, his faith slowly left him. When he had almost despaired of finding shelter, he saw a small clump of trees, from which came a large, black dog. Supposing the animal came from some habitation Elder Powell ran after him as quickly as he could and was nearly out of breath when he almost ran over a man, whom the gathering darkness did not permit him to see.
>
> This forcible introduction caused the stranger to say, "Hello, where are you going?"
>
> "The same way you are," was the answer.
>
> While walking along, Brother Powell asked his companion

> if he belonged to any religious body and was told by the stranger that he had been a "Mormon."
>
> Bro. Powell then told him who he was, and what he was doing. Arriving at the domicile of his new-found friend, Elder Powell was surprised to hear the man greet his wife with the words, "Wife, here is the Elder you dreamed was coming here."[28]

Inexplicably, the dog that had led Elder Powell to the stranger was not seen again.

Another early Church history story tells about Morgan, a recent convert to the Church who was living in North Wales. Morgan became seriously ill, and although her family and friends did all they could to nurse Morgan back to health, her condition worsened. Then Morgan had a dream showing her what she needed to do to recover. When Morgan woke, she insisted on seeing Elder John T. Evans, a missionary who was serving in the area. The account relates:

> When she (Morgan) had grown so bad that the persons waiting upon her expected her to die almost hourly, she fell asleep and dreamed that Elder Evans came and laid his hands upon her and she recovered immediately.
>
> On relating the dream to her friends, they tried to find out where Brother Evans was, and sent to different parts of the country in search of him, without finding him, however; but during the day Elder Evans happened to call at the house where the sick woman was.
>
> She saw him as he passed the window before he entered the door and she declared afterwards that the sight of him caused her pain to vanish, and when he laid his hands upon her head she was healed instantly, and arose and ate her supper.[29]

Yet another story tells about Lolie, the oldest girl in a family, who was expected to do much of the housework and help tend the younger children. Sometimes Lolie felt that she worked harder than her own mother and father. When household chores left her little time to play,

Lolie became sad and irritable. To make matters worse, her mother was often sick, which meant that Lolie had to work extra hard.

One day her mother fell ill again. But this time, she was unable to eat or even sit up. Lolie became frightened and felt guilty, remembering that she had not been very kind or thoughtful during the past week. Now that her mother was confined strictly to bed, Lolie realized that her mother did indeed do much of the housework. As her mother lay in bed, looking so pale and listless, Lolie became alarmed. That night, troubled about the way she had acted, Lolie prayed that God would make her mother well. The account records:

> When she slept, she dreamed that she stood beside her mother's bed, weeping. An angel, very bright and beautiful, and with a loving smile, came and stood beside her.
>
> "Why are you crying, little girl?" asked the angel.
>
> "Because my mother is so sick," answered Lolie.
>
> "She will not be sick much longer, nor have to suffer much more," said the angel, "I have come to take her away, to a peaceful, quiet home, where no one is ever sick."
>
> "Oh! Don't take my mother away, oh! Please don't!" sobbed Lolie, wringing her hands in great grief.[30]

The angel reminded Lolie that she sometimes sulked and was angry when her mother asked her to help. Lolie admitted this but said, "I'll try so hard to be good every way, always after this, if you will only let my mother stay and get well."[31]

The angel then told Lolie that her mother would live. Although she was sick for a very long time, Lolie's mother did eventually recover.

In November 1941, Gertha Bishop, along with her husband, Henry, and their three children, left Buhl, Idaho. They planned to spend the winter harvesting vegetables in Imperial Valley, California. The Bishops had just enough money for their journey and towed a small house trailer, where they planned to sleep each night.

Unfortunately, when they reached Nevada, their car broke down. It cost most of their savings to repair it. Once the car was fixed, the family set out once more. They had just driven past Sacramento, California, when a tire blew out on their trailer house. They could not afford a new tire, so instead, they bought a used tire and a new tube.

The next day, the Bishops had not been on the road longer than about an hour when another tire blew. Gertha and Henry left the trailer at the side of the road with two of their daughters, Shirley and Valair, and went back to Sacramento to get another tire and tube. They did not have enough money to pay for both, but the shop owner kindly allowed them to take the tire and tube anyway.

They were now completely out of money. The couple decided their only option was to take the trailer back to Sacramento, sell it for whatever they could get, and travel on to Imperial Valley. That night they pulled onto a sandy strip of land by a long, trestle bridge to have their evening meal. Gertha relates:

> Many times in my life I have had dreams which seemed to have a definite meaning. My family, of course, knew this and that night just before retiring, my husband, half joking and half in earnest, said I had better get busy with one of my dreams and find out where we might find work or get money to go on our way. We were still hating to sell the trailer house, but we could sleep in it for one more night.
>
> Some time before midnight I dreamed that upon arising in the morning my husband and I were standing near the left wheel of the trailer house when I looked down and saw, folded, up, laying right in the wheel track almost under the front wheel a folded greenback. In my dream I picked it up and my husband remarked that if he had pulled the trailer up one inch the bill would have been ground into the sand and we would never have found it. I unfolded the money and found it to be a five-dollar bill and a one-dollar bill folded together.
>
> I awoke and found my husband lying awake worrying about what we should do. I told him of my dream and we finally fell asleep again. I continued to dream about finding money, and just before I awoke at dawn, I dreamed I was with my sister just older than I, and I told her how badly I needed some money. She said she was very sorry and wished she could help me but that it was impossible at that time. She then said, 'If you will go out of your trailer house and take five paces straight out from the left side of it and come back at an angle to it, then look under the front of the left wheel, you will find some money.'"[32]

When Gertha woke, she related her dream to her family. Then Gertha said:

> I got up and started dressing and happened to look through the glass in the door, when I saw a man sauntering away about one hundred feet from us. He seemed ordinary enough in his dress and slow walk and had I not been thinking of the directions given me in my dream by my sister, I would have paid no further attention to him. As it was I stooped to pick up a piece of clothing and looked out again only to find him gone. He had apparently just disappeared as there was no place he could have gotten out of sight in that length of time."[33]

Gertha went outside and began looking for the money her sister had told her about. She said:

> I followed her directions and coming back to the left wheel of the trailer house I dropped on my knees and there in the track of the wheel and just in front of it lay a folded greenback and just under the house trailer near the wheel were three one dollar bills, slightly crumpled but swaying back and forth.
>
> I gave a cry, calling my husband's name. I gathered the bills into my hand and stumbled into the trailer house where I dropped on my knees at the foot of the bed too overcome to do anything but cry.[34]

Her husband and girls came running in and saw that she had found the money exactly as she had dreamt. Tears streamed down their faces as they looked at the money: a one-dollar bill folded inside a five-dollar bill and three one-dollar bills.

Gertha added, "The wind was blowing that morning with so much force that had those bills not been held by a stronger power than the eye could see, they would have been carried away at once. It was and always will be a question as to the identity of the man who was walking away from our trailer house, and where did he go?"[35]

Using the money for gasoline, the Bishop family made it to their destination. They were nearly out of money again when they stopped in Indio, California, at an employment office to inquire about work. They were sent to see an employer in Mecca, California. When they arrived in Mecca, the manager told Gertha and her daughters that they could start working that afternoon.

"We now learned why we had not been forced to sell our trailer house," Gertha concludes her story. "There were no living quarters to be had at any price and no other work to be had for many miles.

We felt we were truly guided. Even though our funds were gone, our employer was kind enough to advance us what we needed. We were, indeed, grateful and humble before our Heavenly Father and pray that we may always live to be worthy of such a great blessing and testimony."[36]

Wonderful stories like this abound. Elizabeth Horrocks Jackson Kingsford was born on 5 August 1826 in England. She was the oldest of eleven children and began to work in a silk factory when she was only seven years old. Perhaps it was this early entry into the work force that toughened Elizabeth enough to survive the trials she faced later in life.

Elizabeth became a member of The Church of Jesus Christ of Latter-day Saints when she was fifteen. Years later she married Aaron Jackson. The couple had three children when they decided to immigrate to the United States. They joined the ill-fated Martin Handcart Company to travel across the plains. During the journey, the entire family faced extreme hardships, but in the midst of incredible suffering caused by being caught in a frigid early-winter blizzard, Elizabeth was blessed to see an angelic visitor in a dream. Hearing an angel's comforting words helped Elizabeth hold on until help could arrive from Salt Lake City.

Elizabeth's worries began early in the journey when the handcart company's provisions began to run low. As their rations were cut, the pioneers' strength began to wane. When they were near Ft. Laramie, an anxious group of Saints went to the fort and sold their watches and other jewelry in order to buy cornmeal, beans, and bacon. The handcart company pushed on, but before before long, food ran low again. The daily pound of flour each member was allowed was cut to three-fourths of a pound and then to a half. Then it was cut again.

Lack of food was not the only cause for alarm. Elizabeth states, "The trip was full of adventures," Elizabeth observed, "hair breadth escapes, and exposure to attacks from Indians, wolves and other wild beasts."[37]

During the difficult crossing of the Platte River, Aaron's strength gave out. A man on horseback helped him across the river while Elizabeth's sister helped Elizabeth pull the handcart, which carried her three children, across the river.

Then a terrible storm descended.

The company of Saints was pummeled by snow, hail, and fierce winds. They suffered intensely from the cold, having left much of their extra bedding and clothing behind because they had been too weak to carry it along.

Records state that on 20 October, the company wallowed through the snow for ten miles. Three more days of snow followed. All the while, Elizabeth's husband continued to sink. Around October 25, Elizabeth tried to prepare a little food for him, but Aaron didn't have the strength to swallow anything. That night he died.

The next morning, Elizabeth wrapped her husband in a blanket. He was piled with thirteen others who had also died. The pioneers could not bury the bodies, so they left them covered with snow.

Elizabeth said, "I will not attempt to describe my feeling at finding myself thus left a widow with three children, under such excruciating circumstances," Elizabeth recalls. "I cannot do it. . . . My sister was the only relative I had to whom I could look for assistance in this trying ordeal, and she was sick."[38]

Matters worsened. The few men left alive were so weak that they could not raise the poles and pitch the tents at night. This meant the survivors camped out in the open in the bitter cold, with several inches of snow on the ground and the wind whipping around them.

"It will be readily perceived that under such adverse circumstances I had become despondent," Elizabeth continued. "I was six or seven thousand miles from my native land, in a wild rocky mountain country, in a destitute condition, the ground covered with snow, the waters covered with ice, and I with three fatherless children with scarcely anything to protect them from the merciless storms."[39]

Then came the comforting dream.

"When I retired to bed that night," Elizabeth wrote, "being the 27th of October, I had a stunning revelation. In my dream, my husband stood by me, and said, 'Cheer up, Elizabeth, deliverance is at hand.' The dream was fulfilled, for the next day [October 28, 1856] Joseph A. Young, Daniel Jones and Abel Garr galloped unexpectedly into camp, amid tears and cheers and smiles and laughter of the emigrants."[40]

These three men were an advance group, coming ahead of a larger relief effort sent from Salt Lake City. Although the survivors continued to suffer until they arrived in Salt Lake, the worst was over.

Elizabeth was always grateful that her husband had come back and given her much-needed encouragement in her hour of desperation.

Helen Mar Whitney, the daughter of Heber C. and Vilate Kimball, grew up among such prominent Latter-day Saints as Brigham Young, Joseph Smith, Newel K. Whitney, and Eliza R. Snow. Helen was a skilled writer and wrote a series of reminiscences for the *Woman's Exponent,* a semimonthly newspaper for women. In the following account, Helen recalls a special dream she received that taught her that angels are frequently nearby and at least some angels are aware of everything that happens on earth. Helen wrote:

> I dreamed, a few nights ago, of being led by circumstances into a room, or office, where I found myself in the presence of a number of our aged brethren, some apostles, and one brother, who occupied a chair near the centre of the room and attracted my attention most, was from the spirit world. Though I did not know his name, I kept my eyes upon him, while listening with deep interest to the conversation, which was upon common topics or the scenes which most deeply concern the Latter-day Saints. After a little he spoke as follows, emphasizing every word so that it impressed itself the stronger upon my memory:
>
> "Why," said he, "we (spirits from the other side) are around here all the time, and know everything that is transpiring," meaning among our own people and the Gentiles, and that there were many more beside himself, who were similarly engaged."[41]

Charles D. Evans served as a patriarch in Springville, Utah, when he received a powerful manifestation. At the time, Elder Evans was worried about the social and economic problems the United States was facing; he was also concerned about the conflicts the country was experiencing with other nations. Elder Evans was comforted by his extensive dream, even though it showed many great and terrible things occurring in the latter days. Elder Evans recalled:

> As I gazed upward, I saw descending through my bedroom roof, with a gentle gliding movement, a personage clothed in

> white apparel, whose countenance was smoothly serene. . . . My whole being was inbued with a joy unspeakable. All feelings of sorrow instantly vanished. . . .
>
> By some intuition or instinct, I felt he had something to communicate to me to sooth my sorrow or allay my apprehensions. Thereupon addressing me, he said:
>
> "Son, I perceive that thou hast grave anxieties over the perilous state of thy country, that thy soul has felt deep sorrow for its future. I have, therefore, come to thy relief and to tell thee of the causes that have led to this peril. Hear me attentively!"[42]

The angel then showed how apostasy covered all the earth and, without prophets to enlighten the people, all nations had become shrouded in spiritual darkness. Brother Evans was shown how, through the restoration of the gospel through Joseph Smith, the United States in the future will have "reached an unparalleled prosperity. Wealth abounded, new territory was acquired, commerce extended, finance strengthened. . . and people abroad pointed to here as a model nation."[43]

The messenger then told Elder Evans that, in time, there would be a change in prosperity and that confidence in the government would be lost. Although the land would still abound in plenty, problems would occur between labor and management and there would be strikes and lawlessness. In addition, there would be earthquakes, floods, and wars. He was told that a foreign power would threaten the nation and the Constitution. However, the light of the gospel would go forth, and the landscape of the country would be filled with beautiful buildings, lovely gardens, and many schools and universities.

Elder Charles D. Evans concluded his account by saying, "After seeing these things and gazing once more upon the beautiful city, the following sounded in my ears: "Out of Zion, the perfection of beauty, God hath shined!"[44]

Mercy Rachel Fielding Thompson and her brother-in-law, Hyrum Smith, both lost their spouses. After Hyrum's first wife, Jerusha, passed away, Hyrum married Mercy's sister, Mary. Mercy's husband, Robert, died in 1841. Mercy was still a widow when, two years later, she and Hyrum each had the same dream. What makes this experience remarkable is not only that both of them had the same dream but that they had it on the same night. Mercy and Hyrum both saw their deceased spouses and were informed that marriage can be an eternal bond. In telling about her dream, Mercy said:

> I was sleeping with my Sister Mary Smith, Brother Hyrum being absent on business when I dreamt that I was in a garden and my late dear Husband Robert B. Thompson came to me and the Marriage vow was repeated by someone I cannot tell who. . . . I awoke in the Morning deeply impressed by this Dream which I could not interpret. . . .
>
> Brother Hyrum came home in the Evening being somewhat in rather a meditative mood he said he had had a very remarkable Dream. He said his late Wife Jerusha Barton [Barden] and her two Children, viz. Mary and Hyrum [all three deceased] were brought and presented to him on his arrival at home he found a Message had been sent from his Brother Joseph requesting him to come to his house immediately.[45]

Hyrum went to Joseph's home and "to his amazement found that a Revelation had been given stating that Marriages contracted for time only lasted for time and were no more one untill a new contract was made, for All Eternity and for those who had been sepperated by Death a Proxy would have to be obtained to Act for them."[46]

Mercy writes about what transpired next:

> Of cource no time was lost by those who had an opportunity of securing their Companions and the first presidency and as many of the Twelve as were [available] and the Presiding Bishop of the Church were all invited to meet in an Upper Room in the Prophets House each Man bringing his Wife of course. . . .
>
> Such a wedding I am quite sure never witnessed before in this generation. Of course my case was a singular one and had to be considered but the Prophet soon concluded that his Brother Hyrum had the best right to act for Robert B. Thompson. My Sister Mary Smith of course standing with Hyrum for Jerusha Barden. . . . Perhaps some may think I could envy Queen Victoria in some of her glory. Not while my name stands first on the list in this Dispensation of women seal(e)d to a Dead Husband through divine Revelation."[47]

In 1831, Electa Peck was told by her nephew Newel Knight that she needed to move. Newel explained that Joseph Smith had asked him to move his entire extended family to Ohio. While Newel made the necessary arrangements, Electa and the rest of her family made preparations to leave their homes in Colesville, Vermont. Electa did not question the move. She had a testimony that Joseph Smith was a prophet of God and knew that her nephew Newel was one of his most trusted friends.

On the appointed day of departure, Newel started out with the large group and, then left them to travel on by themselves while he returned to Colesville to take care of some unfinished business. The group had only traveled a few days when Electa was badly injured in an accident. Although a doctor cared for Electa, she remained in significant pain.

One day Electa fell asleep and dreamed that Newell returned to the group and gave her a blessing. Of course, when Newel actually did catch up with his family, Electa begged him for a blessing. He did as his aunt requested, and Electa was miraculously healed.

Newel later wrote about this experience:

> Soon after I left, my aunt, Electa Peck, fell and broke her shoulder in a most shocking manner; a surgeon was called to relieve her sufferings, which were very great. My aunt dreamed that I returned and laid my hands upon her, prayed for her, and she was made whole, and pursued her journey with the company. She related this dream to the surgeon who replied, "If you are able to travel in many weeks it will be a miracle, and I will be a Mormon too."
>
> I arrived at the place, where the company had stopped, late in the evening; but, on learning of the accident, I went to see my aunt, and immediately on my entering the room she said, "O, Brother Newel, if you will lay your hands upon me, I shall be well and able to go on the journey with you."
>
> I stepped up to the bed, and, in the name of the Lord Jesus Christ, rebuked the pain with which she was suffering, and commanded her to be made whole; and it was done; for the next morning she arose, dressed herself, and pursued the journey with us.[48]

Lorena A. Wilson dreamed several times that her mother, who had died three months earlier, returned to see her. However, each time she woke from one of these dreams, Lorena was disappointed to find that, once more, she had only *dreamed* of her mother's return.

Then her mother appeared again, only this time it was in a vision. She told her daughter that she actually *had* come to see Lorena in her dreams and that Lorena should not have discounted those visits simply because they had been in the form of a dream. Lorena's mother explained that it was easier to contact Lorena through her dreams than in any other way. Lorena relates her vision:

> I had retired to bed between nine and ten o'clock at night. My husband was out to a High Council meeting which usually kept him to a late hour. A baby, six months old, was by my side, and twin girls two years older, lay in a crib in the same room. The latter acted restless and I was about to arise and look after them. There was rushing, as of wind, and a rustling as of autumn leaves, that filled me with a kind of timid fear.
>
> Just then the room lighted with a soft white light, and I wondered how the moon could be so bright, as the room seemed lighter than at midday. At this point I saw mother enter the door, looking as natural as life, she came directly to my bedside and greeted me. I had dreamed of mother visiting me and was disappointed when I found it was only a dream. Now I told her I was glad she had come while I was awake. She answered that she did come although it was a dream. As she was in spirit form she could more easily converse with my spirit while my body was at rest.[49]

Dreams can truly deliver comfort and peace. Nola was going through a difficult time when she had a comforting dream that left her with a sense of peace that sustained her during her trials. Nola tells about her experience as follows:

> During a very troubled part of my life when my health was poor, my marriage floundering, and I was struggling with a wild teenager, I became quite depressed. Then the news reached me

that my father was ill, perhaps dying. At that point when I had sunk to the lowest ebb of anxiety, I had this dream.

I was entering a lovely room with high ceilings and arches. . . . The home was spacious, but it was also connected to many long hallways, doorways, walls and corners. The architecture was beautiful, different from anything I had ever seen or have seen since. There were long, curving corridors with couch-seats built into the walls that you could sit on and look out the lovely windows into gardens and far-away landscapes. I was going to see my father, and suddenly, I found him there.

He was very happy to see me and gave me a big smile and said, "Come over here, I want to show you my big house." It was his custom in life to show me his house whenever I would come to visit. . . . It was a familiar feeling for me as I followed him on a tour. I also saw a machine, run by a keyboard, that gathered material at people's request. . . . I had never seen nor heard of a computer at the time, but this machine was similar to one.

A wonderful organ projected colors and patterns along with the music played on it. My father played it with great skill and joy, and the organ and the colors it projected related to the décor of this wonderful building. We had a wonderful time as my father showed me around. . . . I was thrilled to see this wonderful place. I knew that my children, my grandchildren, all my grandchildren's children, and everybody could come to this family institution, which seemed to be Daddy's place, only it was related to many groups of people in the same way as the halls and rooms branched off throughout it. Then I thought, "Wow, this is a lot of stuff to manage, to clean, to maintain," and I started thinking about it all in a worldly sense.

I asked my father, "How do you take care of all of this?"

He smiled and his eyes were bright as he said, with the most airy attitude, "Oh, we *can* and we *do*." And I didn't worry about it anymore. . . . We went on, and there were many windows in the curved corridors that became rooms, and through others we could see landscapes, beautiful simple scenes in lovely color combinations. Some were of the mortal world and some looked onto higher planes.

My dream ended, but I awoke with my personal anxieties gone. I felt content that when my father did pass away, this would be his place in paradise. It would be a lovely family home where we would all go until we settle into wherever we will be through the eternities. Here we would be able to contact our loved ones and extended family. We would talk with them, get reassurance, and be satisfied. It is to be a place of luxury and grandeur for extended family; yet cozy to individuals. This dream was a great comfort to me, a hope for the next life, and a motivation to live this mortal life the best I can."[50]

Darwin R. Smith was a United States soldier fighting in Vietnam when he began having the same dream over and over. Finally, the chilling dream came true. The account states:

> A very dramatic story is that of PFC Darwin R. Smith from Idaho Falls who was serving in Vietnam. He dreamed the same dream for six nights in a row. Then one day while in combat he came to a turn in the trail, he being the point man. This turn he had seen in his dream, and as he proceeded around it, the events of his dream came to pass exactly as he had seen them.
>
> He was shot in the chest by an enemy sniper. The bullet hit him in the Book of Mormon which he carried in his fatigue pocket. The bullet indented the word God in Alma 44:4: "Now ye see that this is the true faith of *God*; yes, ye see that God will support, and keep, and preserve us, so long as we are faithful unto him, and unto our faith, and our religion; and never will the Lord suffer that we shall be destroyed except we should deny our faith."[51]

Lila Guerra was overjoyed to travel from Uruguay to Salt Lake City with her husband, Cesar, to attend general conference. While there, the couple planned to go to the temple and be sealed together for time and for all eternity. However, Lila's joy was tinged with sadness because they did not have enough money to take their five children with them. As it was, Cesar had had to take out a loan to buy his wife's ticket. Lila knew it would take a long time to pay the loan off.

Still, Lila and her husband were excited about their upcoming trip. They wrote to friends in the United States about their joy at being able to attend conference and their faith that the Lord would give them another opportunity to come and bring their children.

One night in July, Lila had a dream that they received the money to take their children with them on the upcoming trip. She wanted to tell her husband about it, but when Cesar came home, he was very excited about something and said he needed to talk to her.

Lila interrupted him and said, "Before you tell me your story, let me tell you about my dream last night. I dreamed that we received the money to take the children with us."[52]

Cesar then pulled out a letter and gave it to her. Lila read it with wonder. Friends of theirs in the United States—former missionaries, mission presidents, and their families—had initiated the "Guerra Family Temple Trip." They had collected enough money for the Guerras to bring all five children with them to the temple. Lila's dream had come true.

During her childhood, Cora M. Pratt always felt like an outcast. She shed many tears of loneliness because she was not invited to activities with most other children. Then Cora had a comforting dream that let her know that although her peers did not accept her, she had a true, enduring friend in the Lord. Cora tells about her experience:

> When I was going to school some time ago there seemed to be a class distinction among the school boys and girls. I was one of the unfortunates, and wasn't invited to most of their parties, and was slighted in general. I felt my position very keenly, and thought over it, and wept in my private moments, until one night I prayed that I might either be put on an equal with others or be able to bear my burden.
>
> I then fell asleep sobbing and crying. That night I had a dream, or almost a vision, for I am sure that no vision could be grander. I dreamed that I went to a party where there were many boys and girls, and when I arrived they would not speak to me. They were all going horseback riding, so I sprang upon a white horse, when another girl came and ordered me off, for she was going to ride on it. By this time I had almost lost all courage, so I stood for a moment to decide whether I had better get on another horse or not. I soon decided to try again, but a boy came and took that one away.

They all rode away, leaving me alone, feeling as though I had not a friend in the world. While thus musing I looked up, and behold I saw a cloud of light in the east, and looking around me, I saw that it was dark with the exception of this light. In the light there appeared a grand temple that was of pure white marble glittering like diamonds. As I stood gazing at this beautiful picture, the door opened, and the Lord, followed by the ancient apostles, came through the door out on the steps, which were round and leading down from the temple.

The persons were clad in snowy white raiment, which was made loose, and hung from the shoulders, after the ancient pattern. Now I did not feel lonely, for the Lord seemed to say, "If all the world turneth against you, I will still be your friend."

This ended my dream, and I awoke feeling almost as if I were in heaven, and wondered how it could be that I was so foolish as to care for the friendship of such boys and girls. This dream has taught me a lesson, never to say or think that I am friendless, for the Lord will never forsake us.[53]

Shortly after the pioneers arrived in the Salt Lake Valley, they began having problems with the Indians. President Brigham Young counseled the brethren not to go into the canyons alone for wood. Daniel Tyler relates a story about four or five men who made arrangements to meet at the mouth of Cottonwood Canyon and go together into the mountains to get wood.

Unfortunately, only one of the men showed up at the appointed spot. He waited for some time and then decided to go on up the canyon a short distance and get some wood, hoping that the other men would catch up with him. "He did so," Daniel noted, "then stopped and waited again; still no one came. This was several times repeated, until finally he concluded to go to the place of loading, and there await the arrival of his comrades. Time moved slowly on, still his team were his only companions."[54]

Sundown came and still there was no sound of wagons. The man took stock of his situation. He had gone several miles into the mountains, against the advice of the prophet, and was now alone and in dangerous circumstances. There was only one thing to do. The story continues:

He went away from his team and bowed down before the Lord, committing himself to His protecting care, and pleading innocence of any desire to disobey counsel, but as he seemingly had done so, he asked forgiveness, and retired to rest. He fell asleep and dreamed that he awoke; daylight had arrived, and he finished loading his wagon and drove down out of the canyon unmolested, taking a little different route at one point from where he went up.

About the time he started down the canyon, in his dream he saw a man dressed in white near him to the right, on horseback. This created such a feeling of joy and safety within him. As he descended with his load this man kept just about the same distance from him. At one time his ax dropped from the wagon, and he did not want to leave the ax, nor did he want to get out of the presence of the welcome visitor or companion. So he ran back, letting the team go on, thinking perhaps the personage would keep along with the team and not miss him for half a minute; but as he picked up the ax and rose up behold his companion was just to his right.

Then for the first and only time he (the angel) spoke, saying, "Do you think you can get out of my sight? No, not for one moment; I am always right by your side." . . .After getting out of the canyon and all danger . . . he awoke, and behold he was still in the mountains, with all things as he left them when he retired to rest. All fear, however, had left him, and after completing his load which he had commenced the evening before, he drove down the canyon, taking the road indicated in his dream or vision, and arrived home in safety. . . .

All of us have just such pure, holy beings watching over us, although we may not see them, nor even dream of their presence; yet if we do not grieve them from us, they are our guardians "from the cradle to the grave."[55]

In another story from early Church history, Elder John M. Bohn and his companion, Elder Poulsen, were serving in Lolland, Denmark, in 1852. The elders frequently experienced tense situations there, and occasionally people hostile to the restored gospel sought to mob the missionaries.

One night the elders were at the home of Brother and Sister Jensen when five men knocked at the door. When the men entered, they were openly scornful of the missionaries. Some of them were carrying thick sticks that appeared to have been recently cut.

Although apprehensive, Elder Bohn recalled a scripture, "Behold, I send you forth as sheep in the midst of wolves: be ye wise as serpents yet harmless as doves" (Matthew 10:16).

In an attempt to diffuse the potentially explosive situation, Elder Bohn talked about the restoration of the gospel. He showed the men verses in the book of Revelation that recorded how the Apostle John saw an angel bringing the everlasting gospel, along with the plan of salvation, once again to the earth. Elder Bohn explained that in order to have continued revelation from God there had to be prophets and apostles, such as was found in The Church of Jesus Christ of Latter-day Saints. "After answering some questions," Elder Bohn observed, "there seemed a more calm spirit to enter into the men, so that the three of them became friendly towards us."[56] However, the other two men remained antagonistic.

Elder Bohn "gave them a warning not to fight against the truth, and to do no harm to God's servants, and especially not to thrash us with their heavy oaken sticks, which no doubt they cut in the forest for that purpose."[57]

The men left without incident, but a worried Brother Jensen reminded the missionaries that the men probably wouldn't harm them while they were in his house, but he warned them that they might wait for them outside, planning harm. Brother Jensen invited the missionaries to stay with them, an offer the grateful missionaries accepted. That night Elder Bohn had a dream:

> "In the night I dreamed that I was alone and traveling in an open field; but looking back I beheld a great carnivorous monster, something like a bear, coming after me. As I turned my head again I noticed a close growth of trees at a distance in front of me, and then I ran with all my speed for that clump of trees, thinking that if I could pass through them I would be safe; but coming in among the trees I found myself entangled in snares and strings twined all over and from one tree to the next, so that I had to use all my strength to break them. I then came out and pursued my journey gladly. . . . I awoke from my dream and thought I had the interpretation of it."[58]

The next morning, Elder Bohn told his companion that snares would be laid for him by enemies of the Church but that the Lord would protect him and deliver him from harm. The elders left the Jensen home and headed to Thoreby, a village on the east end of Lolland. They held several well-attended meetings and, the following Saturday night, baptized eleven people.

The next Sunday morning, Elder Poulsen went with another missionary, Brother Swenson, on a special assignment. Elder Bohn was left alone to hold fast and sacrament meeting with the twenty members of the branch. The meeting proceeded well enough, until a local minister showed up with a sizable group of people. Elder Bohn was concerned, sure that they had come to disrupt the service. However, the group listened intently while Elder Bohn spoke for an hour on Christ, the Atonement, and their duty to love one another.

When Elder Bohn was finished, the minister asked to speak. He walked to the front of the congregation, accompanied by four men holding large brandy bottles and carrying long oak sticks. The minister chided those in the congregation who had been converted. He told them they had been led astray by "vagrant Mormons."

As the minister spoke, the men beside him responded by hitting their sticks on the floor and occasionally shouting out exuberantly. The minister continued to chastise the converts, saying, "When you die, you cannot have a Christian burial but must be cast outside and put in the potters' field, among murderers and suicides."[59]

Elder Bohn promptly responded. "Listen my friends; it will not profit a man if he gains all worldly honor and riches, if he loses his soul. . . . But those who are reckoned as the outcasts of the world, yet have walked in the straight and narrow way to the end of their mortal lives, will be raised out of their graves to meet their Redeemer in the clouds of heaven."[60] Some of the people in the audience whispered that the Mormon priest was right.

The minister continued to throw out accusations and inflammatory allegations, firing up the anger of his followers. Finally, after one particularly incendiary comment, one of the burly men shouted, "We will baptize that Mormon priest in his own blood."[61]

Someone outside the building hurled a rock through a window, knocking the candle over. Inside, some of the men began pounding their oak clubs on the table. As Elder Bohn faced the room, he suddenly realized that he was seeing a fulfillment of his dream. Before him was a mob and, like the thick growth of trees in his dream, it was threatening and tied into priestcraft, and he didn't know how to get through it.

A friend hurried to Elder Bohn's side, warning him to leave or he would be killed. The missionary pushed his way through the darkened house and went into a small room. Forcing open the window, he jumped outside. It was easier to see outside than in, for the moon was full, but his heart sank when he saw that the yard was also full of mobbers.

Elder Bohn found some straw bundles and pulled them over himself. As he lay hidden, he could hear the mob yelling as they ransacked the house, "Where is the Mormon? Where is he?"

Then there was a rattle of a wagon pulling into the yard. The driver called out, "What is going on here? Is it murder or robbery?"[62]

The mob fled into the night. Elder Bohn came out from his hiding place. He found the Jensen family, bruised and bleeding but alive. After making sure the Jensens would be all right, Elder Bohn set out to return to his place of residence, a seven-mile walk through the snow.

The trip was difficult, but Elder Bohn was strengthened by the Lord. He arrived home safely and, like the dream had foretold, was able to come out of the frightening experience all right.[63]

Emma Somerville McConkie was living in Moab, Utah, when she had a dream that changed her attitude, abolished her fatigue, and boosted her sagging spirits. Emma's son relates his mother's experience:

> Mother was president of the Moab Relief Society. [A non-member who opposed the Church] had married a Mormon girl. They had several children; now they had a new baby. They were very poor and Mother was going day by day to care for the child and to take them baskets of food, etc. Mother herself was ill, and more than once was hardly able to get home after doing the work at [their] home.
>
> One day she returned home especially tired and weary. She slept in her chair. She dreamed she was bathing a baby which she discovered was the Christ Child. She thought, Oh, what a great honor to thus serve the very Christ! As she held the baby in her lap, she was all but overcome. She thought, who else has

> actually held the Christ Child? Unspeakable joy filled her whole being. She was aflame with the glory of the Lord. It seemed that the very marrow in her bones would melt. Her joy was so great it awakened her. As she awoke, these words were spoken to her, "Inasmuch as ye have done it until one of the least of these my brethren, ye have done it unto me."[64]

Emma's grandson, Oscar McConkie Jr., said he once asked his father about this story. He wanted to make sure he had all the facts right because he wanted to retell it at a family reunion. Oscar admitted that, like others who had shared the story, he wanted to "water down" the story of the angelic visitation. In talking with his father, he mentioned that his grandmother "seemed" to hear a voice. Oscar said, "My father corrected me," Oscar noted, "saying, 'She did not *seem* to hear a voice. She *heard* a voice.'"[65]

Horace G. Whitney had a consoling dream in which he saw a good friend, Fera L. Young, who had died a short time before. By all indications, Fera was going to have a successful life. He had gone to an eastern college and graduated with honors. Then he was called to serve a mission. While traveling to Mexico to begin his mission, Fera passed away. President Heber J. Grant shared Horace's dream during the funeral services.

In his opening remarks, President Grant said, "It always seemed to me a strange thing that a boy with all the education he (Fera) had, who had made a wonderful success, should be taken from us. . . . I thought that with his faith and knowledge, and with all the information he had gained, it was too bad he had to lay down his life while in the Lord's service."[66]

President Grant then said that one of his dear friends, Horace G. Whitney, had seen Fera in a dream and that Fera was preaching the gospel in the next life. "Horace asked him what he was doing," President Grant noted, "and received this reply:

> I am here working, Horace, with the wayward boys and girls of the Church, who are drifting away from it, and I am trying to turn their hearts back to the truth. That is my calling, and it is of far greater importance that it would have been for me to remain upon the earth. I have a great influence with them.[67]

Chapter 5

Angelic Visits that Testified of Truth

Ever since the glorious First Vision, those who have faith and earnestly seek for knowledge have been privileged to receive divine manifestations about the truth of the restored gospel. The Church of Jesus Christ of Latter-day Saints was founded on a vision received by a young, uneducated boy who faithfully inquired after the truth. His humble prayer for knowledge was answered when, in 1820, the heavens were opened and Heavenly Father and Jesus Christ appeared to Joseph Smith.

Elder Joseph G. Romney believed that many dreams are meant to increase a person's faith "We have many other examples wherein men who received dreams from God, and were obedient to their teachings, realized blessings at his hands," he said. "Dreams are great and glorious gifts of God to man, and they are given for his benefit, or his holiest and most deserving servants would not alone receive them. . . . They are given to strengthen the faith of individual Saints."[1]

President Wilford Woodruff said that after one of his dreams, his testimony was strengthened. He then spoke about the purpose of dreams, declaring, "And what is it all for? It is to teach us a principle. We may never see anything take place exactly as we see it in a dream or a vision, yet it is intended to teach us a principle. My dream gave me a strong testimony of the resurrection."[2]

The Spirit of God has touched people on numerous occasions and prepared them to receive the gospel. In a general conference session, Elder Orson Pratt spoke to missionaries when he declared, "Those who have been sent on missions to the nations of the earth have had abundant proof that the Lord is ready and willing to pour out His blessings upon them. You were promised that the angels should go before you, and open the hearts of the people to receive you; and when you have gone among a strange people, some of them have recognized you through the dreams and visions given them from the Almighty, and they have said: 'I know you are a servant of the Lord, for you were shown to me in the night vision.'"[3]

Elder Pratt further stated that the Spirit of God would work upon people, and they would then seek out the missionaries so they could be baptized. Elder Pratt said, "Who told them to come and be baptized? They say that men came to them in their dreams, and spoke to them in their own language, and told them that away yonder was a people who had authority from God to baptize them."[4]

God promises us that we will receive a testimony of the truth if we will ask. "If any of you lack wisdom, let him ask of God, that giveth to all men liberally, and upbraideth not: and it shall be given him. But let him ask in faith, nothing wavering" (James 1:5–6). If we are sincere and ask in faith, we are entitled to receive inspiration from heaven, which will then help us know the truth of all things. "Men and women by the hundreds, yes by the thousands, have had visions regarding the divinity of this work," observed President Heber J. Grant, "and every honest soul who has embraced it has had the testimony of the Holy Spirit."[5]

Many conversion stories testify to this. Through an amazing series of three separate dreams, two missionaries found the first woman convert in Mexico, a Sister Yanes, who was waiting to hear about the gospel. Her son, Jose, told his mother's story to Church leaders who visited the area many years later.

The account states:

> Desiring to hunt up some old Mormons that the ancient mission records located near Tula, President H. S. Harris and

> Elder A. L. Taylor took a train for that place. As the country was new to them and the people strangers, they could only rely upon the Spirit of the Lord to dictate and to guide them to the right place.
>
> Accordingly they alighted at a town called Nopalo, and began what proved to be a six-mile walk. At its termination they arrived in a little town named San Sabastian, and found a rather wealthy and influential man named Jose Yanes, who, with other members of his family, had been baptized many years before.[6]

At first, Brother Yanes treated Elder Harris and Elder Taylor very coolly but after talking with them for some time became friendlier. Rubbing his old, stiff hands together, Brother Yanes invited the elders to sit and stay with him while he told them about his mother's conversion.

Brother Yanes said, "Shortly after the arrival of the first Mormon Elders in Mexico, my mother had a dream, in which it was manifested to her that in the City of Mexico were some men publishing a pamphlet called 'Voz del que Clama en el Desierto,' and that this tract contained information highly important to her spiritual welfare. The following day she sent me to the city to find these men and to bring her a copy of the paper.

> I searched unsuccessfully for two days, then sat down in the Alameda, somewhat discouraged, to decide what to do. A man came and sat down by me. In the conversation that followed between us, he said there were some men in Hotel San Carlos who were publishing a pamphlet by that name. This strengthened my faith, for I admit that I did not expect to find either men or paper.
>
> I went to the hotel, and was received kindly by the Elders, who informed me, unasked, that the literature I sought was at hand. To test their faith and knowledge, I denied being in search of any literature and told them that my mother had been dead many years.
>
> The Elders replied, that it all had been made known to them; that my mother was living; that she was a descendant of Guatemozine, who succeeded Montezuma II as ruler of the Aztecs; and further, that she would be the first woman to embrace the Gospel and be baptized in Mexico.
>
> I then accepted the literature and returned home. When

my mother saw me coming she ran to meet me, her face radiant with joy. She said, "You found the men; let me have the pamphlet."

Desiring to test her still further—for I was still skeptical—I said. "You were mistaken, mother: there are no such men and no such pamphlet in all Mexico."

Her countenance fell and she looked very much disappointed as she said, "You are trying to deceive me. In a dream I saw you talking to the men, and I saw you receive the literature." Then I gave it to her.

After very carefully reading the papers brought her, she sent me to the city again this time to bring the Elders. They returned with me and baptized her according to their vision.[7]

In January 1950, President and Sister Wagner of the Central American Mission gave a tour of the area to Elder Milton R. Hunter and his wife, who were visiting the mission. Shortly after the Hunters arrived in Guatemala City, President Wagner told them the story of Daniel Mich, who lived in Patzicia, Guatemala.

A few years earlier, there had been a rebellion when Indians tried to overthrow the government, which consisted primarily of people of Spanish descent. The rebellion failed, and the government decided to execute all those who had participated. They vigorously rounded up anyone they thought had any part in the rebellion. Many innocent people were jailed.

Although Daniel and his brother had not participated in the rebellion, others implicated them in the act. A friend warned Daniel that he and his brother were in danger. Daniel felt inspired that he and his brother should flee to the mountains and hide in a particular place or else they would be killed. The brothers fled and hid in the spot that Daniel had been told about. Cautiously, they watched from a ledge as soldiers searched the mountainside for them.

Daniel and his brother stayed in hiding for two years before they were captured. However, government officials were not as strict as they had been two years earlier. Instead of being executed, Daniel and his brother were merely thrown into prison. They spent four long years imprisoned under terrible conditions. The men had little clothing and practically no bedding. There was no heat, and they suffered greatly from the cold. They were given so little food that they nearly starved to death. Worst of all, Daniel found out that his wife and six children were destitute and almost as bad off as he was. His wife could not find enough work to provide food for his children, and they were close to starvation.

Daniel could hardly bear the thoughts of his suffering family. In desperation, he knelt and begged God to be merciful and let him and his wife and children die so that they could be released from their misery and suffering. Then Daniel had a dream.

"But God did not let them die. Instead, Daniel Mich had a vision, or a dream, or whatever it might be called. He was going up the side of a steep mountain on a definitely defined trail. He came to a place where a side trail forked off the main trail. A man stood on the side trail and said, 'Follow me.'

"Daniel Mich replied, 'No, I cannot follow you. I must follow this trail straight ahead.'

"He went some distance farther, and another man stood on another side trail. He also said, 'Follow me.'

"And again Daniel Mich replied, 'No, I cannot follow you. I must go straight ahead.' This experience repeated itself three or four times.

"Daniel Mich explained. 'Finally I came to the summit, and there standing in front of me was a tall, handsome man, with beautiful white hair. He had a very kindly and beautiful smile. This man said to me, 'Daniel, follow me.'

"I replied, 'I will follow you,' because as I made that remark, the Spirit of God whispered to me and said, 'That man has the truth.'"[8]

When Daniel woke up, he did not know what to make of his unusual dream. He soon forgot about it when news came that he and his brother were to be released from jail.

Shortly after Daniel and his brother were freed, missionaries from The Church of Jesus Christ of Latter-day Saints came to Patzicia, Daniel's hometown. The mayor was concerned when he learned of the missionaries' arrival and sent for them. He was not the only one disturbed by the coming of the Mormon elders. When the missionaries approached the mayor's office, they saw that a large crowd of approximately two hundred people had gathered. As the missionaries walked toward the building, the throng parted, leaving the elders to thread their way between two long lines of people to reach their destination.

Once the missionaries were inside his office, the mayor bluntly asked them to leave the city, saying he had a petition signed by the community requesting their departure. The elders calmly stated that they wished to stay and preach to anyone who would listen. They stated matter-of-factly that they would not leave until their mission president told them to go.

The mayor had not expected anything but acquiescence and was unsure what to do next. Finally, one of the missionaries suggested he telephone the governor.

The mayor placed the phone call immediately. After the governor heard what was happening in Patzicia, he chided the mayor, saying, "Let those Mormon missionaries alone. They have a right to teach their religion in your town or in any other town or city in Guatemala, because we have religious freedom in our country."[9]

When the missionaries left, the crowd parted again and once more the elders passed between two long lines of people. At the end of the line was Daniel Mich. He stepped forward and asked the elders if they would go with him to his home and talk with him and his family.

After listening to the first lesson, Daniel was eager to hear more. The missionaries made appointments to come back and teach his family the gospel. During one of the lessons, one of the elders opened a book and Daniel saw a photograph of a tall, handsome man who had beautiful white hair.

Daniel excitedly proclaimed, "This is the man! It is he whom I saw!"[10]

After telling the missionaries about the dream he had while in jail, Daniel asked, "Who is this man whose photograph you have in your book?"

"'His name is David O. McKay,' the missionaries replied. 'He is the president of The Church of Jesus Christ of Latter-day Saints. He is God's holy prophet, seer, and revelator upon the earth at the present time. He is the man who holds the keys of the kingdom of God and stands as Christ's representative in the true Church and the leader in spreading the true gospel of Jesus Christ.'

"In deep sincerity Daniel Mich replied, 'I know that all of the things you have told me are true. I know that you missionaries have the true gospel of Jesus Christ.' Then he asked, 'Do you know why I invited you to come to my home that day as you came out of the mayor's office?'"[11]

They did not.

It was another part of his dream, Daniel said, and went on to explain. "At the time that tall, handsome man, with beautiful white hair—whom you have told me was President David O. McKay—said to me, 'Daniel, follow me,' the Spirit of the Lord whispered to me and said, 'This man has the truth.' The Spirit also said, 'Two young men will bring you the truth,' and when you came into our town and began to teach your religion, I became curious. I had been watching you and attempting to find out all about you that I could. When the citizens of Patzicia signed the petition to have you thrown out of town and when you called to see the mayor, I joined the crowd in front of the mayor's office to see what would take place. And now, all the things that I believed have been verified. I know that David O. McKay is a prophet of God. I also know that you have the true religion of Jesus Christ."[12]

An unusual dream prepared J. W. Crosby to hear the message of the restored gospel. He writes:

> A little before the Elders came to my home in New York State, in a vision of the night I saw my body and spirit separated, and they were in features, form and size, exactly alike. I was calm and composed, and the recollection is with me today, just as vividly as forty-two years ago. [This was written in 1881].
>
> When I came out of my vision, fear seized me, and my heart beat quickly. In a short time, however, a happy train of thought came to my mind, and I saw that the vision was given to show me that the immortal spirit is exactly like the tenement it lives in. This gave me joy, and while in this happy mood, word came that the Latter-day Saints were going to preach at my old familiar school-house.
>
> This was the first time I had heard of Saints in our day, and the very name brought conviction to my mind. . . . Faith sprang up in my heart that these Saints were the people who possessed the truth and could teach it to me; and at that one meeting I learned more of the Bible, and more of God and His ways, than I had learned in all my life before.[13]

After he was converted, J. W. Crosby went on a mission himself. He soon discovered that other people were being prepared to receive the missionaries through their dreams. "And what is quite remarkable, many people have seen the Elders in dreams and visions, and recognized them on sight," Elder Crosby noted. "Others have heard beautiful music in their rooms at night, just before the Elders came to their neighborhood to preach."[14]

David John's parents share another touching dream story. The two were devout members of another religion, and one of their greatest desires was to see their son become a minister in their faith. To this end, David's parents sent him away to school to receive the education he needed to become a minister. However, while he was at college, David had a dream that altered his life forever.

When missionaries from The Church of Jesus Christ of Latter-day Saints began teaching in Wales in 1847, many people, including David, listened to their message. He gained a testimony of the truthfulness of the gospel and asked his parents for permission to be baptized.

His parents were shocked, grief stricken, and angry. Not only did they refuse to give their permission, his father demanded that David be placed under bonds in order to keep him away from the Mormons until he became of age. Outraged at his father's actions, David went to talk with Elder Orson Pratt, president of the European Mission. Elder Pratt counseled the young man to obey his father.

David heeded Elder Pratt's advice and cut off all contact with the Latter-day Saint people. He also gave in to his father's request that he spend four years at a religious college in South Wales, preparing for the ministry.

Then, in January 1856, David had a dream. David writes:

> I dreamt that I saw an angel of the Lord. . . . His eyes were of a dark brown color, but full of glory. His voice was clear but full of power and authority. . . .
>
> The angel asked, "Why are you spending your time in vain here? How is it you will not join the Church of Christ and spend your time there?"
>
> I replied, "I hope I am in the Church now, am I not?"
>
> "You know better," he said.[15]

The angel showed David a glimpse of heaven. David was even allowed to see Christ in all His glory, sitting upon His throne. He also saw people being gathered together to be judged.

"The Saints seemed lovely, and all smiled," David observed. "But the other line seemed miserable and full of discontent, sorrow and grief, turning their faces from Jesus . . . (as though they) could not abide His presence."

After this dream, David knelt down and prayed. As he did, the angel came to him again, saying, "Thou wert foreordained before the foundation of the world to come forth in this age to assist to build the kingdom of God upon the earth."[16]

The words of the angel sank deep into the young man's mind. He spent many hours in deep meditation. Although David rejoiced in his dream and the angel's visit, he felt a responsibility to act upon the truth that had been made known to him. Still, David was anxious about how his parents would react if he joined the Mormons.

The following day, David could not concentrate on his studies. His teacher, supposing him to be ill, excused him from class. David walked to the home of a nearby friend, Elder John Griffiths, who was a member of the Church. He asked to see some literature. After studying "Voice of Warning" by Parley P. Pratt, David felt prepared to face his family and friends. He informed his parents, friends, and teachers that since he was now twenty-three years old, his father could no longer force him to act against his wishes. He told everyone that he was going to quit college and dedicate his life to The Church of Jesus Christ of Latter-day Saints.

His classmates, teachers, and family were appalled. Although they tried to get David to change his mind, he would not. David was soon baptized and ordained to the office of a priest. Later he became an elder and in June 1856, he was set apart to go to a mission in the Pembrokeshire Conference. The following December, David was appointed to preside over the Flintshire Conference, where he remained for one year before being called as a second counselor to the president of the Welsh Mission. David John continued to earnestly build the kingdom of God for the rest of his life.

Because Sister Miller saw a missionary, Elder Walter G. Paul, in a series of dreams before he arrived, she was prepared to accept the truth of the gospel when it was presented to her. However, Sister Miller was not the only one to see Elder Paul before he arrived in Kentucky in 1882. A fellow missionary, Elder Louis A. Kelsch, also saw Elder Paul in a dream.

Elder Paul says of the experience, "One spring morning . . . while I was walking through the woods, I met a gentleman with grip and umbrella. On seeing me he exclaimed: 'Hello, Brother Paul. I know you, I dreamed about you last night.'"[17]

The man with the suitcase and umbrella was Elder Louis A. Kelsch. After his dream, Elder Kelsch had set out to walk seventy-five miles to meet Elder Paul. The two elders were soon fast friends. Then Elder Kelsch told his new companion that someone else, a Sister Miller, had also dreamed about him.

Elder Paul wrote, "He told me that for months past a Baptist preacher's wife [Sister Miller] of Gracon Country, Kentucky, had been dreaming all about me. She knew my name, and could describe me accurately." Furthermore, Elder Kelsch told him, "She will not be satisfied until she sees you. She claims that she will know you even among a thousand."[18]

Elder Paul was astonished to hear this, especially when he learned that Sister Miller had been told that there was no missionary by his name or matching his physical description. Despite the missionaries telling her all this, Sister Miller continued to have great faith in her dreams.

She merely retorted sharply, "Well . . . there is, and I am going to see him."

Elder Paul said, "I was therefore told to get ready for the seventy-five mile walk, which I did. We walked forty miles the first day, twenty the second, and finished the journey on the third. It made me very footsore and tired. Within a short distance of the Miller house a halt was made."

At this point, the elders thought they would have some fun. They decided to test Sister Miller's dream by introducing Elder Paul by some other name.

They did so, but Sister Miller could not be deceived.

Elder Paul states, "She laughed as we greeted her, and she said to me, 'How do you do, Brother Paul? I have been dreaming about you for months past.'

"We next went out into the cornfield and endeavored to play the same trick on Mr. Miller; but he had listened to his wife's description of me so often that he recognized me at once."

Elder Paul continued, "I wanted to accompany the Elders on their journeys to fill appointments, but nothing would do but I must stay with the Millers. The children (there were fifteen of them) were dispatched to the neighbors with an invitation to come and see the long-looked-for preacher from Utah.

"I tried to be sociable but I was very much embarrassed upon being invited to talk to them. I tried to entertain them on home and other topics as I could not discuss freely the principles of the Gospel. In this providential way I was led to this family. It certainly was not chance. My first mission call was for Great Britain, which was changed to the Southern States. Then my appointment was to the exact locality where I had been seen in dreams by this woman."[19]

As part of the legacy Mary Magdelaine Cardon Guild wanted to leave for her children and grandchildren, she wrote her personal history. An important part of this legacy was her testimony, which included a special experience she'd had as a child while growing up in a remote, mountainous part of Italy. Mary wrote:

> I was but a young child, between six and seven years of age. One morning, while in bed, I had a wonderful dream, or vision, which has proved to be one of the greatest blessings that my aged parents and family could ever have received on this earth.
>
> It seemed to me that I was grown up into young womanhood, instead of being a small child. I thought I was out by my father's vineyard on a small piece of meadow taking care of some of my father's milk cows so that (they) would not go into the vineyard. I thought I was sitting down on the grass reading a book, and as I raised my eyes I saw three men standing before me and looking at me. I dropped my eyes instantly as they were strangers to me. I felt somewhat alarmed, and as I raised my eyes again and looked them in the face.
>
> One of the strangers said unto me, "Fear not, for we are the servants of God and have come from afar to bring unto you and all who desire to be saved into the Kingdom of Heaven the Gospel. We are sent to reveal the everlasting Gospel of Jesus Christ.

> It is re-establish (ed) upon the earth never to be taken away, for that it should be re-established in its fullness was revealed to the Prophet Joseph Smith Jr., a boy of fourteen or fifteen years of age, he being very desirous to know which of different sects or churches was the right one. He asked God, in humbleness of heart, that he might know the true religion, and while in humble prayer he heard a voice speak to him, saying, 'There are none that are right at present, but the true Gospel will soon be revealed in its fullness.'"
>
> These three strange (personages) spoke of many future things which would come to pass. They handed me two small books, one with a pale blue cover and the other a pale green and they asked me to read them carefully and said that if I would obey the commandments of God, I would be saved. They said the day was not far off when my parents and family would embrace the Gospel of Christ, yea, and all of the House of Israel would be gathered together. The first step to this Gospel was faith, repentance, baptism by immersion, and the laying on of hands after baptism for the gift of the Holy Ghost. They said many things concerning our departure from our home and of our journey in the wilderness and that God would be our guide throughout our journey to Zion, and they then departed and disappeared out of sight.
>
> I awoke and felt very frightened and weak and somewhat strange. I walked into the kitchen where my mother was busy getting breakfast. She looked at me and saw that I was very pale and strange. She asked me if I were sick and I said, "No." She tried in vain to find what was the matter with me. . . . Soon my father came in and . . . he took me on his knees and talked to me for a while. Finally, I told him all that I had seen and heard and what those three strangers had said to me."[20]

The years passed. Then one day, when Mary was between seventeen and eighteen years old, her father came home greatly excited. He told his wife to get his best suit of clothes ready, for he wanted to change and be off quickly. He had just come from talking with a friend who told him that some strangers were preaching a very strange doctrine. His friend had explained some of what the strangers had said. Mary's father was struck with amazement because everything these strange men were saying was exactly what the three men in Mary's dream had told her years before. After her father got dressed in his best clothes, he started off for La Tour, walking the rest of the day and arriving the next morning.

Mary's father located the three men and attended their meeting. Afterward, he asked them to come to his home and make it their headquarters. The missionaries were glad to accept; they had been having a hard time finding people who were interested in hearing their message. In fact, only the day before, the three missionaries had gone into the mountains to fast and pray that the way might be opened up for them to find people to teach.

As the men walked, Mary's father told the missionaries about the vision his daughter had had so many years ago. He also told them that he had not been able to rest one moment after hearing about their message from his friend.

Mary was tending the cows when the men arrived. When her father walked over to introduce the three missionaries to her, she was speechless, for they were the same men she had seen in her dream so many years before. Their names were Elder Stainhouse, Elder Toronto, and Elder Lorenzo Snow. The missionaries handed Mary several small books, which contained the Articles of Faith and other doctrine. Mary looked down at the books in wonder. The books were identical to the ones she had been given in her dream. Her father became the first member of the Church in Italy, and soon after, Mary and the rest of her family were baptized.[21]

Mother Teasdel, as she was often called by her family and friends, also saw a missionary, Elder Thomas Smith, in a dream long before he appeared in person. Sometime after her dream, Mother Teasdel saw Elder Smith walking along the road. She recognized him and stopped and invited him to come to her home. Although she didn't know it at the time, her actions paved the way for missionary work to proceed in the Norwich area.

Hannah Last Cornaby, a friend, writes of Sister Teasdel's experience. "Inseparably connected with this happy time, were the occasions when we were guests under the hospitable roof of Mother Teasdel and her son, Brother Samuel P., listening while Sister Teasdel told, among other incidents connected with the commencement of the Latter-day work in Norwich; and how, long afterwards, she saw and recognized the same man on the street, in the person of Elder Thomas Smith; and, as directed by the spirit, accosted the stranger, telling him of her dream, and inviting him to her house; thus being the first to open her house to a Latter-day Saint Elder in the Norwich Conference."[22]

A woman not only was shown two missionaries in a dream, but learned about their individual personality traits long before they knocked at her door.

Two early Church history missionaries, Elder T. Lafayette Hatch and his companion, Elder Leo J. Neville, were the subjects of another dream—a happy event they recorded in their missionary record. The two were supposed to go to Dublin, but because Elder Hatch became ill, the pair was reassigned to the town of Lurgan. When the elders arrived in Lurgan, they began making inquires about lodging. One of the shopkeepers directed the missionaries to a nearby boarding house. When a woman answered the door, she appeared greatly astonished to see them but offered no explanation as to why she was so dumbfounded. She invited them in to see the available lodging.

Elder Hatch and Elder Neville liked the accommodations but asked if they could look further before making a commitment because those were the first rooms they'd seen in the town. Later that day, they returned, having decided to stay there. At that point, they found out why the landlady had been so astonished to see them. Elder Hatch writes:

> We then learned that the whole incident of our coming had been shown to the lady in a dream two nights before our arrival, or the night previous to the changing of our appointment. She recognized our dress and our features to be the same as those shown to her in the dream, hence the cause of her being startled at our appearance at her door. She had been shown the exact positions we would take on entering the room, and she was even shown the difference which she now actually knows exists in our dispositions.
>
> This, together with the fact that we were advised to come directly to her home, is a strong testimony to us that the hand of the Lord is over His servants. This is the same work in which the prophets of old were engaged; this is the work which Jesus Christ set up; this is the same gospel which was preached by Peter and Paul and other apostles. The same spirit which

directed them directs God's servants to-day, and if we are faithful we will not fail to enjoy the gifts of the Spirit.[23]

Sister Cottom also saw the missionaries in a dream before they arrived at her door. In fact, she dreamed of the missionaries on three separate occasions. Sister Cottom's dream was so vivid, she even noticed that one was carrying an umbrella while the other had a Bible tucked under his arm. Sister Cottom was no stranger to important dreams. Because of a dream she had received previously when she had been thinking about joining another church, Sister Cottom already had a testimony that the Church was true. Elder Brimhall recorded her dream experiences in his journal:

> Friday, August 27, 1897. Revisited Brother Cottom [and] explained [the] Gospel. Sister Cottom testified that she saw us three different nights in a dream before we came and had described us to her husband, even to the parasol carried by Elder Mann and the Bible which I carried under my arm; and that she knew us as soon as we came to the door although we had neither of us ever met her before.
>
> She is a young wife of 17 years. [She] had received a testimony that the Mormons were right in this wise: She had been baptized when a child but had taken no thought about her religion until lately. She had been visited, however, by a Presbyterian minister and through his personal influence thought some of joining that creed; when one night she saw in a dream a young Presbyterian lady come out of her grave and tell her not to join the Presbyterians. . . that the "Mormons" were right.
>
> Curious to know whether such a lady was really buried or not she sought the graveyard and went directly to the place and saw on the tombstone the name of the lady who had visited her in a dream, as the visitor was known in the dream by the name found on the tombstone which Sister C. had never seen before.[24]

After he heard missionaries from The Church of Jesus Christ of Latter-day Saints preach about the restoration of the gospel, Benjamin

Brown was converted and wanted to be baptized. However, he decided to wait until his wife—who still felt unsure—could gain a testimony of her own. One night, as he was waiting, Benjamin prayed to find out if what the missionaries had said about the judgments that were supposed to come upon the earth was true. In answer to his prayer, Benjamin had a vision.

"I was shown, in answer, by a vision, the various scenes described in the revelations of the ancient prophets," Benjamin writes. "The inhabitants of the earth appeared before me in their various occupations—plowing, sowing, fishing, and engaged in mechanical business. I saw them, under the infliction of the plagues, etc., lift their eyes towards heaven, curse God, and die. I also saw many other things as predicted by ancient prophets. Thus do I *know* the truth of the Bible as well as of the Book of Mormon, and am witness for both!"[25]

After this vision, Benjamin waited patiently for over a year and a half for his wife to gain a testimony. Unfortunately, her initial interest faded. Then she became opposed to the Church and even threatened to leave Benjamin if he was baptized. Despite this threat, Benjamin decided he had waited long enough to become a member and was baptized in May 1835.

His wife did not leave him, and after much earnest prayer, Benjamin was reassured by the Spirit that one day she would join the Church. He continued to wait. Then, about a year and a half after his baptism, Benjamin's wife had a simple dream that gave her a special witness about the truthfulness of the restored gospel. Benjamin relates it as follows:

> She dreamed one night that a large company of visitors had come to her house, for whom she had to prepare supper. On going into her buttery to procure the necessary food to cook, she could only find a small potato, about the size of a robin's egg, lying on a wooden trencher. However, with this small stock she commenced, and by some wonderful means converted this little affair into a splendid preparation of pies, puddings, etc.
>
> When they were ready she stood still, wondering how it had all been done, for, as may be supposed, it puzzled her sorely to conceive how, from a small potato, and that on a wooden trencher, she had produced such an elegant entertainment.
>
> Just at this moment while she was thus marveling, I was awakened from my sleep, with a command sounding in my ears that I was to say to my wife, 'Don't you remember hearing that

you should not despise the day of *small things?*[26]

Since Benjamin had been told to tell this statement to his wife at once, he woke her and repeated the sentence. This declaration, coming on the heels of her dream, had a great effect on Sister Brown. She had always felt that the Church was not important, since it was poor. But the dream and her husband's words caused Sister Brown to experience an immediate change of heart. With that change came confirmation through the Spirit that the gospel was true.

Brother Brown concludes his story by stating that his wife "was baptized, and has remained firm to the Church ever since."[266]

When local leaders would not allow Elder Benjamin Brown and his companion, Elder Crosby, to preach in Nova Scotia, the two elders decided to go to Quebec instead. They did not know until later that the Lord was sending them to Quebec to answer the prayers of a group that had been praying for a preacher. In fact, the Lord had already shown them to one of the group members in a dream.

Before they went to Quebec, Benjamin recorded the following in his journal: "I prayed the Lord to show us, in vision, those people among whom he wished us to stop and confine our efforts, for our mission to Nova Scotia had been assigned to us at the request of Brother Crosby, whose friends lived in that part, and was more to comply with his desire than from any prior intention the Presidency had with regard to the place."[28]

The two missionaries set off down St. John's River. When they overtook a man on a raft, they struck up a conversation. When the man learned they were preachers, he invited them to speak at his house the following Sunday.

When the missionaries arrived on Sunday, the man's wife seemed overjoyed—even jubilant—to meet them, but they had little opportunity to talk as people were arriving for the meeting. As the senior missionary, Elder Brown stood up first to speak. He taught the audience the basic principles of the restored gospel. Then Elder Crosby stood and bore his testimony.

Afterward, the man's wife told the missionaries that she and her friends and neighbors had been praying for several months for the Lord to send them a preacher. Their previous minister had left three months earlier. She also told them that she had had a vision, one that explained her extraordinary joy at seeing the elders at her door.

The vision came when she had been praying, as usual, for God to send them a preacher. Benjamin said that while the woman was on her knees "thus engaged, she was shown in a vision two men, the elder of whom was preaching, but the other delivered an exhortation of a different kind. The doctrine, she said, was new to her, but it seemed true. She also recollected distinctly the clothes and appearance of these men, and, to her great surprise and pleasure, recognized them in the persons of Elder Crosby and myself, directly we entered the room. Of course our hearts were cheered at hearing this, and we felt assured that the Lord was working in the vineyard with His servants."[29]

Sometime between 1890 and 1895, Polley Ann had an unusual dream that left an indelible impression. Later, when missionaries came to her door, Polley realized that they were there in fulfillment of her dream.

Ruth Spears Cruze, a granddaughter, relates the experience:, noting that "Polley Ann and William lived on a side road, off the beaten path. I don't think people traveled this road as much. Polley Ann was a religious woman. I don't think she belonged to any church. But one night she had a dream. In her dream she was standing at her front door looking out down the road from her house. She saw these two large birds flying towards her house. She thought they were eagles. They flew down and they lit on the road. After they lit on the road they changed into men. She got a good look at them as they walked up towards her house. The idea was put into her mind that they had a message to give her."[30]

When Polley woke up, she didn't know what to make of her dream.

"A few days later she was standing at her front door looking up the road. She saw two men coming up the road. When they got closer she recognized them as the two men she saw in her dream. When they walked up to her house, she remembered they had a message for her. They told her they were missionaries of the Church of Jesus Christ of Latter-day Saints."[31]

Polley told the missionaries she knew they had a message for her and that she'd seen them in a dream and was anxious to hear the message.

"They came in and taught the family the Gospel," the record continues. "They had eight children—7 girls and 1 boy. They were all baptized into the Church. My mother was the second oldest, Frances Joanna Sherrell. Polley Ann and William and their family were the only members of the Church at that time, in their area."[32]

Although Gaston L. Braley enjoyed talking to the missionaries of The Church of Jesus Christ of Latter-day Saints, he was not certain their doctrine was true. Because he had never been much for praying, he hardly knew how to go about obtaining a testimony. However, when Gaston decided to give prayer a try, he received a vision that convinced him that the Church was true.

The night before he had the vision, Gaston spent the entire evening talking with the missionaries. After they left, he prepared for bed, but his thoughts kept returning to their discussion. The next morning, Gaston headed outside to plow one of his fields. He writes:

> While I was cultivating my crop in the forenoon I resolved to pray for a divine manifestation. . . . I must say that I was an amateur in that kind of thing, but I tackled it anyway, having faith. I seemed to lose track of things about me and was carried away into a mental state, which I haven't a name for. I was transported from where I was, across the broad Kansas plains. . . over the Rocky Mountains and into the valleys occupied then by the Saints. I saw them happy and very busy, and somewhat prosperous as I went about. . . . Then I saw the Church in dire trouble. I saw the leaders of the Church hunted and persecuted. And I wept as I saw this. I saw some of them thrown into prison. . . . Later I saw a change come, a great change. The field became ripe to harvest, there was plenty everywhere; confidence was restored; the Elders went about unmolested; the brethren were no longer in prison. . . . I saw the Church overcome her adversaries and come into her own. I saw Salt Lake City and her beautiful Temple.
>
> It was about 5 P.M. when I discovered that I had been there all day, without food or drink for myself or horse and had been plowing constantly. I was on the point of exhaustion. I unhooked my horse and went home, pondering upon the astonishing things I had seen. And thus practically the first prayer I

> had addressed to Almighty God was answered in very deed. I lived to see that vision all come true.[33]

After this experience, Gaston joined the Church and moved to Salt Lake City, Utah. From there, he moved to California, where he served as patriarch of the San Francisco Stake.

Daniel Tyler was born in New York City in 1816, into a large and religious family. When he was sixteen years old, two missionaries, Samuel H. Smith and Orson Hyde, began preaching in the area. However, Daniel's story actually begins long before the arrival of these two elders.

When Daniel was a boy, his father and grandfather become unusually interested in the scriptures because of a religious furor sweeping across the nation at that time. As they read and studied, Daniel's grandfather said many times that he felt sure that somewhere there had to be a group of people following the true church of Christ. Then he had a vision that he was going to die soon; sure enough, he passed away a short time later.

Daniel's father continued to study the scriptures on his own. He was a man of strong opinions and came up with his own particular views on exactly what doctrine the true church of Jesus Christ should have. He was eager to the point of belligerence to discuss his views with any preacher he came in contact with and soon discovered that none of their doctrine stood up to what he believed was the truth.

Wryly, Daniel said of his father, "He never allowed a traveling minister to leave the neighborhood without an argument if he could avoid it, and his arguments were in no instance refuted."[34]

Then Samuel Smith and Orson Hyde came to town. They held a meeting to explain the doctrine of The Church of Jesus Christ of Latter-day Saints. Daniel records, "At the close of the first meeting my father, as his custom was, sprung his usual question about the spiritual gifts and was quite surprised to hear Elder Smith say, 'That is our doctrine, and we have those gifts in our Church.'"[35]

Daniel's father accepted a Book of Mormon, which he took home and read. Daniel was interested in the book himself and also began to read. However, he was unsure and frightened by the stirrings of the

Spirit he felt while reading. When Daniel's older brother insisted that the Book of Mormon had a spirit of witchcraft and that those who read it would become bewitched, Daniel set the book aside.

Before Elder Smith and Elder Hyde left the area, they had baptized three new members—and found a bitter enemy in Daniel's father. Although he admitted that the Mormon doctrines corresponded with his own beliefs, Daniel's father claimed that the Mormons had only adopted them to cover up other frauds. He listened to and believed people who told outlandish tales such as "Old Joe Smith walking on the water, pretended miracles, angels being caught, etc."[36]

Although Daniel finally did finish reading the Book of Mormon, and came to believe the restored gospel was true, he did not have the courage to stand up to his dynamic father. He continued to pray daily and finally promised the Lord that if his sister would agree to be baptized, he would too.

At the time, Daniel's sister was living and working at a neighbor's home. When Daniel went to talk with her about the Mormons, he discovered that not only had she already heard about the gospel, she had been taught its principles and planned on being baptized.

When she informed her father about her decision, he was very angry and said, "'If you do join them, you must never darken my door afterwards."[37] Although saddened by her father's attitude, Daniel's sister was determined to be baptized, even when her brothers threatened physical harm to any missionary who dared baptize her.

When Hyrum Smith came to the area. Daniel's father sought him out, angrily telling Hyrum that his daughter wanted to be baptized but that "the Elder who baptized her would do so at his peril."

Hyrum replied mildly, "Mr. Tyler, we shall not baptize your daughter against your wishes. If our doctrine be true, which we testify it is, if you prevent your daughter from embracing it, the sin will be on your head, not on ours or your daughter's."[38]

This gentle rebuke pricked Daniel's father to the heart. He began to reconsider his position. Then he stated that he would permit his daughter to exercise her agency. Finally, he declared he was confused and that Mormonism was either the best religion in the world or the worst and he did not know which.

His daughter talked with him about the gospel at length. She bore her testimony that The Church of Jesus Christ of Latter-day Saints was true and that she felt it was her duty to be baptized. Her father acquiesced to her wishes and took her by an ox sled to Lake Erie, two miles away. There, a hole was cut through three feet of ice, and she was baptized and confirmed by Hyrum Smith.

Despite his earlier resolve to be baptized when his sister was, Daniel remained so fearful of confronting his strong-willed father that he did not admit he had also been converted. Daniel stayed at home during his sister's baptism, feeling guilty at having broken his promise to the Lord.

Then Daniel received unexpected help from his dead grandfather.

Shortly after his sister's baptism, Daniel's grandfather appeared to Daniel's father in a dream. He told his son that the Mormon people were the people he had prophesied of when he was alive. This testimony from beyond the grave finally convinced Daniel's father that the restored gospel was true. He and his wife were actually baptized, followed by Daniel and his brothers. Daniel later became a prominent leader in the church.[39]

Newel Knight was one of the first members of the fledgling Church of Jesus Christ of Latter-day Saints and a close friend of the Prophet Joseph Smith. When Joseph convened the first conference of the Church in Fayette, New York, Newel was present, along with about thirty other people. During the conference at Peter Whitmer's home, Newel received a special vision and saw a glimpse of heaven. He was blessed to see the Savior and was told that he would have the privilege of returning to God's presence.

The conference was held on 1 June 1830. On that day, Joseph Smith gathered together members of the Church, as well as those who wanted to learn more about the gospel. During the conference, Joseph confirmed those who had been baptized, ordained men to various offices in the priesthood, and taught the gospel.

Newel records, "Much good instruction was given, and the Holy Ghost was poured out upon us in a marvelous manner. . . . I felt my heart filled with love, with glory, and with pleasure unspeakable. I could discern all that was going on in the room and a vision of futurity also suddenly burst upon me, and I saw, represented, the great work, which, through the instrumentality of Joseph Smith, was to be accomplished. I saw the heavens opened, I beheld the Lord Jesus Christ seated at the right hand of the Majesty on High, and it was made plain to my understanding that the time would come when I should be admitted into His presence, to enjoy His society for ever and ever."[40]

D. M. Bethune Jr. had just gained a testimony of the truth of the gospel when he received another witness to its veracity—recognizing the missionaries who called at his house. He recognized the elders because he had seen them earlier in a dream.

In November 1914, Elder Arthur T. Shurtleff and his companion, Elder D. L. Turner, were serving in South Carolina when they received a letter from the mission office. The mission president wanted them to contact Mr. Bethune, who had contacted his office. Mr. Bethune wrote to inquire if missionaries could be sent to his home because he wanted to become a member of The Church of Jesus Christ of Latter-day Saints

After receiving the letter from the mission office, Elder Shurtleff and Elder Turner finished their business and set off. About five o'clock that evening, they stopped to ask directions and were told that Mr. Bethune lived on that very road. When the missionaries arrived at their destination, they noticed a man chopping wood in the back yard and went around the house to speak with him.

"As I came up, hat in hand, the man looked at me and all color left his face," Elder Shurtleff recalled. "His hand trembled as he shook mine and he was overcome with emotion. He invited us into the house, and there he told us the cause of his shock and emotion at meeting us."

Elder Shurtleff recounts Mr. Bethune's story. "Exactly one year to the day, November 11, 1913, he [Mr. Bethune] related, he had seen two men in vision, who came to him with an important message. These men appeared so realistic that he took careful note of their appearance, dress and what they carried. . . . When we appeared he recognized in us the identity of the messengers whom he had seen in vision one year before."[41]

What makes this experience even more amazing is that at the time of Mr. Bethune's dream, Elder Shurtleff was preaching in Ohio and had no plans to go to South Carolina. Also, at the time of the dream, Elder Shurtleff wore a mustache, parted his hair in the middle, and did not wear glasses.

Elder Shurtleff continues, "And yet, as brother Bethune saw me, I was smooth-shaven, my hair was parted on the side, and I was wearing nose clip glasses, exactly as was the case one year later, when I appeared with my companion in person at the Bethune home.

"The entire Bethune family became members of the Church. And since that time, Brother Bethune has borne his testimony of his vision and its literal fulfillment to hundreds. And he still bears it. Dated June 1, 1936. Arthur T. Shurtleff, First Counselor in the Grant Stake Presidency."[42]

Mary Dunster Chittenden received a witness of the truth of the restored gospel in a dream before she ever heard it in reality. At the time of her dream, Mary and her husband, William, were living on a ranch in Camden, Australia. The account states:

> Mary dreamed that she was lying in her bed asleep. It was, as you might say, a dream within a dream. As she lay sleeping two men, each carrying a satchel in one hand and a cane in the other, came to the foot of her bed. She dreamed then that she awoke from her dream and looked earnestly at these two men; so earnestly that their faces were indelibly fixed upon her memory. One of them held out to her a little book.
>
> "What is the use of my taking the book?" she thought within herself, "I cannot read a line, for I have never learned to read." Then, after a moment's hesitation, she thought, "Why, I can take it and my children can read it to me." So she took the book.
>
> One of the men said these words to her: "We are clothed upon with power to preach to the people."
>
> She awoke in reality then, with those strange words thrilling her with a new power she had never felt before. She roused her husband up and related her dream.[43]

Some time later, William needed to go to Sydney, a distance of approximately one hundred miles away, to sell a load of wheat. After selling the grain, he planned to ask around and see if anyone would hire him to haul a load of freight on his return journey, so he could earn some additional income and help pay for his trip. The account states:

> On his arrival in Sydney after the disposal of his wheat, he walked out to see an old friend named William Andrews who lived in the suburbs of the town. Here he passed the time until evening when Mr. Andrews remarked, "I say, Chittenden, I've got some brothers come from America, and I am going up to see them. Would you like to go along?"
>
> "Oh yes," replied William. "I didn't know you had any brothers in America!"
>
> And so, arm in arm, they entered the little room where several men sat at a table, or pulpit with a strange book in their hands and strange words upon their lips. Here William heard the sound of the everlasting gospel for the first time. From the first William felt the truth contained in the words of the Elders although he knew little or nothing concerning them.
>
> On their way home Mr. Andrews explained to him that these men were his brothers, being brothers in the covenant of Christ.
>
> "And Chittenden," he added, "if any of them go down your way, you'll give them dinner and a bed, won't you, for I know you can?"
>
> "Oh, as to that," replied William, "I wouldn't turn down a beggar from my door, if he was hungry or wanted a roof to cover him."[44]

William found a man who would pay him to take a load of freight to Goulburn, which was south of his home in Camden. Since it was on his way, William decided to stop briefly at his home before proceeding on to Goulburn. As he rode along, William pondered deeply on what the elders had said.

When William reached his home, he told Mary about the missionaries. When she asked William what he thought of them, he answered, "Well, Mary, if they don't speak the truth then I never heard it spoken."[45]

Meanwhile, back in Sydney, the missionaries held a meeting. It was decided that two of them, Elder Fleming and Elder Eldredge, should go to Camden and the surrounding area. However, at the last minute, one of the older missionaries asked Elder Fleming to stay in Sydney, so Elder Graham went in his place.

Meanwhile, William had continued on to Goulburn to deliver the freight. While he was gone, “two dusty, tired, hungry men each with a satchel and a walking-cane in their hands, stopped at the wide open door of the Chittenden farmhouse. And what saw Mary, when she came to the porch? With a queer throb, she saw in her door the very man who came to her bedside in her dream. She even noticed the low-cut vest showing the white shirt underneath. But as he stepped aside, and her eyes fell upon his companion, she saw HE was not the second one of her dream, although he too carried a cane and satchel. She invited them within, and the first one said, ‘We are come, madam, to preach the gospel.’”[46]

The words were almost identical with those the men had spoken in her dream. She invited them inside, and they expressed their gratitude. Elder Eldredge explained that they had traveled from Sydney and, in all that long way, had found no one willing to give them food or shelter. Mary invited them to stay to eat and bustled about, preparing dinner for her guests. The account continues:

> When evening grew near, Brother Eldredge remarked, “Mrs. Chittenden, can you let us remain here over night?”
>
> “Oh,” said Mary, “I am afraid I have no place to put you!”
>
> “Well you can let us sit up by your fireside, and that is better than lying on the ground as we have done lately!”
>
> And then Mary assured them that she would do the best she could for them. So a bed was spread out on the floor of the sitting-room, and here the foot-sore Elders were glad to rest their bodies.
>
> The principles and doctrines of these men fell deep into Mary’s heart, and like her husband she felt they spoke the truths of heaven. One evening in conversation with them, Mary told Brother Eldredge that she had seen him before in a dream. But, she added, you were accompanied by another man, not Mr. Graham.
>
> “Ah, well, that might have been. You may have seen Brother Fleming for he was coming with me, but Brother Farnham altered the appointment at the last moment!”
>
> And it proved so. When Mary afterwards saw Brother Fleming she recognized him as the second one of her dream.[47]

Hans Jorgensen dreamed that his son, Jens, would one day be a savior to his family but never understood exactly what that meant or what it might entail. However, the meaning became clear many years later when Jens returned to his childhood home in Fyen and taught his parents about the restored gospel.

Jens was born in Denmark in 1823. After being introduced to The Church of Jesus Christ of Latter-day Saints and learning about their beliefs, he became a member in 1851. At a general conference in Copenhagen that same year, Jens was ordained a priest and then set apart as a missionary. He and his companion, Elder William Andersen, were sent to the island of Fyen—the place where Jens had grown up—to begin their missionary labors. The men worked hard, holding meetings, selling tracts, and speaking with the people about the gospel.

As soon as they could, the missionaries went to see Jens's parents, who were overjoyed and welcomed the missionaries into their home. They held several well-attended meetings. During one of them, Hans finally understood the meaning of the dream he'd had so many years before. Jens explained:

> One evening, after I had addressed a large gathering, my father went into his garden, where he bent his knees and in earnest prayer pleaded with the Lord to give his understanding and discernment as to whether the message which I was proclaiming was from God.
>
> When he again entered the house, the sign was given him, which caused his whole body to shake terribly and he felt unworthy to enter the room in which I was sitting. With trembling voice and tear-drenched eyes he now requested me to baptize him, which request was granted that same evening. My mother was baptized on the same occasion and a short time afterwards four of my brothers, together with several other people, were also added to the fold by baptism.[48]

Elder Glen Wood was serving as the bishop of his ward when he became very ill. After being taken to the hospital, he was diagnosed with blood poisoning. While in the hospital, he had a dream, which led him to believe he would die. "He seemed to know from the first that he would not recover," noted his father, Edward Wood, president of the Alberta Temple.

While lying in his hospital room, Elder Wood told his father about a dream he had. He dreamed that he was sitting in the temple, in a sealing room, when a messenger came to the room and told him that he would not be healed. But that was not the end of his dream.

Elder Wood also confided that his uncle, who had died some time before, had come to talk with him. And he had also had visits from other departed people. Finally, Glen revealed that he'd already received a call to preach to Samoans in the spirit world; Glen had served a mission in Samoa.

Then, the account states, "He (Glen) began speaking in Samoan to his father and said he was going on a 'malanga fou,' a new journey; whereupon he told his brothers, who were at his bedside, not to delay him, for he had to go. . . . Near the end, he began speaking in Samoan to Saints in the Spirit World, then died."[49]

Teenagers are often unnerved when death strikes one of their own, and Mickey, a young woman, was no exception. Mickey was distraught when Linda, a relative and close friend, died. Before Linda's death, the two girls had often talked about religion, but Mickey had never taken their discussions seriously. However, after Linda's death, Mickey began having the same dream over and over, leading her to believe that everything Linda had told her about The Church of Jesus Christ of Latter-day Saints was true. The following account was written by Lea Hoecherl, Linda's aunt and Mickey's sister.

> Linda Kay Andrus, daughter of my sister Barbara, lay still with death's sleep at age 15 years. Death seemed so unreal to me, so hard to comprehend. I was 16 years old, a junior in high school.
>
> My sister, Mickey, and niece, Linda, had been close companions. Linda often spoke to Mickey and told her about the importance of being baptized. Mickey's thoughts were, "Linda is too religious, and baptism isn't that important." After Linda's death, however, Mickey kept having the same dream over and over again.
>
> In this dream Linda stood in a lake of water, dressed in white. There were other people there being baptized. Linda called to Mickey and motioned for her to come in and be baptized. The dream upset her so that my father spoke to the Bishop, and sister missionaries were sent to our home. We

> studied the Book of Mormon and had discussions given to us. Soon after we were baptized. I knew that the Book of Mormon was true. I knew that this was the true gospel of Jesus Christ. I knew that baptism was essential.[50]

John Galbraith had a dream that stood as a testimony to him that The Church of Jesus Christ of Latter-day Saints held an important key in regard to temple work for the dead. President Wood, mentioned earlier, also related Brother Gailbraith's story. He states:

> Nearby is an Indian reservation. An Indian by the name of Brother Warner, from Parker, Idaho, came up to do missionary work among Indians in Montana. He and a young man named Galbraith went with him.
>
> This Brother Galbraith had a dream. He said he came to our meeting. He saw in the meeting, in his dream, four or five old Indian chiefs sitting on the stand. He knew these Indians were dead and had been for a long time. One of them was his uncle. The highest point on the Rocky Mountains near us was called Old Chief. That was the name of his uncle, the highest chief among the Blackfoot nation. He said as he went into the audience that this uncle of his told him to come up on the stand with him, and he said he wondered how it was, because this man was dead; he knew this.
>
> He went up and he heard his uncle stand up and preach a sermon to the audience there and turn around and say, "This nephew of mine must be our representative among our people."
>
> Brother Galbraith said that his uncle spoke in a language he could understand and marveled at it. Then Brother Galbraith said, "What have I got to do?"
>
> He [the uncle] said, "You see a book on the table;"—and he pointed to a book on the table—"that book contains the history of our people. We are what people call all *dead* and you are in the life, with the book. It will be told to you what to do."
>
> He awoke and after two long years of investigating, he joined the Church.[51]

In another instance, Harold E. Card Jr. gives an account of a man (who is not identified) who was working in his restaurant when he recognized a customer as someone he had seen in a dream, not just once but many times. He'd had the dream at least once a year ever since he was a young boy. In the dream, the customer took him to a large, beautiful building. Since they had never gone inside, this man had never discovered what the building housed. Harold E. Card's account states:

> In the fall of 1964, our mission president stopped in a certain area near Portland, Oregon, because of a referral he had received concerning an Indian of royal blood. He went into a café owned by this Indian and ordered a meal. While he was waiting to be served, the Indian entered the room.
>
> He stared at the mission president and continued staring while crossing the room. He entered the kitchen and gazed (at the president) through a window in the door. After a few moments he came into the room and approached the table at which our president was seated and introduced himself. Then he told of a dream he had been having each year since he had been a small boy.
>
> In this dream he had seen a white man who resembled the mission president and who had, in the dream, taken . . . [him] by the hand and led him up some stairs and each time when they would reach the top of the stairs he would awaken.[52]

When this man was shown a picture of the Salt Lake Temple, he recognized it as the building. Eager to know more about the Church that had been revealed to him in his once-a-year dreams, the man asked the missionaries to teach him and his wife. After nine months, the couple asked to be baptized. Elder Harold E. Card continues:

> My companion and I had been traveling through Southern Oregon and did not return to Portland in time to attend the (couple's) baptismal service from the beginning. As we walked down the entrance hall we realized that there was a light coming from the baptismal room brighter than an ordinary light.
>
> Upon entering the baptismal room we realized there was something different; a different spirit—a good spirit. We sat down while the president spoke. He told us he could feel the presence of the Indian's father in the room and that of the father's father and his father; also his wife's father, grandfather

and great grandfather. These were all were deceased. He also felt the presence of great Indian chiefs.

As these two people of royal Indian blood were baptized, tears came into their eyes and they said that they too felt the presence of their parents and grandparents in the room. The couple was confirmed at this time and when the service was over the lights were turned off, yet the room still glowed with this unusual light and we stood still for a moment until the spirits had all departed; then the room darkened. We are grateful for this experience.[53]

Dreams sent from a loving, concerned Father in Heaven truly are amazing experiences. W. J. Kohlberg was taking the train home when he fell asleep and missed his stop. Although irritated at first, Brother Kohlberg later realized that this misfortune was actually providential and helped shape the rest of his life.

After missing the stop, Brother Kohlberg got off the train, intending to take the first train back home. However, before he could purchase a ticket, he met a man who struck up a friendly conversation. The two men hit it off and his new friend asked if he would like to attend a "Mormon" meeting before returning home. Brother Kohlberg accepted the invitation, was impressed with the doctrine, and returned home with much to think about.

For several years, Brother Kohlberg continued to investigate the Church, as well as other religions, yet he was unable to make up his mind about whether The Church of Jesus Christ of Latter-day Saints was true. Finally, frustrated at his inability to reach a firm conclusion, he decided to travel to Salt Lake City, investigate the Church thoroughly, and make a decision.

Brother Kohlberg relates, "After hearing awful tales about the 'Mormons' and reading for two and a half years all that I could find, for and against the Church, I determined to know things for myself, bade my pleading parents, friends and relatives goodbye, and left my home in tears with a promise of converting either myself or some of the 'Mormons.'

"I arrived in Salt Lake City on New Year's morning, 1903, an absolute stranger," continues Brother Kohlberg, who found himself at Solomon F. Kimball's home. He knocked at the door and "to my surprise I was greeted and welcomed as one he had seen before. I had never seen Brother Kimball before, and I wondered, till he said: 'I saw you in a dream three days ago.'"[54]

Solomon Kimball went on to further astonish Brother Kohlberg by telling his visitor that he would become converted to Mormonism and that he would accomplish a great work.

Brother Kohlberg said he was not sure about these claims "because of my skepticism concerning 'Mormon' dreams and prophecies."[55]

Solomon told Brother Kohlberg about many of his experiences and even his reason for coming to Salt Lake City. Brother Kohlberg was astonished that a stranger could know so much about him. He thought Solomon was an amazing mind reader. Solomon further prophesied that his new young friend would experience a tremendous change through faith and evidence.

Although he still harbored many doubts, Brother Kohlberg stated, "Oh, how I hoped it were true! Faith and evidence one way or the other, was what I had been looking for."

Thankfully, everything came to pass as Solomon Kimball had said, and Brother Kohlberg wrote, "On a sunny morning, the second day in the beautiful month of May, 1903, faith and evidence led me to the waters of baptism. Later I was confirmed with knowledge, and filled with conviction, through the gift of the Holy Ghost. Since then, amid storms and sunshine, I have had ecstatic experiences and mountain-high evidence that so-called 'Mormonism' is the restored gospel of Christ."[56]

Carlos G. Alvarez attended Catholic schools all his life, beginning at the age of three. When he was a boy, Carlos had an experience that served to build his testimony when he became acquainted with The Church of Jesus Christ of Latter-day Saints later in his life. Carlos relates:

> When I was about seven I had a dream, or a vision, or whatever you want to call it. I saw this beautiful, lighted temple. It was a night scene.
>
> This stayed with me and later I made a drawing of it, and then a model. I had never seen a temple before, and the fathers [at parochial school] found out about my model and asked me

what it was. I told them, "It's a temple, and someday I'll go there." The priests smiled and called me loco and "visionary."

But when I started studying the Church, I saw a picture of the Salt Lake Temple, and my drawing was an almost duplicate of the temple in Salt Lake City. Now I know, someday, my dream will be fulfilled.[296]

In 1930, Lorin Grant Carruth was called to serve a mission to Texas. When he arrived in San Antonio, he had to hitchhike four hundred miles to reach the lower Rio Grande Valley. He served in that area for nine months, spending five of them without a companion. He was laboring in a town called McAllen when he was prompted to locate a man who, he was told, wanted to hear about the gospel. The account states:

> On December 11, 1930, Lorin began searching for a Mr. Anderson, also of McAllen. All during the night before, thoughts of this man troubled Lorin so that he could not sleep. He began tracting but could accomplish nothing, his mind being troubled. One of the saints in another town had told of this Mr. Anderson wanting to see the missionaries of the Mormon Church. So troubled was Lorin at the mental disturbance that he returned to his room and petitioned the Lord for guidance. Almost immediately a spirit of sweet peace came over him and he left the room, walking to the east of the city limits.
>
> After walking perhaps a mile from the town he walked up to a house that sat in the rear of a large orchard. He knocked on the door and a somewhat feeble voice told him to enter. In a far corner of the room lay a man on a cot, he knew immediately that it was the man he sought. Mr. Anderson also knew Lorin for he said, "I know you, you are the man I dreamed of last night, you have brought me a new message. I told my wife this morning that a stranger was coming to see me and that I would know him when I saw him."[58]

Mr. Anderson was paralyzed and had been confined to bed for two years when Elder Carruth arrived at his door. After learning more about the doctrines of the restored gospel, Mr. Anderson accepted it and "prayed for the day when he might be baptized."[59]

Although he was a teacher in the Methodist faith, David Rogers, along with many others on the street that day, stopped to listen to two missionaries from The Church of Jesus Christ of Latter-day Saints. When Elder Parley P. Pratt and Elder Elijah Fordham asked if anyone in the crowd would allow them to use their home so that they could more fully explain their doctrine, David volunteered.

Elders Pratt and Fordham were glad of the offer. Indeed, they had been having such a difficult time proselyting that they had almost decided to leave New York and head for New Orleans. However, before finalizing their plans, Elder Pratt felt inspired that they should stay in New York and that the Lord had prepared many people in that city to hear the gospel. They hoped the evening at the Rogers's home would be a successful one.

Many people came to David Rogers's home to listen to the missionaries. The elders were gratified to see a full house, and they preached with power. After the missionaries had finished speaking, David felt a deep longing to know whether or not this new religion was from God. Believing in the power of prayer, he decided to pray unceasingly until he received an answer.

His daughter, Caroline, remembered the first morning her father did not come to breakfast. When Caroline went to his bedroom to check on her father, "she saw her father kneeling in prayer by the side of his bed, so she shut the door carefully and went away. Every little while she returned to look through the door to see if he was still there.

"He was.

"He stayed there four days and nights, seeking a testimony of the truth of the restored gospel which he had been taught by the missionaries and by the scriptures brought forth by the Prophet Joseph Smith."[60]

When he finally came out of his room, David told his family that he had received a vision and had been given a witness of the divinity of the restored gospel. He also said that he knew that Joseph Smith was a prophet of God, for although he had never met the man in person, David had seen him in his vision.

David said of his vision, "During that time, the room was a blaze of light as bright as the noon day sun. I saw Joseph Smith sitting. . . in the corner of the room with a book of Mormon in his hand."[61]

Afterward, David was anxious to meet with Elder Parley P. Pratt and tell him about his vision. When David described Joseph Smith, Elder Pratt said the description matched wonderfully.

John Whittaker Taylor, son of President John Taylor, served a mission to Kentucky in 1881. One night Elder John W. Taylor and his companion visited a family and told them, "We have a message for you from heaven; and if you will entertain us, it shall be made known to you by dreams this very night that we are the true servants of the Lord."[62]

That evening the two elders taught the family some of the basic principles of the restored gospel. Later, as Elder Taylor had promised, the father, mother, and some of the children had dreams testifying that the elders spoke the truth. Ultimately, family members were among the more than two hundred fifty converts Elder Taylor baptized during his many missions.[63]

While Elder Charles E. Robinson was serving on a mission in South Carolina, he had a dream about his own death. The account states:

> About two months prior to his death, Brother Robinson had a dream in which his uncle, Counselor D. H. Wells, appeared to him and said, addressing him familiarly by name, "Charlie, you must hurry up; you have only half an hour left."
>
> He (Charlie) afterwards related it to the Elders with whom he was associated, at a conference held in July, a little over a month before he died. Some of them supposed at the time that it indicated their being driving out of the state, but Brother Robinson, himself, as soon as he was taken sick, accepted it as a premonition of his end. He never expressed any hope afterwards of living, except to remark that nothing but the power of God could save him.[64]

Even though Elder Robinson left mortality, he was still called to preach the gospel. A short time after Elder Robinson's death, Mary Gordon, who was living in the small town where he had passed away, had a dream. Mary dreamed that her departed father appeared to her. He told Mary that Brother Robinson had been to see him and convinced him of the truth of the gospel. After his conversion, Mary's father apparently had a strong desire for his temple work to be done, for in talking with Mary, he "further declared that he depended upon her for his temple work to be done, as his son, who then lived in Colorado, had apostatized, after having joined the Church."[65]

Although Mary had not known that her brother had fallen away from the Church, she learned later that it was just as her father had said—her brother no longer had anything to do with the Church.

Soren Rasmus Nielsen was born in 1845 in Thorsmole, Denmark. He had an unusual dream when he was a boy and later, when he was nineteen, had a vision that bore witness to him that The Church of Jesus Christ of Latter-day Saints was true.

When Soren was eleven, he dreamed that he was on a large ship in the ocean. When the ship began to sink, Soren looked around and saw a body of land to the west. After the ship sank, many people, himself included, made their way through the water until they reached land. When Soren woke, he understood that his dream was symbolic and that the ship represented the world, but he was still puzzled about what it meant.

Years passed.

When Soren was nineteen, Mormon missionaries came to Thorsmole to preach the gospel. This caused a great commotion among the people. Soren's brother was one of the first converts, and in the midst of the uproar, he took time to relate the story of Joseph Smith and the First Vision to the family. He also explained the Church's doctrines. Soren's brother told him that if he wanted to know more, he should pray in humility, God would make the truth known to him. Soren states:

> I obeyed and asked God that same evening. I believe it was 1st January, 1864. After I had prayed I retired to my bed. Whether I slept or it was a vision that I do not know. I saw the earth spread before me as a large field. The people that lived thereon were hunting in different faiths to find a way to heaven. But I saw no way that led from the different faiths to heaven, though I saw the heavens open.

After I looked thereon for a while, I saw a little bank of people, from them was a straight path that led right into heaven. But on both sides was a deep chasm so that those that did not walk the straight path, but went from one side to the other, fell into the deep chasm and they were lost. I saw some that fell therein, but few there were that were saved there from. I myself came upon this way. At first it was easy and as I walked farther and farther it became more difficult.

I awoke and came to myself. I was lying with my eyes open and a voice said to me that the path you saw was a path that was laid by Joseph Smith. It was daytime. I thought of what I had seen. I didn't think that I would leave the ways of the world as long as I was young and I thought that when I was married that I would obey the teachings. And for the time being I was taken into the ways of the world. Through the testimony that had been given to me was preserved by me and I thank my Heavenly Father for it.[66]

In February 1849, just before he heard the message of the restored gospel, Thomas C. Haddon had an unusual dream. Although Thomas's dream is rather unusual, it produced such deep feelings in his heart that he was convinced that it was from God. He felt the dream came to assure him that what the missionaries were preaching was true. "I was standing in a certain place, and saw four round lights in the north all in a row extending from west to east," he writes. "I also saw dark clouds floating over my heard, very dark, And I felt greatly surprised at the sight. . . This dream or vision was given me a few weeks previous to my hearing the princables (principles) of the gospel of Jesus Christ by the Elders of this church."[67]

Thomas was profoundly moved by this dream. Because of the strong emotions that came from it, Thomas was eager to listen to the missionaries. He was soon baptized.

Then, six years later, Thomas had another dream wherein he saw many leaders of the Church. He writes, "Another given October 1856 I saw a very Dark cloud in the west, and above it, it was very bright, and I see Bro. H. C. Kimball, and bro G. A. smith, and A strang (s) man sitting on a mule . . . in a minet (s) they all disappeared, then A very large and splendid looking house appeared, and in a minit (s) or so that disappeared then appeared . . . Then Joseph and Hyrum appeared, and Joseph came to me."[68]

The truth of the restored gospel was made manifest to a young woman and her mother through not one or two, but four separate dreams. Anna Noorlander was a young girl growing up in Holland. When she became interested in a Jewish boy, her parents sent her to a convent because they did not want her to marry outside the Catholic Church. Although Anna was only supposed to attend the school for two years, she liked it so well that her parents permitted her to stay longer.

While Anna was away from home, missionaries visited her mother. Anna's mother believed their message, and after she and two of her children were taught the gospel, they were baptized. When the mother told Anna, she was shocked. Grief stricken, she began praying that her mother, brother, and sister would return to the Catholic faith.

Her parents decided it was time for Anna to return home. Anna was very sad to have to leave the convent. Before she left, Anna shared her worries about her family's conversion with her friends. They were sympathetic and warned her to be on guard against the dreadful Mormons.

Anna's parents prepared a special homecoming for her first night back home. They invited many people to dinner, including some Mormon elders. Although the missionaries were friendly, Anna refused to even shake their hands because she was "positive that they were servants of Satan, and that they were guilty of dragging her own brother and sister and mother to perdition."[69]

Anna was so unhappy about the situation that she finally ran away, heading back to the convent. Anna begged the sisters to let her stay, but since she did not have her parents' consent, she had to return home.

After Anna returned home, her mother tried many times to explain various doctrines of the gospel to her daughter. This only upset Anna, who would place her hands over her ears as she had been instructed—to protect herself from evil.

One day her mother asked Anna how old she had been when she was baptized. Anna replied that she had been three days old. Her mother then asked how old Jesus had been when he was baptized. Unsure where her mother's discussion was leading, Anna answered that Jesus was about thirty or thirty-one. Her mother pointed out that the Bible says that one must first repent and then be baptized. However, since little babies are without sin, they have no need of repentance and do not need to be baptized. Patiently, the mother explained that Mormon doctrine states that babies do not need to be baptized because they are innocent and that baptism is only necessary when a person reaches the age of accountability. The mother quietly told Anna that this doctrine followed the Bible's teaching.

Anna was very confused. Before going to bed that night, she prayed that she would be able to know if the Church was true or at least understand the doctrine of baptism as it related to babies. That night she had an emotionally charged dream. In it some men grabbed her, tied her up with strong cords, and began to beat her. Suddenly an old man appeared and told the men to stop hitting Anna and to let her go.

"Immediately the men cut the ropes that bound her and she stood up," the story goes. "And there before a great multitude of people who gathered about, she raised her right hand and said in a loud voice, 'I know that the Prophet Joseph Smith is a true Prophet of God, and that I must be baptized for the forgiveness of my sins. I know that the Mormon Church is the true Church of Jesus Christ!' Then Anna woke."[70]

At first she was horrified. Positive that the dream was from Satan, Anna prayed for deliverance from evil. Then she began to wonder if the dream had actually come from Satan. Anna knelt again and prayed that if the dream was actually from God that He would bless her to have the same dream again. She went back to sleep and had the very same dream, repeated in every detail. When she woke up, she was still frightened and worried. Once again she prayed for direction, saying it was impossible for her—who had been raised as a Catholic—to believe in the Mormon Church. Once more doubts crept in and once more she begged God for a manifestation of some kind.

Anna fell asleep and received the identical dream. Every detail was exactly the same. This finally convinced her that the dream was from God. Anna ran to her mother's room to tell her about the three dreams and that she now believed the Church was true.

"Weeping for joy," the account continues, "her mother raised up in bed, and unable to restrain herself further said, 'Oh, my daughter,

I, too, saw it all happen in a dream last night. And I saw Sister Coann and Sister Murrin come here to go with us [for baptism]."[71]

A few hours later, without any message being sent, or any pre-arranging, Sister Coann and Sister Murrin arrived at Anna's home, each of the women coming from opposite parts of the city. It was a bitterly cold, blustery day on 15 January when Anna, her mother, Sister Coann, and Sister Murrin, and two missionaries walked from The Hague to the ocean for baptism.

Once they arrived, Elder Kenner, who was going to baptize Anna, looked at the rough ocean and said, "Sister, hadn't you better wait for another time? Look at the sea, how wild and rough it is!"

Anna went a short distance away and knelt to pray, asking the Lord to calm the sea. When she returned, the wind had subsided. She walked out into the water and was baptized. In time she came to America and raised a family.[72]

During general conference, Elder Milton R. Hunter of the First Council of the Seventy related this story, which he called a "modern miracle in missionary work." Elder Hunter said:

> A missionary related an experience that illustrates one method that God has used to bring the searchers after truth into his true church. He (the missionary) stated that he and his companion had knocked on a door.
>
> A woman opened the door immediately, enthusiastically invited them in, and said to them, "You young men have come to my home today in answer to my prayers. For a long time I have been dissatisfied with the church to which I belong, feeling that it does not contain many of the doctrines that Christ taught while here upon the earth. I felt that it was not the true church that was founded originally by our Savior. I prayed earnestly and asked our Father in heaven to send somebody to me who would bring me the true gospel plan of salvation and make it possible for me to find the true church."
>
> The woman continued, "After doing so, I had a dream that two young men knocked on my door and when I let them in they said to me, 'We have come to bring you the true gospel of Jesus Christ.' I recognize that you two young men are the same two young men I saw in my dream, and as in my dream, you

announced yourselves by saying, 'We have come to bring you the gospel of Jesus Christ.' I know that you are the servants of our Master and that you will teach me his gospel."

The two missionaries were happily surprised at this reception and thankful to have the privilege of teaching this good woman the gospel. She eagerly received it and soon thereafter was a baptized member of The Church of Jesus Christ of Latter-day Saints. Thus, another modern miracle in missionary work had occurred.[73]

James Forman Turpin was born on 22 June 1815 and grew up in Tennessee. By chance, he was not at home when Elders Patten, Parish, and Woodruff visited the area where he lived. But when James returned home, a few new converts eagerly introduced him to the gospel. James listened to them and spent some time pondering the doctrine. Shortly afterward, he had a dream. James relates the first part of his story as follows:

> I had a dream in the spring of 1836. While I was laying meditating upon the Gospel and plan of salvation, all at once I was placed in a beautiful mansion. I stepped to the door of the entry where I met a person that I thought was Jesus Christ. He introduced me into another apartment of the house. He then told me I was to act as justice of the peace. All at once appeared before me a writing desk and books.
>
> He gave me a pen and I went to business. I appeared to see him go between two walls. I went to look between them and dropped my pen as I was trying to get it, I awoke. This left the impression on my mind that the gift to me was the priesthood, the Books and the laws of God.[74]

Because of this dream, James began to feel sure that the Church was true. Then he had to go on a trip. While he was away, James spent some of his free time learning more about the gospel. "After I arrived home I felt quite zealous in the things I knew of the Gospel," he observed. "As I was conversing with my father, my stepmother said to my father 'Old Man Jesse is a Mormon.'"

James did not know what to make of his stepmother's scornful remark and said, "It being the first time I had heard the word, I denied the charge, but if believing in the truth made me a Mormon, Amen to it."[75]

Because of his dream and subsequent investigating, James was ready to listen to the missionaries when they returned to the area. "In the course of two or three weeks I heard Elder Woodruff preach and I believed what he said," James recalls. "A few weeks following I heard Elder Patten and Parish preach. I was thoroughly convinced of the truth of their message. I went forward and was baptized by Elder Woodruff and confirmed by Elder Parish on 14 April, 1836. It was not known unto me what my dream really meant until I was immersed into the water for it then came to me very plain and I understood all my dreams for my Spirit told me."[76]

Some time later, James had a second dream. "One evening while I was laying on my bed meditating upon the glories of God," he wrote, "I was cut out and placed in a beautiful mansion. I was there amusing myself when Jesus Christ appeared to me. As I thought, he took me by the hand and led me into a splendid hall. Here he introduced me to the twelve apostles. I enjoyed myself while in their society. I spoke to the Apostle James on the beauties of religion and happiness it afforded one to know that they were doing the will of God. My joy was unspeakable and full of glory."[77]

Brother Pettersson was a well-respected man who lived in a small city in Sweden. Although he was normally an amiable person, he did not have a lot of patience with anyone who did not belong to his faith, which was the predominant religion in the area. He had even less patience with a man named Carlsson, a member of a strange and little-known religion called The Church of Jesus Christ of Latter-day Saints. One day Brother Pettersson decided it was his duty to go talk with Brother Carlsson and point out the error of his ways. He was disappointed when his attempt to convince Brother Carlsson that he belonged to a false religion did not go well.

He made no further efforts to correct his neighbor.

Some time later, on a stormy fall night, Brother Pettersson had a dream. The account states that this dream was the turning point of his life because "he [Brother Pettersson] believed in dreams, and, therefore, the Lord could speak to him in that language. It was one of those dreams that seemed to be realities."[317]

In his dream, Brother Pettersson died. After passing to the other side of the veil, he was met by kind people who took him to meet his family and friends. Brother Pettersson felt very happy to be in such a beautiful place, but it was a shock when he discovered that he was not in heaven but in a place called the world of the spirits. He found that Satan was there, trying with all his powers of deceit and cunning to lead people astray. He also learned that the true gospel was being taught there, as well as to people on earth.

Brother Pettersson was astonished to see Brother Carlsson's older brother there. Although Brother Carlsson's brother had died in poverty some years ago—after being ostracized because he was a Mormon—in this place he was richly robed and was obviously a man of some importance.

Brother Pettersson listened to a sermon and learned more about the principle of repentance. The speaker talked about the trials the Saints had faced in Nauvoo and were currently facing as they crossed the plains to reach the Salt Lake Valley. The speaker also talked about temples, telling the audience that temples would one day "dot the surface of the Earth, in which representative work will be performed, until every spirit in the spirit world shall have an opportunity to enter into some degree of glory."[79] Being unfamiliar with temples, Brother Pettersson did not understand anything about this doctrine. When the sermon was over, he inquired who the speaker was and was told it was Joseph Smith.

Then he awoke.

His wife was standing by his bed when he opened his eyes. At first Brother Pettersson was confused, wondering how she had come to be in the world of the spirits. Then he realized that everything he'd seen and heard had come to him through a dream.

"Herr Pettersson was a changed man from that night," the account states. "He now fully realized that he knew absolutely nothing of God's plan of salvation. . . . He hastened to the home of the . . . Mormon [Brother Carlsson], whose testimony he had despised, but which had, nevertheless, taken hold of his soul, and given to his existence a new meaning. He heard again of faith, repentance, baptism, the laying on of hands, the gathering of the saints, the Millennial reign, judgment, and the glory of the Hereafter. And he drank in every word eagerly.

He and his wife and the other children were baptized, and there was exceeding joy in that home."[80]

In yet another dream experience, a woman saw missionaries coming to her door, bringing her a book that she somehow knew would bring salvation to her and her family. Elder Mark E. Petersen, one of the missionaries who later actually knocked on her door, recalls the story. At the time of this experience, Elder Peterson was serving in eastern Canada with his companion, Elder Henry L. Baker. Elder Peterson recounts:

> As we came to one door, a woman responded to our knock and immediately invited us in—before we had a chance to give the usual door approach!
>
> Hardly had we entered the house when she said, "Where is the book you were to bring me?"
>
> Naturally we were astonished. But she quickly explained. She said that during the previous night she had had a dream in which she saw us come to her home. It was so vivid she said, that when she saw us approaching her door, she recognized us instantly. She was told in the dream that we had a book that would lead her entire family to salvation.
>
> Immediately we gave her the Book of Mormon and discussed it at some length with her. She invited us to return that same evening to meet her family, which we did. After an appropriate period of study, the family joined the Church and all are still faithful and true.[81]

In 1811, Joseph Smith Sr. became greatly interested in religion. However, he would not commit himself to any particular religion, feeling that the true church of God would have the ancient order that had been established by Jesus Christ when He lived on earth, and Joseph Sr. had not yet discovered such a church.

One night as Joseph Sr. was contemplating the various sects of the day, he fell asleep and had a dream. In the dream, he was wandering about in a barren field where there was nothing except for dead timber as far as he could see. There was no life whatsoever, only a death-like silence. Suddenly, an angel appeared by his side. Joseph Sr. and the angel walked together, and as they walked, Joseph asked why they were traveling through such a dismal place.

The angel answered, "This field is the world, which now lieth inanimate and dumb, in regard to the true religion, or plan of salvation; but travel on."[82]

When Joseph awoke, he was trembling. Because of the dream, he was more convinced than ever that no church on earth was correct.

Later that year, Joseph Smith Sr., his wife, Lucy, and their children moved to Lebanon, New Hampshire. There, Joseph had another dream. This one bore an amazing resemblance to Lehi's dream in the Book of Mormon, which he would read about many years in the future, after his son, Joseph Smith Jr., translated the golden plates.

Joseph Smith Sr. says of this dream: "I was traveling in an open, desolate field, which appeared to be very barren. As I was thus traveling, the thought suddenly came into my mind that I had better stop and reflect upon what I was doing, before I went any farther. . . . My guide, who was by my side, as before, said, 'This is the desolate world; but travel on.' . . .

> Traveling a short distance further, I came to a narrow path. This path I entered, and, when I had traveled a little way in it, I beheld a beautiful stream of water [running alongside]. . . . as far as my eyes could extend. I could see a rope, running along the bank of it. . . . And beyond me was a low, but very pleasant valley, in which stood a tree such as I had never seen before. . . . Its beautiful branches spread themselves somewhat like an umbrella, and it bore a kind of fruit, in shape much like a chestnut bur, and as white as snow, or, if possible, whiter. . . . I drew near and began to eat of it, and found it delicious beyond description. As I was eating, I said in my heart, "I cannot eat this alone, I must bring my wife and children, that they may partake with me.[83]

Joseph went and got his family. Returning to the tree, his family ate from the tree, were filled with joy, and praised God. Then Joseph saw a spacious building across the valley. "It was full of doors and windows," Joseph says, "and they were all filled with people, who were very finely dressed. When these people observed us in the low valley, under the tree, they pointed the finger of scorn at us, and treated us with all manner of disrespect and contempt."[84]

Joseph and his family ignored them. He then turned to his guide and asked him why the fruit was so delicious. The guide told Joseph that the fruit was that pure love of God, which was shed abroad in the hearts of all those who loved Him and kept His commandments. The angel then told Joseph to go and bring the rest of his children to the tree. Joseph replied that they were all there.

"No," he replied, "look yonder, you have two more, and you must bring them also."[85]

Joseph looked and saw two small children standing a distance away. He went to them, bringing them to the tree so they could eat with the rest of his family. After feasting for a time, Joseph asked his guide what the spacious building represented.

The angel replied, "It is Babylon, it is Babylon, and it must fall. The people in the doors and windows are the inhabitants thereof, who scorn and despise the Saints of God because of their humility."[86]

In 1840, Ann Booth had a dream so remarkable that Wilford Woodruff wrote it down in his journal. In the dream, Ann saw a man of God and understood that he was an apostle who had been killed for his faith. After she had the dream, Ann heard about The Church of Jesus Christ of Latter-day Saints and found out that they had apostles and that one of them had been killed.

In her dream, Ann states that she was carried away to the place of departed souls. She writes:

> On arriving at the door of the uppermost prision, I beheld one of the 12 Apostles of the Lamb who had been martered in America Standing at the door of the prison holding a key with which he unlocked the door and went in and I followed him.
>
> He appeared to be of a large size thick set, Dark hair Dark eyes and eyebrows of a smileing Countenance, & on his head was a Crown of Gold or sumthing brighter. He was Dressed in a long white robe with the sleeves plaited from the Sholder to the hand. Upon his breast were four stars apparrently like gold and a golden girdle about his loins. His feet were bear from above the ancles downwards, and his hands were also bear.
>
> As he entered the prision he seemed to stand about 3 feet

> from the floor (which was of Marble) as if the place was not worthy for him to stand upon. A vary brilient and glorious light Serrounded him while the rest of the Prision was dark But his light was peculiar to himself & did not reflect upon others who were in the Prison who were surrounded with a gloom of darkness. . . . The Apostle then commenced to Preach the Baptism of repentance for remission of Sins and the gift of the Holy Ghost by the laying on of hands."[87]

Then the apostle began to baptize people. Among them were some of Ann's relatives. After baptizing the people, the apostle confirmed them and "in-stantly the darkness dispersed & they were all Surrounded & envelloped in A Brilient light such as surrounded the Apostle at the first. . . . My Grandfather then Came to me & blessed me saying the Lord bless thee forever and ever (and asked,) 'Art thou come to see us deliverd?' My mother then came to me & clasped me in her arms and kissed me three times. . . . I then awoke out of the Vision & felt so happy & overjoyed that I knew not how to remain in bed."[88]

After Ann woke, she roused her husband and told him about her dream. Together they searched the Bible, reading in the New Testament about the spirits in prison. Ann concludes:

> I would further state that at the time I had this vision I had never herd of the Death of David W. Patten whom I have since learned was one of the Twelve Apostles of the Latter Day Saints in America & was slain in the late persecution in the fall of 1838. But in the Vision I knew it was an Apostle who had been slain in America.
>
> Perhaps many will think lightly of this vision But I hereby sollemnly testify that I actaully Saw & herd in a vision what I have here related & I give my name & set my seal in witness to the Same well knowing that I must stand before the Judgement seat of Christ and answer for this Testimony.[89]

Chapter 6

Ministering Angels

The fact that God can and does penetrate the veil that lies between earth and heaven in order to touch our hearts and enlighten our minds is both intriguing and comforting. The Holy Scriptures, both ancient and modern, relate many glorious occasions when angels have been sent to minister to mortals. One of the ways that God uses to communicate to mankind is through visions and dreams. President Wilford Woodruff said, "But what I wanted to say in regard to these matters is, that the Lord does communicate some things of importance to the children of men by means of visions and dreams as well as by the records of divine truth."[1]

President Woodruff further stated that while people sometimes dream about things that will never come to pass, some dreams have great meaning. "Thus," President Woodruff states, "we may have dreams about things of great importance and dreams of no importance at all. The Lord warned Joseph in a dream to take the young child Jesus and his mother into Egypt, and thus he was saved from the wrath of Herod. Hence there are a great many things taught us in dreams that are true, and if a man has the spirit of God he can tell the difference between what is from the Lord and what is not. And I want to say to my brethren and sisters, that whenever you have a dream that you feel is from the Lord, pay attention to it."[2]

When we have a dream that strongly affects our emotions, we should ponder on it, even if the meaning is not immediately clear. If we feel strongly that a dream is important, it usually is. God may be trying to help us, perhaps by guiding us to make good choices in the future. Elder Orson Pratt stated, "I have been blessed with some revelations and prophecies, and with dreams of things that have come to pass."[3]

Heavenly Father can use dreams to communicate with people whenever they demonstrate sufficient faith and when circumstances warrant divine mediation. "I have had the administration of angels in my day and time, though I never prayed for an angel," President Woodruff said. "The Lord revealed to me by vision, by revelations, and by the Holy Spirit, many things that lay before me."[4]

During a general conference address, Elder Carlos H. Amado noted that after we are converted and believe in God, "he will answer our petitions in accordance with our sincerity. After you are baptized, if you remain worthy and faithful to your covenants, you will have the constant guidance of the Holy Ghost, through whisperings, impressions, feelings, dreams, and warnings."[5]

One father experienced this very thing. When Elder Henry Ballard was called to serve a mission, his wife, Margaret McNeil, was pregnant. Their son, Melvin J., was born 9 February 1873, while Henry was on his mission. When young Melvin fell ill, Sister Ballard wrote her husband about the baby's illness. Although Sister Ballard and the doctors did all they could, the baby's condition worsened. Finally, he became so critical that the doctors lost hope and told Sister Ballard that her infant son would soon die.

But Melvin's father was a man who had great faith. The account states:

> When Elder Ballard learned of its (his son's) critical condition, full of sorrow and anxiety, he went alone into the woods to plead with the Lord to save his first born. Under this weight of grief, he fell asleep and in spirit he came home and blessed the child, rebuked the destroyer and when he awoke, he had the assurance that all would be well with his son.
>
> On this particular night, Sister Ballard, the mother of Melvin J., was taking care of the little one. The doctor told her he

could do nothing further; that the child would probably pass away before morning. During the night the child took a sudden change for the better and while Mrs. Ballard did not see anything, she felt the unseen presence of Elder Ballard and knew something miraculous had happened. The change took place the very hour he went into the woods to pray."[6]

Melvin grew up to be an inspiring Church leader, serving as a stake president, mission president, and apostle.

Elder Rowberry, a stake patriarch, also experienced an unusual dream. Although he did not understand the dream, he could not forget it. The dream was on his mind when he was asked to go to the train station in Tooele, Utah, pick up Elder Orson Pratt, an apostle who was coming to attend conference in Elder Rowberry's stake.

> During the ride to the meeting, Elder Rowberry confided to the Apostle. "Brother Pratt," he said, "I have had a rather remarkable dream. I can't understand it. I wish you would tell me the interpretation of it.
>
> Brother Pratt said, "Tell me the dream and I will pray about it, and if I can get the interpretation before I go back to Salt Lake I'll tell you what it is."
>
> Brother Rowberry said, "I dreamed that I was on a big ship on the ocean, and as we traveled along the way people began to fall off that ship one after another. And finally I fell off and fell into the water and made my way to the shore. And lo and behold, when I got there I met a man." [Coincidentally, the man happened to be Orson Pratt, but Elder Rowberry didn't tell the apostle that.]
>
> Elder Rowberry continued, "I met a man, and he showed me around the place where we were, whatever it was, the spirit world, I suppose. And, oh, it was such a beautiful place. Brother Pratt, he said, this man said to me, this guide, 'Is there any place you would like to see especially?'
>
> "I said, 'Yes, I have always had a great love for the Prophet Joseph, and I would appreciate it if I might see his home.' And so he showed me the Prophet's home and other places."
>
> Brother Pratt said, "I'll pray to the Lord about it, and if I get the interpretation I'll tell you."

> As Brother Rowberry was taking him to the train after his visit in the stake and visiting the wards, Brother Pratt said to him, "By the way, Brother Rowberry, I have the interpretation of that dream for you." He said, "The ship that you saw was the world, and the people who fell off were people dying, and," he said, "if you'll make a record of those who fell off the ship, in the order that you saw them fall off, as nearly as you can, they will pass away in that particular order." And he said, "When your time comes and you meet the man whom you saw in your dreams, he will tell you that the dream was of the Lord and so also was the interpretation."[7]

Brother Rowberry shared this dream, as well as Elder Pratt's interpretation, with Elder Heber J. Grant, who was later called to be a stake president. One day Brother Rowberry approached him and said, "Brother Grant, you remember my dream. Well, I wrote down the names of those people in the order in which they fell off that ship and," he said, "they've done it. They have died just in that order."

More time passed. One day President Grant received a request from Church headquarters. He was told to ask the people in his stake to pray for Brother Orson Pratt, who was very sick. The stake presidency decided they would say a prayer themselves before conference and went to a quiet room where they often met to pray and ponder.

As they were walking to the prayer room, Elder Rowberry asked, "Brother Grant, do you remember my dream?"

President Grant replied that he did.

Elder Rowberry said, "It's all right to pray for Brother Pratt, but it's his turn next."

A short time later, they received word that Elder Pratt had died, just as Elder Rowberry had seen in his dream.

In time, Elder Heber J. Grant was called to be an apostle. During one of his visits back to Tooele, he met privately with Brother Rowberry.

The account states: "Brother Rowberry reminded him (Elder Grant) of that dream and he said those people had passed away in just the order that they had been listed. And he said, "Brother Grant, it's my turn next. I just can't wait to get over on the other side to meet Brother Pratt and to meet the Prophet Joseph and your father." He said, "I'll tell them what a wonderful work you are doing as an apostle of the Lord."[8]

Elder B. F. Johnson , a missionary serving in the Sandwich Islands (Hawaii), also received a powerful dream. At that time, the people in the area were protesting against a government leader, Dr. Judd. The political situation worsened when the king ignored his subjects' concerns and did not dismiss Dr. Judd. The king hesitated to demote Dr. Judd not only because the man was one of his good friends but because the doctor had given him large donations.

As time went on, the people became increasingly incensed at the king's lack of action. "It seemed, at times, as though the people would break out in tumult and insurrection," Elder Johnson wrote. "And no answer was given to their petitions."[9]

Elder Johnson had listened intently to the people's concerns, attended their meetings, and finally decided to get involved. Feeling he had some grasp of the problem, Elder Johnson wrote a lengthy letter to the king. In it he explained his reason for being on the island and a little about the gospel.

The letter had such a strong impact on the king that he had it published in a government journal, in both English and Hawaiian. The king also sent a message to Elder Johnson, saying that he would give the missionary an audience when he had time.

Shortly after this, Elder Johnson had a dream. In it he stood on an outcropping of rocks near a large mountain. Below him he saw a building under construction. As he watched, dense smoke began rising from this building, and he heard people crying, "Fire!"

A strong wind blew towards the building and the mountain, yet people were coming up the side of the mountain to put out the fire, which made it so the people were blinded by the smoke which blew in their faces. Elder Johnson recalled:

> I thought how foolish they were to thus stay on the opposite side from the wind, to be blinded with the smoke. Looking, I saw a bucket with a rope attached on a flume through which the water ran. I quickly took it up, drew it full of water, looked for the center of the fire, dashed it in, and, all at once, the flame was extinguished. I thought a multitude of people came crowding into the building, wondering by whom the fire had been extinguished. Although I was with them, they appeared to

> comprehend nothing of my agency in the matter. . . . They calculated that the damage the building had sustained was about fifty thousand dollars.[10]

Elder Johnson then awoke. Although he did not understand the dream, he felt that it was important and related it to his companion, Elder Nathan Tanner.

"That morning," Elder Johnson continues, "Brother Tanner called on one of the native Saints, who was living with Halalea, one of the highest native chiefs. He was a special friend of, and a counselor to, the king, and the man who carried him my letter. He told Brother Tanner that the king had appointed him to come with Prince Rehoreho, to meet us that night at our rooms, lay before us the king's great political trouble, and get their counsel."

Elder Johnson continued, "It came plainly to me, then, that therein would be the fulfillment of my dream."[11]

That evening, Elder Johnson and Elder Tanner met with Prince Rehoreho and Halalea. The Hawaiians explained that the king was deeply troubled about the alarming condition of the government and was uncertain what to do about it. The king was loath to turn Dr. Judd out of office, for he had been his friend for a long time, had been a good advisor, and in times of need, had supplied him with money.

Elder Johnson said, "While Halalea and the prince were delivering their message from the king, I was continually praying in my heart that the Lord would give us wisdom to say such things as would do honor to His cause, for I felt very small for such an important occasion."[12]

When it was Elder Johnson's turn to talk, he said, "I arose and told them that we were not sent to meddle with governments, nor to teach political science, but to preach the gospel of Christ as now revealed. But, inasmuch as the king was our friend, and desired counsel of us, we would give him such as the Lord would put in our hearts.

"I told them the Bible said, that 'when the wicked rule the people mourn'; that if Dr. Judd was really a good man and a true friend to the king, as the king had believed him to be, he would not now allow the king to be in such great trouble on his account, but, like a true friend, would resign his office for the sake of peace between the king and his subjects. The fact that he was disposed to hold on to his office, at the expense of peace to the king's realm, showed, conclusively, that he was influenced by other motives that the peace and welfare of the kingdom."[13]

Elder Johnson further stated that the political trouble had come about not because Dr. Judd was not a good man but because he was holding onto his office against the wishes of the people. The missionary reminded the prince and Halalea that there were many men of equal ability whom the king could appoint as Dr. Judd's successor.

When Elder Johnson finished talking, the prince and Halalea shook his hand gratefully. They said, "The things you have told us we had not thought of, and they are true. The king will be glad when we tell him what you have said, for we can see it plainly, now."[14]

The next morning at ten o'clock, the heralds were heard proclaiming the dismissal of Dr. Judd. The news created wonder and astonishment among the people, and they hurried together with public demonstrations of joy. They greatly marveled and queried by what agency, or through whom influence this long delayed, though most desirable, object had been attained.

Elder Johnson concluded by saying, "As I had dreamed, so I saw the people greatly rejoicing, and, although I was daily among them, they had no thought that a Latter-day Saint could have had any agency in so important a matter. . . . In a settlement with Dr. Judd, as I had dreamed, the government found that it had lost fifty thousand dollars. Thus my prophecy and my dream were fulfilled together and peace returned to the people. Joy came to our hearts that the Lord, through the inspiration of His Holy Spirit had made us, His humble Elders, the means of giving saving counsel to princes."[15]

Who knows exactly what characteristics we need to receive a dream or vision from the Lord. Lorenzo Dow Young, a brother of Brigham Young, gives his mother credit for being a good influence on him, saying, "She . . . trained me to trust in God."[16] Perhaps it was this trust in God that allowed Lorenzo to have a powerful dream. Lorenzo states:

> In the autumn of 1816, when about nine years old, I had a peculiar dream. I thought I stood in an open, clear space of ground, and saw a plain, fine road, leading, at an angle of 45° degrees, into the air, as far as I could see. I heard a noise like a carriage in rapid motion, at what seemed the upper end of the road. In a moment it came in sight. It was drawn by a pair of

> beautiful, white horses. The carriage and harness appeared brilliant with gold. The horses traveled with the speed of the wind.
>
> It was made manifest to me that the Savior was in the carriage, and that it was driven by His servant. The carriage stopped near me, and the Savior inquired where my brother Brigham was. After informing Him, He further inquired about my other brothers, and our father. After I had answered his inquires, He stated that He wanted us all, but He especially wanted my brother Brigham. The team then turned right about, and returned on the road it had come."[17]

When Lorenzo awoke, he was frightened, thinking that the dream meant that he and his brothers and father were going to die. He told his father about the dream, and his father assured him that Lorenzo's interpretation was incorrect.

The Savior did indeed "want" his brother Brigham but not to return to heaven as Lorenzo feared. The family was introduced to The Church of Jesus Christ of Latter-day Saints in 1830. After studying the gospel at length, Brigham Young was baptized in 1832. He was called to be an apostle in 1835, and in December 1847, he was sustained as the second prophet of the Church.

Before he even knew about The Church of Jesus Christ of Latter-day Saints, Benjamin Brown dreamed he would be called to preach the true gospel. When he told his wife about his dream, she scoffed. Benjamin then told her that in his dream an angel said that his mother-in-law had been given a similar dream and would be able to convince his wife that Benjamin's dream was from God. Benjamin recorded this dream in his journal as follows:

> I had been called to preach the gospel, and the first time I thus officiated, it was in a school-house, in an adjoining town, with which I was well acquainted. I saw all the members of the congregation, which was small, and, when I awoke, I could distinctly remember the position each person occupied in the room.
>
> This so impressed my mind that I told my wife of it, and said I believed it would be realized; but she scouted the idea. What was I, a working man, to do with preaching? Well, at other times, it would have appeared equally foolish to myself,

> but it had been given to me that her mother, living at the place, knew by a dream the same thing, and I told this to my wife. At last she promised that, if it turned out to be the case, she would believe the dream to be true.
>
> In a day or so, we paid her mother a visit, and found that she had dreamed, that night, that I was coming to preach in the town where she lived, and we learned, from her friends, that she had been entreating one of her relatives to carry her to my residence, that she might tell me of it.[18]

However, there was one problem. Benjamin did not know which church had the true doctrine. Although he had investigated many religions over the years, he did not fully agree with any of them. Benjamin continued his investigation, looking into different religions. Five years passed, and still Benjamin could not find a church that followed the same doctrine that Christ taught.

Finally, in one last effort to find the truth, he began attending what were called "protracted meetings." These meetings were put on by various sects and were very popular at the time. These meetings lasted for days, sometimes weeks. But even after attending many of these, Benjamin still felt unsatisfied.

Finally, he met two missionaries from The Church of Jesus Christ of Latter-day Saints. Although he usually was quite open to new doctrine, Benjamin felt unusually scornful of the Mormons. When the missionaries asked him to read the Book of Mormon, he took it home but, after reading only a few pages, decided that the book was nonsense. He vowed to read no more.

Then a depressing feeling came over him. The thought came to his mind that the Bible was just as useless as the Book of Mormon. He was astonished at such thoughts. This strange and unusual change in Benjamin's feelings, when he had always been a devout believer of the Bible, alerted him that something was wrong. After pondering, Benjamin decided that Satan was trying to deceive him. He vowed to read the Book of Mormon from cover to cover. After Benjamin finished the book, he prayed to receive a testimony of its truth. Benjamin's prayer was answered in a way that left no doubt in his mind that he had finally discovered the true Church. Benjamin was baptized in May 1835. Shortly after, he was ordained to the priesthood and sent to preach the true doctrine of Christ, fulfilling his dream.

True courage is going forward even when you know the path will be difficult. Such was the case with Brother George Cannon and his wife, who became members of the Church while living in England. Brother Cannon was the father of George Q. Cannon, who became an apostle in 1860.

Before he was married, Brother Cannon had a disturbing dream. Although he was not married at the time, he dreamed that he and his wife left England to go to America but that his wife did not survive the trip.

Even after Brother Cannon was married, he remembered his dream. Then he and his wife were introduced to The Church of Jesus Christ of Latter-day Saints. They were taught the gospel by Sister Cannon's brother, Elder John Taylor, and his companion. Brother and Sister Cannon believed the gospel was true and were baptized. Despite Brother Cannon's troubling dream, the couple decided to immigrate to the United States. Although she believed in her husband's dream, Sister Cannon felt it was important for her children to be with the Saints and did not shrink from going on the journey. The account states:

> Long before his marriage, the father of the family (Brother Cannon) had a dream concerning the death of his wife, and when emigration was talked about, they both seemed to be aware that she would not live to reach Zion. Her relatives remonstrated with her for going with the saints, but in reply she said to them, that though she knew she never would live to reach the body of the Church, she was determined to undertake the journey for the sake of her children, and she never shrank at the prospect before her. The manifestation that they had received proved to be true. They started for Zion, sailing from Liverpool in the ship "Sidney," Sept. 17, 1842, but she died and was buried in the ocean.[19]

William Hobbs was a kind but poor man who lived in the small village of Hersham, England. Because of his dream, Elder Thomas Phillips, who was in England serving a mission, learned how mindful the Lord is of His children, even about small matters. Elder Phillips relates the story:

One night Brother Hobbs dreamed that a personage came to him and told him that (a) Brother Phillips would be at his house on a certain day, naming the time, which I think was four or five days from the time he dreamed. He was further told that he must get a new hat for Brother Philips; for the one he wore was very shabby.

This dream was very much impressed on the mind of Brother Hobbs, and troubled him sorely, for it found him without money and some miles from any town where he could buy a hat.

Brother Hobbs was the overseer of a small number of men, whose work was to keep some miles of railroad in repair for the safety of the trains. When the day came that I was to be at his house in the evening, he went to his work very low-spirited, not having obtained the hat. While at work on the track, a long train of cars came along, and when passing the place where Brother Hobbs and his hands were at work, a hat, suitable for the finest gentleman in the land, flew out of one of the windows.

Brother Hobbs shouted, "That's the hat for Brother Phillips! Thank God!"

When Brother Hobbs came home in the evening, I was there, it being the time specified in the dream. He walked up to me and said: "Brother Phillips, I was to give you a hat, and here it is." To our surprise, it fitted me well.

As a matter of course I was anxious to know who was so thoughtful for an Elder of the Church of Jesus Christ of Latter-day Saints; and, in answer to my questions, Brother Hobbs told me the dream.

Then I knew, and still know, that the providences of our heavenly Father were, and are, working in favor of the servants and Saints of the Most High.[20]

The following experience is another interesting account of a person who saw a missionary in a dream before he actually arrived. The missionary, known only by the initials J. H. H., was in England when he wrote the following account in his journal:

I will here relate an adventure that occurred on the 23rd of Aug., 1831. On leaving Saint Laurence in the morning, I took the road to Saint Aubins by way of Saint Peters. I was walking

> along ruminating on the great latter-day work, and almost lost in my reflections, when on looking around I found myself in a narrow road where I had never been before. Seeing a house of some distance I enquired my way.
>
> A man came to the door who proceeded to direct me to my destination when his wife requested him to ask if I was an Elder of the Church of Jesus Christ of Latter-day Saints, and that I had books with me setting forth its doctrines. When I entered, the lady said she had been expecting me for over two weeks, for she had a dream or a vision in which she saw me come to her house with the books just as she then saw me.
>
> Addressing her husband, Mrs. Bartlett said, "This is the gentleman I have been talking to you about during the last two weeks."[349]

Mrs. Bartlett had been visiting with a friend when Elder H. arrived. After introductions were made, the missionary did his best to explain the basic doctrines of the gospel to the two women. They were eager to hear more, so he made a series of appointments to teach them the gospel.

Over time, the women gained testimonies of the truthfulness of the gospel and wanted to become members. Elder H. arranged to take Mrs. Bartlett and her friend down to the sea where he baptized and confirmed them members of The Church of Jesus Christ of Latter-day Saints.

Sister Bartlett's baptism had more of an effect on her than she expected. For several years, she had suffered from a chronic disease. She had gone to many doctors, but none of them had been able to help her.

Elder H. writes, "Before being baptized, she had prayed earnestly that God would give her another evidence that this work was true, and heal her of her sickness in and through the ordinance of baptism. She then testified that the Lord had answered her prayer, and had made her whole. All this was the Lord's doing and marvelous in our eyes, and tended to strengthen our faith."[22]

Because of a dream, Amanda W. Anderson believed that President Joseph F. Smith and President Anthon H. Lund would soon leave mortality. During her incredible dream, Amanda was also allowed to see the Savior. Amanda writes:

In a dream I was in a front room on the first floor of a large building. Glass doors reached from the ceiling to the floor, and they opened on a porch. Then it seemed that a boy, about fourteen years of age, came running through a large hall, calling out: "The Savior is coming!"

And then the Savior came into the room where I was. He came toward me, smiling. I knew it was He, and as He stood before me, He spoke to me, and a shining light radiated from Him. However, I was not permitted to remember what He said. But how happy I was to think that the Savior would honor me with a visit! I can't describe the happy and heavenly feeling that rested on me.

Then the Savior said to me, "Go to that door, and tell the usher to send word upstairs that Joseph F. Smith and Anthon H. Lund are wanted down here." I did as I was told, and while the door was open I could see that the building was a spacious one; the hall was very wide, and so was the stairway. The usher made a bow, and I closed the door and turned back to the Savior, and saw that He still smiled at me. Then the thought came to my mind: "Just think if President Smith and President Lund will not know that this is the Savior, and will act distant on account of being disturbed."

The Savior read my thoughts, for he said: "Don't worry; they will know me."

The door opened. President Smith came in first, and he looked the Savior in the eye, and they shook hands like old friends. Then he stepped aside, and President Lund shook hands in a very friendly way, with that smile of his. Then the Savior took two chairs and placed them between the glass doors, and indicated that the brethren were to sit down. He stepped behind them, and while in that position His glory encircled all three of them. I saw the Savior's lips moving, but could not hear what he said, though it seemed much as if He were setting them apart for some mission. His right hand was on President Smith's head, and his left on President Lund. Then my dream ended. Some time later President Smith answered his final summons, and not very long after President Lund left us. (signed) Amanda W. Anderson[23]

Thomas Briggs received several dreams. The first one prepared him for that which was to come, and the second one prompted him to act. However, the third, more surprising dream was the one his wife had but did not tell him about. Thomas learned about her dream from his children, years after his wife had died.

Thomas was born in England in 1832. He was baptized when he was eighteen and then traveled to America, where he married some time later. His youngest child was four years old when his wife became ill. Sister Briggs was diagnosed with dropsy. Then Thomas injured his leg, which became badly infected. When his wife's condition grew worse, Thomas had the first of several dreams.

The record states, "About this time he (Thomas) had a dream, which indicated to him that he would have to part with her, and when, on the 15th of July following, she suddenly died, the circumstances were in fulfillment of the dream, thus confirming what was predicted in tongues in 1849: that his trials should be shown him beforehand."[24]

After the death of his wife, Thomas took over the running of the household. Although he was diligent in his efforts to be both mother and father, he was hampered by the suffering he endured because of the open, oozing wound in his leg.

A few years after his wife passed away, the temple in St. George was finished and dedicated. Thomas remembered his father's dying admonition to "never forget the dead"[25] and felt impressed to go to St. George and have temple work done for his ancestors. However, Thomas was still afflicted with running sores on his leg and worried that this might prevent him from working at the temple. He discussed his problem with his bishop, Anson Call, who advised him to talk with Brigham Young.

Then Thomas had another dream.

In this dream, he found himself traveling with his wife's sister, Sarah. As they continued their journey, it grew dark, and they became separated. Then Thomas saw a light in the distance. As he went toward it, it became brighter, and he could see that the light was emanating from a large white building. Everything around the building was as white as snow. When Thomas entered the building, he saw a flight of steps. At the top of the steps stood a woman whom he recognized as one of his neighbors; she moved towards him and embraced him.

When Thomas awoke, he pondered at length upon this dream. Finally, he came to the conclusion that the Lord had another wife for him—the woman who stood at the top of the stairs. Her name was Ann Ashdown. She was a widow and lived nearby. In the dream, Ann had appeared to be waiting for him.

In keeping with his bishop's advice, Thomas also went to talk with President Young about doing temple work for his ancestors. When President Young found out that Thomas had only seven names, he asked, "And have you faith to travel to St. George, over three hundred miles distant, to do the work for seven dead persons?"[26]

Thomas assured him he had.

"Well, the Lord bless you for your faith!" President Young replied. "Go to St. George, and have the work done for those whose names you have. . . . You shall be blessed on the trip."[27]

Thomas began making preparations for the journey. Before he left, Thomas visited his neighbor, Ann Ashdown. Spurred by his dream, Thomas impulsively asked Ann if she would go with him to St. George, marry him in the temple, and be a mother to his children. Thomas told Ann to think about it overnight, and he would return the following day for her answer. When he returned, Ann agreed to marry him.

Later that day, Thomas went to the home of his son Ephraim to tell him that he was going to get married. He told Ephraim that he would never guess who his new bride was going to be.

However, Ephraim already knew. In fact, he told Thomas, before she died his mother had said that someday Thomas would marry Sister Ashdown.

Thomas then went to see his oldest daughter, Emma, to tell her the news. "She too was prepared for it, and informed him that her mother, some time before her death, had predicted to her that Mrs. Ashdown would yet become her father's wife, either in time or eternity, as it had been made known to her in a vision."[28] Thomas felt that his first wife's vision or dream was confirmation that he was doing the right thing in marrying again.

Many people have received dreams predicting something will happen at some point in the future. When Philo Dibble had a dream that Joseph Smith was arrested, it came true only a few days later. Philo was a good friend of Joseph and Emma Smith and saw them frequently.

One night Philo was at the Smith home while Joseph and Emma were making preparations to go up the river the next day to visit friends. That night Philo had his dream. Philo records:

> The night before they started, I had a dream, in which I saw Joseph taken prisoner and guarded by two men, who after awhile left Joseph in Nauvoo and went off cursing and swearing. The next morning I related my dream to Joseph; he listened to me but made no reply.
>
> While visiting at Dixon he was taken prisoner by a sheriff of Missouri and an officer of Illinois, but instead of getting him over into Missouri as they had planned to, he was brought to Nauvoo. There they left Joseph and went off cursing and swearing, just as I had heard them in my dream.[29]

Dreams have all sorts of consequences. One Church history experience records a missionary who had a dream, which he related to Church members in order to chasten them when they unthinkingly hindered his missionary efforts. The elder, whose name is not given, had just finished giving a sermon when he was approached by a minister and two of his friends. The minister asked if he and his associates could talk with the elder to discuss the gospel, saying they would appreciate learning more.

"What saints there were gathered round to listen," the missionary noted, "and as the minister and his associates were very talkative, and would seldom give me an opportunity to answer their many questions, the Saints became impatient, and abruptly broke in . . . and thus took what little opportunity I might have had for replies."[30]

As minutes and then hours passed, it became clear that the minister and his friends were more interested in speaking than in learning. Finally, the missionary asked to be excused.

That night he had a symbolic dream.

He wrote, "I fell asleep, and dreamed that I was rowing and guiding a boat across a large body of water, with no other oar or helm than a walking stick. There were twelve or fifteen passengers with me in the boat, who kept. . . moving from side to side. . . near causing the boat to upset. I talked to them, and tried to persuade them to sit still, and keep a balance on the boat. . . Many times the top of the boat was about even with the surface of the water, which made it very difficult for one to manage to keep the boat erect." Despite his difficulties, he said, "I succeeded in bringing them all safe ashore."[31]

In the morning, the missionary shared his dream with a married couple who had been present the previous evening. The husband and wife each offered the same interpretation of the dream, saying that they had been guilty of taking the conversation away from the missionary. Although they had only been trying to help, the couple could see now that they had been rocking the boat from side to side and if they had simply sat still and let the elder do his work, he might have had an easier time.

During the day, every one of the members who had been present the night before visited the missionary. He told each one about his dream. They all said, "I will remember the rocking of the boat next time, and be still."[32]

Although many of his friends had been called to serve missions, C. V. Spencer felt he personally was unqualified for such work. Therefore, he was surprised to hear his name announced in the April 1850 general conference. Elder Spencer did accept the calling, however, and during his mission, he received another surprise when a woman recognized him from a dream she'd had and welcomed him to her house.

Elder Spencer left for his mission near the end of April. When he arrived in New York City, he paid $10 for passage to Liverpool, England. After arriving there, he was sent to Colchester, a place known as being difficult for missionaries to make any headway. Elder Spencer said wryly, "It was a hard place and in order to have raised any life there in relation to 'Mormonism,' one would have required the power to resurrect the dead."[33]

Still, Elder Spencer determined to do his best. "You were sent to this land by God's highest authority to preach the gospel," he said to himself, "and it is your duty to do it."[34]

One day, with his carpetbag in hand, he set off to walk twenty miles to a distant town. The roads were wet, making it a difficult trip. Then Elder Spencer had a special experience that reminded him that the Lord was mindful of him and those who with whom he would share the gospel.

"I came in sight of the place, on the top of a long hill, and noticed a woman crossing the road with two pails," Elder Spencer records. "She filled them with water and started back, but as she saw me walking towards her, she dropped both pails and came to me, saying, 'I knew you would come: I saw you in a dream. Come into my house; I have a room all fixed nice and clean for you.'"[35]

While there, Elder Spencer baptized his first converts of his mission. He continued to work hard and was able to bring the light of the gospel to many people.

The year was 1918 and the place was Verdun, France: a terrifying location to be during the war. Charles A. Shirley, along with the rest of his company, took up their position at the front, on top of a high hill. From there he and two of his comrades watched the movement of the enemy. At 10:00 PM, the trio decided that one of them should watch, while the other two slept.

Brother Shirley took the first turn watching. As he did, the clouds in the night sky suddenly broke apart, letting the moon shine through. The light was bright enough to allow Brother Shirley to see several objects lying nearby. He supposed they were packs, but when he went to examine them found that they were the bodies of dead men. Then Brother Shirley had what he supposed was a vivid dream, although he felt that he was awake at the time. He states:

> A strange feeling came over me, one that I cannot describe. . . . I looked down upon my sleeping comrades. Then, all of a sudden, I discovered someone was sitting by my side. Where he came from or how he joined me without my hearing him I did not know. I did not ask him his name.
>
> Without any explanation on the part of either of us, we began to talk. He spoke to me, saying, "Three days you will fight in a battle at Verdun, and you will fall critically wounded. If you were given your choice, on what part of your body would you choose to be wounded?"
>
> I thought a moment and then answered, "If I were shot in my legs, no doubt I would lose them and be a cripple for life. If I were shot in my right arm, perhaps I would lose my arm." I paused a moment and continued, "If I am to be given my choice, let me be shot in the left side, in the shoulder, the arm, or the hand." Without comment the stranger replied, "You have your choice."[36]

Brother Shirley then glanced at his companions, who still lay asleep. When he turned back, his visitor was gone, vanished as mysteriously as he had come. Because of this strange vision, Brother Shirley had lost all desire for sleep and did not wake his companions.

At sunrise he washed and tried to ready himself for the ordeal that was coming. Brother Shirley took his mess kit and extra clothing down the hill to a rolling kitchen, as he felt he would not need the clothing. He could not make himself eat but brought back food for his comrades.

He was unable to shake off his depression and said, "Oh, what a dreadful thing it is to wait in suspense for some terrible calamity to come upon you."[37]

Brother Shirley recalled how he had recently written his brother, advising him to register for the army, and "if necessary, to go and defend our country, even if it cost his last drop of blood. And now I was waiting, as it seemed to me, for the hour to come when I would in all probability make the supreme sacrifice. I might be blown to pieces. Oh, what a dreadful fear gripped my sad heart!"[38]

That night his company began an offensive. Brother Shirley states:

> We were crawling on the ground like an army of worms while the enemy was mowing down our ranks with deadly fire. I heard the sickening cries of many as the shells tore through the air or struck the ground, tearing the bodies of my comrades to pieces. The hill was in a tremble. . . . I found myself caught in the deadly trap of scissor fire and, being in the front rank, I realized my danger. While I lay upon the ground, I prayed to my Father in Heaven to spare my life and promised Him that if he would do so, I would dedicate myself to His service forever if He could use me.
>
> On both sides of me I could see a stream of melted steel, just a few feet away. I knew that in just a few moments I would be in eternity. I gasped and cried, "Oh God! Spare me! Thy will be done!"
>
> The fire ceased at that instant around me. I saw a shell hole a few feet away and crawled into it quickly. Once in the bottom, I thanked God for this protection. This was the fifth time I had been spared during the war.
>
> Three days later we were making another attack. I had carried a message a mile back to headquarters and was standing

watching the charge while waiting for my return orders. As I waited, a shell burst near me. Another passed over me. Then I heard another shell coming. Something seemed to tell me that it would get me. I tried to get into a dugout, but it burst almost on top of me. I was wounded in the left side, shoulder, arm and hand, just as I had chosen to be.

If it had not been for God's answer to prayers, I would not be here today, but would be sleeping in Flanders field. Dated August 10, 1934. Charles A. Shirley.[39]

Sarah Pea's dream wasn't nearly as terrifying as Brother Shirley's, but it was unusual. In her dream, Sarah Pea saw two missionaries, who had recently visited her family in Looking-Glass Prairie, Illinois, return to her home. Interestingly enough, the missionaries who had stopped at Sarah's home on their way to Kirtland dreamed that they traveled over five hundred miles in order to return to the Pea home. Sarah writes:

> In the summer of 1835, two Mormon elders came to preach in our home, by request of my father. . . . At that time I, together with my parents, was a member of the reformed Methodist Church. The two elders came and held a meeting and preached on the first principles and the gospel, and related to the people about there being a prophet in their church, and told us about the *Book of Mormon* and the angel appearing to the Prophet. . . . It was in the afternoon that they held their meeting; so my father asked them to stay all night—which invitation they accepted. They were on their way to Kirtland, Ohio, some five hundred miles from where we lived.
>
> After supper was over a number of neighbors gathered, to hear these strange men talk. Feeling anxious to see the Book of Mormon they had told us about, I asked one of the elders if I could see the book, and I asked the company to excuse me for the evening. I retired to my room and spent the rest of that evening and most of the night reading it. . . . The book left an impression on my mind never to be forgotten. . . . The next morning the men left for Ohio . . . We did not think we should ever meet with the men again.[40]

However, six weeks after the missionaries left, Sarah dreamed about them. She continues her account:

> I dreamed on Friday night that they would come to our house the next evening, just as the sun was going down, and that they would first come in sight at the end of a long lane in front of the house. I also dreamed that I met them on the porch and of a remark made by them and one made by myself in answer—which I will relate later on.
>
> In the morning father and mother went to Belleville. At breakfast I had asked father if he would not try to be home early.
>
> He answered, "Why are you so particular? Is your young man coming?"
>
> I said, "No, father, but those two Mormon elders will be here to-night."
>
> "Why," asked father, "have you heard from them?"
>
> I said, "No, but I dreamed last night that they would be here, and I feel sure it will be so."
>
> Father said I must be crazy, for those men were hundreds of miles away. But I insisted: "Father, hurry home this evening, for I am sure they will come." He only laughed, and he and mother went off to town.
>
> Then I said to my sister, "Let's prepare, for those men will surely be here." She, too, laughed at me. But as it was Saturday, we went to work baking and preparing for Sunday, as was our custom.
>
> As the day passed, I began to look, once in a while, down the lane for those men. Sure enough, just as the sun was setting, they made their appearance, just where I dreamed I first saw them. I met them on the porch, and bade them the time of day.
>
> "I have been looking for you to come," I said.
>
> "Why," one of them answered, "had you heard we were coming?"
>
> "No," I said, "I dreamed last night that you would come, and I felt sure you would be here."
>
> "Well," said one of the elders, "we had a dream that we were to return here and baptize you and build up a church in this region."
>
> I answered, "Well, that is something in the future." I bade them take chairs and be comfortable, for my parents would soon be home.
>
> In a very short time my father and mother drove into the

> yard. As I was standing on the porch, my father said to me, "Well, Sarah, where are your Mormon elders?" I told him they were in the house, at the same time they stepped out on the porch, to meet him. Father was struck with astonishment, as he remembered what I had told him in the morning about my dream.[41]

After dinner, they all spent the evening talking about religion. Sarah said, "The more they told us, the more we were interested."

The next morning, a Sunday, her father rode around to his neighbors and told them that two Mormon elders would be preaching at his house that night. Sarah relates:

> When the time arrived, the house was filled. All listened attentively to a beautiful discourse upon the coming forth of the Book of Mormon. After the meeting, a great many stayed and spent the evening asking questions until a late hour. Before the meeting was dismissed it was agreed that the elders should preach again on Tuesday evening at the same place. When Tuesday evening came, people arrived from all the settlements; the house and the porch were filled. On the dismissal of the meeting the missionaries had many invitations to preach in different places.
>
> By this time I was convinced that their doctrine was of God. So the next morning I was baptized. I had made it a matter of prayer, that the Lord would show me whether what these men had said was true; and he did so. I was convinced that it was the work of God, and never have I for one moment doubted it since; and it is now fifty-four years since I embraced Mormonism. It was the fifteenth of December that I was baptized, and they had to cut the ice in order to baptize me. The two elders remained here till they had built up a church of seventy members, my father, mother, and sister being among this number.[42]

Certainly, Sarah's dream, as well as the two missionaries' dream, foretold true events. When Martha Cragun Cox had a dream that her mother died, she was sure her dream also represented a true event. Martha writes:

> In December, 1901 the night before Christmas I dreamed

that I stood before my mother's door in St. George. My sister, Teresa, drove into the yard in a carriage. My mother came to the door to greet her. My mother looked so frail, so thin and white, that she advanced slowly to the carriage where my sister sat. She could not lift her foot to the step and I was powerless to help her. My sister took my mother's hand and immediately she floated into the carriage, and turned towards [me].

Her face was so young, so beautiful, and smilingly happy. My brother stood on the doorway weeping because his pleadings to go with Mother was not answered. My sister had said to him, "You cannot go now, Jim, you must wait till your turn comes." When I awoke I knew my mother had gone home, and I told the family of her death. In due time I had a letter from Frank telling of her death on the very Christmas eve."[43]

After spending six weeks without friends and money, Elder M. F. Cowley dreamed that he returned home from his mission before his time was up. "Any Elder who has such a manifestation knows what remorse and sorrow rests upon him while in the dream," Elder Cowley writes, "and what joy and peace fills his soul when he awakes and finds himself still far away from home and kindred where duty casts his lot. In one of these dreams I saw President John Taylor, and was very fearful of meeting him lest he should chide me for being home too soon; but when he spoke, he smiled and in terms of kindness said, 'Well you're home, are you; you can go to Georgia now.'"[44]

It was a prophetic dream. "I finished my mission, was honorably released, and was home a little less than six months, when I was called again to the Southern States," Elder Cowley continues. "Having been so greatly blessed in Virginia, having so many friends there, I naturally inclined to go there on my second mission, but President Morgan did not want me to return to that field but assigned me to the State of Georgia to labor with Brother John W. Taylor [son of President John Taylor]. Thus fulfilling my dream, though President Morgan knew nothing of the dream until after its fulfillment."[45]

Elder Cowley's dream made him determined to fulfill an honorable mission. He states, "The manifestation of being home before the right time so filled me with chagrin and sorrow, that I was constantly buoyed up with courage to discharge my duty and be contented in my field of labor until honorably released to return to my mountain home."[46]

Elder Cowley's dreams motivated him and so did the two dreams received by Evan Molbourne Greene. In both of them, Brother Greene saw glimpses of heaven. Brother Greene relates the first dream as follows:

> On Tuesday morning, the 1st day of Feb. between the hours of 2 ocl. and 4 ocl not having slept any all night, I fell asleep and dreamed that as I was traveling to the south; I was passing down a corridor with doors opening on my left into beautiful rooms of pure white finish—whiter than any alabaster that my eyes have ever beheld—of the same pure white finish was the corridor—no tongues can tell the beauty of that whiteness: of the same clear transparent whiteness was every object that I beheld: no shining of the sun, for the Lord God was the light thereof: I saw no person and no object that seemed to possess animal life: but the joy and peace that filled my soul and thrilled through every fiber of my existence was beyond description:
>
> Having passed a great many of those rooms. . . I entered a room running to the west with another group: as I entered that room I discovered that I was dressed in my temple clothes, which I had not noticed before; in this room was a large company, all females and all dressed in their temple clothes—all was of the same pure white. . . even the skin of the persons whom I saw. This was the lecture room for the instruction of those spirits who receive the gospel by proxy after they are dead. . . in the middle of which and some distance to the west stood Sister E. R. Snow. . . and a few feet in front and a little to the left stood Sister Zina Young. A little further to the left and nearly on a line with Sister Snow stood my wife Susan Kent Greene, to the right of Sister Snow and in about the same positions were others, and so behind as far as my eye could penetrate stood others.[47]

Brother Greene also heard melodic singing and then when he awoke, "my soul filled with a joy not to be expressed!" He also received a second dream. He records:

> [This dream occurred] on Tuesday night, the 1st day of February, 1881, between the hours of 10 ocl. and 12 ocl. P.M.

> after having been coughing all the fore part of the night, I fell a sleep and dreamed I was traveling to the south in a very wide road that was filled with pedestrians of all nationalities who were traveling some each way: all seemed to feel well, and looked pleased: all were dressed in the same kind of a bag or coat: which seemed to be made whole, the body reaching from the neck to the feet: fitting tight. . . . And presently I saw a large pavilion in front and the sides of the road converged so as to meet the sides of the pavilion. . . . I saw the road entered there: the interior from the door or open end, was seated with three tiers of seats, running across the interior of the pavilion. . . .
>
> As I was passing up the right hand aisle a man sitting on the end of one of the seats, between me and the wall slapped me on the leg, to draw my attention, at the same time saying, "Seems I ought to know your story."
>
> As I looked down upon him I saw a man whom I knew when I was a boy, whose name was Redman . . . he replied "Well, who would have thought that we should have met here."
>
> After passing him a young man rose from the back seat on my right, and said in a few minutes Mr. Stranger will lecture from this stand, and the singers are requested to hasten to their seats: I then discovered a large company of female singers entering a side door just back of me, which door I did not before observe: and passing with a hurried step up the aisle in which I was passing, so to give room for them I stepped down into the aisle next to the center seats:
>
> The singers were all dressed in white: their garments were of the same material and made in the style as the main congregations but were pure white. . . . The male singers entered also at a side door and passed up the aisle on that side. . . . [I then heard] the voice of Prest. B. [Brigham] Young. I looked and saw his face surrounded by a heavy dark main [mane] like a lion's main, and his voice was like that of a heavy trumpet, which filled the whole pavilion.[48]

Then Brother Greene heard a voice announce, "The place where Brigham the Lion of the Lord speaks from the Holy of Holies to the people." Brother Greene concluded his account by saying, "Here I awoke much strengthened both in mind and body."[49]

Johannes Hasler was critically ill when he dreamed that a spirit came to persuade him to leave his home and family. Johannes related his experience:

> In the fall of 1872 a severe trial overtook us. I was suddenly taken down with typhoid fever, which later developed into rheumatic fever. I was laid low all winter. My life hung on a thread for months. My body was reduced to a skeleton. The cords of my limbs were drawn together. In those days, there was no medical help obtainable. We had to depend entirely on the Lord, much faith being exercised by my family and the brethren of the Holy Priesthood.
>
> I was for months delirious. In the first days of my illness I told my wife of a dream I had. I dreamed I was working in the field when a personage dressed in a military suit came to me and wanted me to follow him. He promised me work that would be to my liking in music and I could be a good leader. This was very tempting to me, but I thought then of my wife and family who so much depended on me. I pleaded with him to let me then go to town to consider it. I was thinking of gaining time and that I could get the help of the Priesthood.
>
> I told my wife if I would get delirious again to get my brethren to help me, for fear this man would come back and overpower me. I did not want to go with him. My wife told the dream to those who came to administer to me mostly every day. Some of them got weak in the faith and felt that it was almost a greater blessing to pray to our Father in heaven to take me and release me from the misery, for I suffered much. Many of them were faithful and fasted and prayed for my recovery. I was not able to help myself in the least for months. My wife carried me from one room to another so she could be near me and help me while doing her household duties.[50]

Through Louise's diligent nursing and the faithful prayers of friends and family, Johannes did slowly recover, although it took him three years before he could walk without crutches. When Johannes was well enough to travel, he and Louise and his wife sailed from Liverpool to New York then boarded an emigration train that took them to Ogden. From there they traveled to Mt. Pleasant, where they made their new home.

In the later part of 1844, Mephibosheth Sirrine was chosen by Brigham Young to preside over branches of the Church in Connecticut and Michigan. Then, when the Saints began their trek west, he was asked to serve as a pioneer captain. Some time later, Elder Sirrine served a mission to England. While there he had an unforgettable dream. He wrote about this dream in a letter to a friend and later gave permission for the letter to be printed in *The Millennial Star.* The letter states:

> Dear Brother Hyde, I take the opportunity to drop these few lines to you. I am not in the habit of repeating dreams or visions, but in consequence of the heavenly impression that a certain dream or vision left on my mind, I thought I would relate it to you.
>
> I preached in Bolton (England) on the evening of the 16th of December (1864), on the resurrection of the dead. After (the) meeting I . . . retired to bed. . . . I had not been in bed long before this singular occurrence took place. I viewed myself traveling in company with two or three of my brethren. . . . All at once, a very fine looking man fell in company with us.
>
> He said, "Well, brethren, how do you all do?"
>
> We looked at him, and said, "You have got the advantage of us, for we do not know you."
>
> He said, "If you will keep it to yourselves whilst I am with you, I will tell you who I am." We told him we would. . . .
>
> Said the stranger to us, "My name is James. I am one of the twelve apostles that was on this earth in the days of our Savior, and you now see my resurrected body. Handle me, and see; for a spirit hath not flesh and bones as you see me have.' We then viewed him very closely, but, oh, the beauty and glory of that body; would to God that I had language to describe it. His flesh and skin looked so beautiful and pure, and his cheeks like the rose.
>
> Said I, "Brother James, how did the people treat you and the rest of the Saints in that age of the world?"
>
> Said he, "Very much the same as they treat you and the twelve at the present time; they mocked and derided us, our names were cast out as evil; the priests contended with us, they told the people we were false prophets, imposters, and not fit to live on the earth, just as the people say at the present day about the twelve that God has sent in this dispensation.

> "The truth is," continued he, "the people are the same now that they were then, and the pure principles of Christ they will not receive, any more at the present day than they would when we told them the truth; and in that day only a few believed our testimony, and but a few will receive the truth at the present day."[51]

Elder Sirrine then mentioned that a nearby chapel had been built and dedicated to James. He invited James to go and preach there. James replied that the people would not let him speak there because his preaching would directly oppose all of their false traditions. James further stated that the plainest part of his writings had been taken away and what little of his writings the people had they did not practice.

James continued, "So all that can be done is to preach where you can get an opportunity, and gather out the honest."

Elder Sirrine said, "I then asked him what he thought of the twelve apostles that we had now with us, that are the leaders of the Church of Jesus Christ of Latter-day Saints.

Said he, "They are good men, and if the Saints will follow their counsel they will be exalted in the kingdom of God."

Elder Sirrine commented, "They have learned many great and glorious principles since the organization of the church.

"'Yes,' says he, 'but they are all but babes yet to what they will be when they get their immortal bodies, as you now see me have.'

"Said I to him, 'I wish that I had my immortal body, as I see you have; how glad I should be.'

"Says he, 'It will not be long, if you are faithful, before you and all the rest of the Saints will have just such a body as you see me have.'

"At this (said Elder Sirrine,) I awoke, and behold, it was a dream. Some may think that it was nothing but a phantom of the brain, but to me it was something glorious and tangible, and which I never shall forget in time nor in eternity; for it is verily true, just as I have related it, and it makes my heart rejoice very time I think of it. Oh, the beauty and glory of that body! Language cannot describe it; therefore I feel willing to pass through sorrow and affliction whilst in this mortal body, that I may obtain a glorious resurrection."[52]

Frederick Hurst was born in 1833 on the Isle of Jersey. Six years later, his family moved to New Zealand. When Frederick was a young boy, he heard a voice from heaven pronouncing on him a special promise, one which he never revealed to anyone. Years later, when he was called on a mission, Elder Hurst was given a blessing by President George Q. Cannon, who promised him the same exact thing the heavenly being had. Then eighteen years after his mission, Elder Hurst had a remarkable dream where he saw two important personages.

Elder Hurst recorded these experiences when he began writing his memoirs in 1890. He wrote:

> I felt like I would like to leave the following facts on record. What I am about to relate transpired in New Zealand. I was about eight years of age and entirely alone, as all the folks were to meeting, and I was left to mind the house.
>
> Being very fond of reading the Bible I took it on my lap and sat down in the center of the room, and I read the beginning of the 14th chapter of Revelation. I was deeply interested in the one hundred and forty-four thousand men chosen for their virute [virtue]. . . . They sang a new song, etc. In my childlike simplicity I full believed every word of it. Also the holy angel having the everlasting Gospel. I raised my eyes from the sacred book and exclaimed aloud: "Oh! I would like to be one of that glorious throng."
>
> To my utter and unspeakable astonishment the Spirit and Glory of God filled the room where I was sitting and I distinctly heard a voice from Heaven saying: "You shall be one of that number if you live a pure life."
>
> I was filled with joy that I cannot describe, and though a mere child I resolved to love God and keep His commandments, and to do all in my power, through the mercy and blessing of the Lord, to be worthy of so great a blessing. I never told my parents but kept the circumstances locked up in my heart, but I have never forgotten it. It has been a beacon or guide to me through life.
>
> I will now relate something very remarkable in connection with that most glorious promise to me. Please bear in mind, I had never told a single soul of this heavenly manifestation to me. I attended the conference of this Church in San Francisco, April 6, 1857. Being set apart with some other young Elders, President George Q. Cannon was mouth, I was very much

astonished to hear him say: "Brother Fred, that you should be one of the one hundred and forty-four thousand that should stand upon Mt. Zion and sing a new song, and now by virtue and authority of the Holy Priesthood, I seal and confirm that promise on your head."

Oh! How vividly everything was brought to my mind. I felt like it would be impossible for me to thank the Lord enough for all of His blessings to me. Hunger, thirst, hardship of any kind, even my life if necessary for the Gospel's sake should not be withheld, and then how could that compare with such a great promise. Not a drop in the bucket compared with the vast ocean.

Still farther I had a dream in 1875 as follows: I found myself in front of one of the grandest buildings I had ever seen. The front was open to quite an extent, supported on immense columns or pillars, and about twelve steps to ascend to the open court. Altogether the building was magnificent and glorious. I saw two persons standing by a desk upon which lay an open book they were looking at. As I raised my right foot to ascend the steps the thought occurred to me, "Am I worthy to enter such a glorious and beautiful place?" upon which they both looked at me (they were both tall fine-looking men).

One of them (Brother Parley P. Pratt) ran down the steps, took me by the right hand and led me up to the desk, then took me by the shoulders with both his hands, immediately facing the book. The other person still stood with the forefinger of his right hand nearly half way down the column of names, pointing to my name in full, FREDERICK WILLIAM HURST.

Brother Pratt said: "Brother Hurst, we were looking over the list of the one hundred and forty-four thousand and had just got to your name when we saw you." I was so full of joy I was moved to tears. They talked to me for a short time, but what passed between us passed from me. There was one of the brethren that I was well acquainted with came out of the building. . . . He said: "Do you know those brethren you have been talking with?"

I replied, "I judge one to be Brother Parley P. Pratt."

He said, "Yes, and the other is John the Revelator." I then awoke.[53]

Dreams often reveal reassuring things. In one interesting instance, a man, whose name is not given, was allowed to see some of the judgments that would come upon the earth in the future. He also saw that during those calamities the Saints would be protected. Writing about this experience, the man recorded, "Some two or three years ago, I had retired for the night, when suddenly a glorious messenger appeared at my bedside and awoke me from my slumber. The light of his presence filled the room, so that objects were discerned as clearly as at noonday. He handed me a book, saying, 'Look, and see what is coming to pass.' I took the book in my hands and, sitting up in bed, examined it carefully and read its contents."[54]

The book showed a series of pictures and writings reflecting the death and destruction that would come in the latter days. The man stated that these judgments matched the revelations given to the Prophet Joseph. "Plagues will come and the wicked must suffer," the man wrote, "but Saints will be preserved by the very principle for which the wicked persecute them, which is present revelation from the Almighty."[55]

Albert Hamblin, the adopted son of Jacob Hamblin, the famous apostle to the Lamanites, was accustomed to having dreams and visions. When Albert was twenty-two years old, he had a dream that let him know that he would soon be called to do missionary work—in the next life.

In March 1863, some Moqui Indians came to visit with Jacob and his family. When they concluded their visit, Jacob made preparations to escort them home. Jacob planned on being gone for some time, so he talked with Albert about running the farm before he left. Albert was already knowledgeable about the farm; he'd been in charge of the sheep, horses, and cattle ever since he had arrived on the Hamblin farm twelve years earlier. As they talked, Jacob observed that the weather had warmed up and that the peach trees were beginning to bloom.

Albert replied, "Yes, and I shall bloom in another place before you get back. I shall be on my mission!"

Jacob asked, "What do you mean by that?'

He replied, "That I shall be dead and buried when you get back."

Jacob returned home two months later. He wrote, "I found on my return home that my Indian boy, Albert, was dead and buried, as he had predicted he would be when I left home."

Jacob continued, "Some time before his death he (Albert) had a vision, in which he saw himself preaching the gospel to a multitude of his people. He believed that this vision would be realized in the world of spirits. He referred to this when he said that he should die before my return home, and be on his mission. He was a faithful Latter-day Saint; believed he had a great work to do among his people; had many dreams and visions, and had received his blessings in the house of the Lord."[56]

Marie Weiss had an unusual dream the day before her husband, Henry, came home from his mission to the Northwestern States. Marie was disturbed by the dream because she thought it meant her husband would soon be called to leave mortality.

In the dream, Marie saw a great number of people gathered together in a large valley, talking earnestly among themselves. At the front of the crowd was a man dressed like an old-time schoolmaster in Bavaria, the land of Marie and Henry's ancestors. The schoolmaster went over to Marie's father-in-law, who was standing nearby. The account states:

> The schoolmaster . . . said to him (Marie's father-in-law): "We have heard that upon earth some labor has been performed in our behalf which will bring us great happiness. Can you tell us about it?"
>
> The father-in-law answered, "I am sorry, but I cannot. I only heard of the Gospel once before I died. You should have my son, Henry Weiss, here as a missionary. He could tell you all about that."
>
> The group discussed the matter and decided to get up a petition asking for Henry Weiss to be called to the Spirit World on a mission to preach to his numerous kindred.[57]

When Marie awoke from this dream, she was deeply troubled. It was a great relief when Henry arrived home in good health. Later, she told him about the dream. He replied, "I suppose it means that I should redouble my efforts to gather records of my relatives."[58]

Henry then began spending a great deal of time checking over his family's records. Prior to leaving on his mission, Henry had worked diligently and had gathered more than thirty thousand names of German Saints. Henry, Marie, and their married children frequently went to the temple to do the temple work for these people.

After he had been home about six months, Henry began having unusual pains and went to see a doctor. After an examination and x-rays, the doctors discovered Henry had cancer. The doctor operated as soon as he could, but a few days later, Henry died. Marie wrote the following after her husband's death:

> The interpretation of the dream is very clear to me now. My husband's father was the last who died in his family without having accepted the Gospel. The oldest man, dressed like a schoolmaster, was the earliest ancestor on our pedigree chart, who emigrated in 1620 from Silesia into Bavaria as a soldier and school teacher. The Gospel had to be preached to them and so they looked for someone in mortal life to be called on a mission over to the Spirit World to instruct them. My husband was the only one out of a big family of fifteen children to hear the Gospel message and accept it, and was ready to go over as a missionary to his father's household and preach to his own kindred in the Spirit World the glad tidings of the Gospel.[59]

Sally Knight and her husband, Newel Knight, lived in Colesville, New York. One night Sally dreamed that the Prophet Joseph Smith would stop and visit the Saints in Colesville on a specific day. She felt assured of his arrival, even though it was common knowledge that Joseph was traveling constantly, often without prior plans, in order to avoid being arrested and thrown into jail by enemies of the Church.

Joseph Smith himself relates the experience:

> After our departure from Colesville, after the trial, the Church there were very anxious, as might be expected, concerning our again visiting them, during which time Sister Knight, wife of Newel Knight, had a dream, which enabled her to say that we would visit them that day, which really came to pass, for

a few hours afterwards we arrived; and thus was our faith much strengthened concerning dreams and visions in the last days, foretold by the ancient Prophet Joel; and although we this time were forced to seek safety from our enemies by flight, yet did we feel confident that eventually we should come off victorious, if we only continued faithful to Him who had called us forth from darkness into the marvelous light of the everlasting Gospel of our Lord Jesus Christ.[60]

While Sister Sherwood, a new convert, didn't see the prophet in her dream, she did see an angel. Sister Sherwood related her experience to Elder John Sims Carter, who recorded it as follows:

> April 18th, 1833. Heard Sister Sherwood relate her vision of seeing an angel which was last Monday. We conversed with her as she supposed about 15 minutes and told her that he should come again. She has had many wonderful visions. She relates that she heard a voice soon after she came into this work telling her that if she would be faithful she should see many grand and glorious things. This she has already proved, which commenced by seeing an unusual light, the night upon which her eyes were opened and saw visions of God concerning that which must come hereafter purporting indeed, that the hour of God's judgement has come and astonishing things soon are to take place.[61]

W. Rider's dream was published in 1851 in *The Millennial Star.* The editor of that newspaper, usually a member of the Quorum of the Twelve Apostles, wrote the following preface to Brother Rider's dream: "It is often both interesting and profitable to contemplate the cogitations of the mind which occur during the slumbers of the night. . . . Important secrets are often revealed by dreams and visions of the night, not only in relation to the present, but of the future, and of the past."[62]

Brother Rider then shared his dream, saying, "Methought I beheld a female in a white robe, with an olive branch in her hand. . . . With an air that expressed majesty and affection, she pointed to a temple that stood at some distance. . . . I went towards it. As I approached I observed that the avenues were declining, and that they were bespread with roses, and perfumed with fragrance, which rendered the way not only easy but agreeable."[63]

Brother Rider went inside the temple, where he saw people performing various tasks. After watching the people for some time, Brother Rider suddenly awoke, feeling grateful that God had restored His gospel to the earth in the latter days.

Dreams sometimes reveal little-known facts or secrets. One woman, known in this account only as M. S., found out through a dream that she had been adopted through a dream. Her adoptive parents had discovered a basket containing a baby girl on their front porch and raised the infant as theirs, never telling their daughter that she had been abandoned.

However, M. S. received a dream—three times in one night—revealing that she had been adopted. In the dream, M. S. saw her biological mother sitting at a spinning wheel. The dream even showed her where the woman lived.

The next morning, M. S. shared the dream with her husband, who ridiculed her. Despite her husband's scorn, M. S., had such strong feelings about the dream that she decided to go to the street she had seen in her dream.

When she reached the street, M. S. easily found the house. As she stared at the house, M. S. saw framed in the window a woman sitting in front of a spinning wheel—the same woman the dream had revealed was her mother.

M. S. knocked on the door. When the woman came to the door, M. S. asked if the woman had given birth to a baby girl in May 1804 and if she had left that baby in a basket at a home on a particular street.

The older woman did not hesitate, replying firmly that she had not. She then asked M. S. what had put such a strange idea in her head. M. S. briefly related her dream. The account so shocked the older woman that she fell backwards into a chair and admitted that she was M. S.'s mother. The woman told Sister S. that her biological father had forced her to banish her infant. He was an influential man and felt that a public scandal would ruin his reputation.

M. S. was grateful that the dream had revealed the truth.[64]

One last touching story of a dream sent from heaven to guide and direct the faithful. Elder Peterson had been sent by Church authorities to Emery County to organize a branch. He was serving as stake president when he experienced a spiritual manifestation. The story states that Brother Peterson was sleeping in a wagon when what he called a dream passed.

"A company of men were coming towards him, of whom he felt afraid at first, and then in consideration of his business there, he resolved to stand his ground boldly. When they came up to him he found that they were a band of musicians dressed in their regalia, or costume."[65]

The men began to play, and Brother Peterson said the music was exquisitely sweet. They used instruments that differed from any he had seen before.

> Brother Peterson asked them, for what reason they had come to serenade him. The leader, of the two answered, that he [Peterson] was the first man for a great many hundred years who had come into that country to organize any part of the Church that they belonged to or believed in. They mentioned the number of hundred years, which was over a thousand, since any man had been there on that business, and they had come to play for him because they were so glad he had come among them. That they had lived there many hundred years ago and were a band of musicians then. They played three more times and then left.
>
> A few nights after that, a couple of young men stopping about half a mile from there, heard the same music near the same place and the same number of tunes, but could not see any one. They were wide awake.[66]

Notes

Chapter 1

1. James E. Talmage, *A Study of the Articles of Faith* (Salt Lake City: The Church of Jesus Christ of Latter-day Saints, 1924), 226.
2. Wilford Woodruff, in *Journal of Discourses,* 26 vols. (London: Latter-day Saints' Book Depot, 1854–86), 22:331.
3. Boyd K. Packer, "A Thought from the Scriptures," *Church News,* 20 December 1997, 16.
4. Harold B. Lee, *Stand Ye in Holy Places, Selected Sermons and Writings of President Harold B. Lee* (Salt Lake City: Deseret Book, 1974), 141, 143, 145.
5. Elder H. Ricks, "Dreams," *The Millennial Star*, 51:18.
6. Lee, *Stand Ye in Holy Places,* 142.
7. David A. Bednar, "The Tender Mercies of the Lord," *Ensign,* May 2005, 100, 101, 102.
8. George F. Richards, as quoted by Spencer W. Kimball, "The Cause Is Just and Worthy," *Ensign,* May 1974, 119.
9. *The Millennial Star*, 15:600.
10. Brigham Young, in *Journal of Discourses,* 8:148.
11. Heber C. Kimball, in *Journal of Discourses,* 10:245.
12. Parley P. Pratt, as quoted in Lee, *Stand Ye in Holy Places,* 142.

13. *The Millennial Star*, 26:636.
14. Ibid., 26:293.
15. Ibid., 29:369.
16. Boyd K. Packer, "Revelation in a Changing World," *Ensign,* November 1989, 14.
17. Vaughn J. Featherstone, "In the Dream of a Night Vision," devotional, 28 September 1979, Salt Lake Institute of Religion, University of Utah, 19.
18. Joseph Smith, *Teachings of the Prophet Joseph Smith,* sel. Joseph Fielding Smith (Salt Lake City: Deseret Book, 1976), 204.
19. Ibid., 209.
20. Ibid., 213–14.
21. Ibid., 214–15.
22. Joseph Smith, *History of The Church of Jesus Christ of Latter-day Saints,* ed. B. H. Roberts, 2d ed. rev., 7 vols. (Salt Lake City: The Church of Jesus Christ of Latter-day Saints, 1932–51), 3:381.
23. Joseph G. Romney, *The Millennial Star,* 26:293.
24. Wilford Woodruff, in *Journal of Discourses*, 22:332–33.
25. *The Millennial Star*, 15:291.
26. Packer, "Revelation in a Changing World," 14–15.
27. *The Millennial Star*, 29:369.
28. Featherstone, devotional, 7.
29. Talmage, *A Study of the Articles of Faith,* 226.
30. Erastus Snow, in *Journal of Discourses,* 19:273.
31. Joseph Smith, *Personal Writings of Joseph Smith,* comp. Dean C. Jessee (Salt Lake City: Deseret Book, 1984), 175.

Chapter 2

1. Harold B. Lee, *The Teachings of Harold B. Lee*, ed. Clyde J. Williams (Salt Lake City: Bookcraft, 1996), 426–27.
2. Charles A. Callis, in Conference Reports of The Church of Jesus Christ of Latter-day Saints (Salt Lake City: The Church of Jesus Christ of Latter-day Saints, 1898 to present), October 1930, 15.
3. Wilford Woodruff, *Leaves from My Journal, Third Book of the Faith-Promoting Series* (Salt Lake City: Juvenile Instructor Office, 1882), 94.
4. "Stepping Stones to Faith," *Young Woman's Journal*, December 1916, 27:701.

5. James E. Talmage, *A Study of the Articles of Faith* (Salt Lake City: The Church of Jesus Christ of Latter-day Saints, 1924), 229.
6. Melvin J. Ballard, *Melvin J. Ballard, Crusader for Righteousness* (Salt Lake City: Bookcraft, 1966), 138–39.
7. Bryant S. Hinckley, *The Faith of Our Pioneer Fathers* (Salt Lake City: Bookcraft, 1956), 225.
8. George Q. Cannon, "A Dream," *Juvenile Instructor* 32 (1 November 1897): 656.
9. Vaughn J. Featherstone, "In the Dream of a Night Vision," devotional, Salt Lake Institute of Religion, University of Utah, 28 September 1979, 8–9.
10. Heber J. Grant, "President Grant Relates Incidents to Promote Faith," *Church News*, 21 November 1931, 2.
11. In *The Forefather Quest, A Lesson Book for Third-Year Junior Genealogical Classes* (Salt Lake City: Genealogical Society of Utah, 1937), 19–20.
12. Ibid., in Bryant S. Hinckley, *Heber J. Grant: Highlights in the Life of a Great Leader* (Salt Lake City: Deseret Book, 1951), 247–48.
13. Bryant S. Hinckley, *The Faith of Our Pioneer Fathers*, 234.
14. Orson F. Whitney, *Life of Heber C. Kimball* (Salt Lake City, Bookcraft, 1888), 120.
15. In Joseph Smith, *History of The Church of Jesus Christ of Latter-day Saints*, ed. B. H. Roberts, 2d ed. rev., 7 vols. (Salt Lake City: The Church of Jesus Christ of Latter-day Saints, 1932–51), 4:203.
16. *Wilford Woodruff, History of His Life and Labors, As Recorded in His Daily Journals*, comp. Matthias F. Cowley (Salt Lake City: *The Deseret News*, 1909), 376.
17. *Cherished Experiences from the Writings of President David O. McKay*, comp. Clare Middlemiss (Salt Lake City: Deseret Book, 1976), 59–60.
18. Ibid., 129–30.
19. *Times and Seasons* 5, no. 2 (15 January 1844): 414.
20. Franklin L. West, *Life of Franklin D. Richards* (Salt Lake City: Deseret News Press, 1924), 81–82.
21. In Conference Report, April 1974, 173–74.
22. *Wilford Woodruff, History of His Life and Labors*, 60.
23. Ibid., 59–60.

24. Boyd K. Packer, "Elder Petersen Is Eulogized," *Church News*, 22 January 1984, 10.
25. William W. Phelps, *Messenger and Advocate* 1 (October 1834–September 1835): 66.
26. Adah Roberts Naylor, "An Immigrant Mother and Her Son," *The Relief Society Magazine* 21 (January 1834): 3–8.
27. Robert Leatham Simpson, *The Lord Is Mindful of His Own*, BYU Speeches of the Year, 4 April 1962, 9–10.
28. *Wilford Woodruff,* 199.
29. *History of the Church,* 6:461–62.
30. Joseph G. Romney, "Dreams," *The Millennial Star,* 26:293.
31. William Wines Phelps, *Joseph Smith's Last Dream*, unpublished manuscript (Salt Lake City: LDS Church History Library), 1–9.
32. Joseph F. Smith, *Gospel Doctrine*, 14th ed. (Salt Lake City: Deseret Book, 1966), 541–53.
33. Eliza Roxey Snow Smith, *Biography and Family Record of Lorenzo Snow* (Salt Lake City: Deseret News Company, 1884), 17.
34. John Taylor, in *Journal of Discourses*, 22:354.
35. Ibid., "Nauvoo Journal of John Taylor Found," *Church News*, 30 January 1983, 12.
36. Orson F. Whitney, *Through Memory's Halls, The Life Story of Orson F. Whitney* (Independence, Missouri: Zion's Printing and Publishing Company, 1930), 81–82.
37. Ibid., 83.
38. Whitney, *Through Memory's Halls,* 81–83.
39. *Wilford Woodruff,* 51–52.
40. Ibid., 52.
41. Ibid.
42. Ibid., 51–53.
43. Ibid., 189.
44. Ibid., 234.
45. Ibid., 227.
46. Wilford Woodruff, in *Journal of Discourses,* 22:332.
47. Ibid.
48. Ibid., 333.
49. Wilford Woodruff, in *Journal of Discourses,* 21:299–300.
50. Ibid., *Journals 1833–1898*, 31 December 1893 (Salt Lake City: LDS Church Archives).

51. *Wilford Woodruff,* 529.
52. Wilford Woodruff, in *Journal of Discourses*, 21:318.
53. *Wilford Woodruff,* 531.
54. Wilford Woodruff, in *Journal of Discourses*, 21:317–18.
55. *Wilford Woodruff,* 505. 50.
56. J. Watson, *Manuscript History of Brigham Young 1846–1847* (Salt Lake City: LDS Church History Library), 528–30.

Chapter 3

1. Elder H. Ricks, "Dreams," *The Millennial Star*, 51:17.
2. Wilford Woodruff, *The Discourses of Wilford Woodruff*, comp. G. Homer Durham (Salt Lake City: Bookcraft, 1946), 217–18.
3. Harold B. Lee, *The Teachings of Harold B. Lee,* ed. Clyde J. Williams (Salt Lake City: Bookcraft, 1996), 425.
4. Ibid., 424.
5. Bryant S. Hinckley, *The Faith of Our Pioneer Fathers* (Salt Lake City: Bookcraft, 1956), 242.
6. Ibid., 243.
7. Ibid., 242–44.
8. Castle H. Murphy, *Castle of Zion—Hawauum Autobiography and Episodes from the Life of Castle H. Murphy, Missionary to Hawaii* (Salt Lake City: Deseret Book, 1963), 46.
9. Ibid., 46.
10. Oscar W. McConkie Jr., *Angels* (Salt Lake City: Deseret Book, 1975), 117.
11. Ibid., 116–17.
12. *Links of Forever,* comp. Connie Rector and Diane Deputy (Salt Lake City: Bookcraft, 1977), 135.
13. Ibid., 135–37.
14. William J. Facer, "A Dream Fulfilled," *The Millennial Star,* 64:750.
15. William M. Palmer, "Answer to Prayer," *The Contributor,* 17:430
16. Ibid., 430.
17. Ibid.
18. Ibid., 430–31.
19. *Helpful Visions, the Fourteenth Book of the Faith-Promoting Series* (Salt Lake City: Juvenile Instructor Office, 1887), 59–61.
20. Norma Clark Larsen, *His Everlasting Love* (Bountiful: Horizon, 1977), 99–100.

21. Ibid., 100–101.
22. “A Remarkable Testimony,” *The Elders’ Journal of the Southern States Mission of The Church of Jesus Christ of Latter-day Saints*, 2:291.
23. Ibid., 291–92.
24. Rex, “A Sunday Morning Dream,” *The Contributor* 6 (1885): 142.
25. Ibid., 141–44.
26. William Daybell, “A Dream Fulfilled,” *The Improvement Era*, 2:686.
27. Ibid., 2:686–87.
28. Larsen, *His Everlasting Love*, 101–2.
29. Ogden Kraut, *A Gift of Dreams* (Salt Lake City: LDS Church History Library), 84.
30. Ibid., 85.
31. Ibid., 84–86.
32. Larsen, *His Everlasting Love*, 105.
33. Ibid., 105–6.
34. Claudius Spencer, “A Dream,” *Juvenile Instructor*, 19:95.
35. Ibid.
36. J. D. C., “From the Other World,” *Liahona*, 6:519.
37. Ibid., 520.
38. Ibid., 519–21.
39. *Heroines of Mormondom, Second Book of the Noble Women’s Lives Series* (Salt Lake City: Juvenile Instructor Office, LDS Church History Library, 1884), 78–79.
40. Joseph Heinerman, *Memoirs of Henry Savage*, as quoted in *Spirit World Manifestations* (Salt Lake City: Magazine Printing and Publishing, 1978), 135–37.
41. Kevin Stoker, “Green Street Conversion,” *Church News*, 10 February 1985, 16.
42. *Juvenile Instructor* 19 (15 January 1884): 29.
43. Milton R. Hunter, in Conference Reports of The Church of Jesus Christ of Latter-day Saints (Salt Lake City: The Church of Jesus Christ of Latter-day Saints, 1898 to present), October 1959, 91–92.
44. Marilyn S. Bateman, “Lay Hold of Every Good Thing,” *Brigham Young University 2000–2001 Speeches* (Provo, Utah: University Publications, 2001), 101.

45. *Mary Elizabeth Rollins Lightner, 1818–1913,* comp. Jennie Lee Adam (Salt Lake City: LDS Church Archives), 16–18.
46. M. F. Cowley, "Fulfillment of Dreams," *Improvement Era*, 2:264.
47. Ibid.
48. Ibid., 265.
49. Ibid., 264–66.
50. David L. and Georgia Hardy, personal interview, 5 January 2005; see also "Warned in a Dream," *Ensign*, June 1985, 32.
51. Ibid.
52. Ibid.
53. *Scraps of Biography, Tenth Book of the Faith-Promoting Series* (Salt Lake City: Juvenile Instructor Office, 1883), 12–13.
54. *Helpful Visions, Fourteenth Book of the Faith-Promoting Series*, 49.
55. Ibid.
56. Ibid., 50.
57. Ibid.
58. Ibid., 51.
59. Ibid.
60. Ibid., 64.
61. Ibid., 65.
62. Ibid., 66.
63. "The Night Side of Nature," *The Millennial Star*, 10:107.
64. Ibid.
65. Lewis Stewart, "What Came of a Dream," *The Contributor*, 16:616.
66. Ibid.
67. "Joseph Smith, the Prophet," *Young Woman's Journal*, 16:522–23.
68. Joseph Heinerman, *John H. Thorpe Manuscript Journals*, as quoted in *Spirit World Manifestations* (Salt Lake City: Magazine Printing and Publishing, 1978), 115.
69. Ibid., 114–17.
70. "Some of Our Composers," *Juvenile Instructor* 37 (15 July 1902), 429–31.
71. Gary Fuller Reese, *Uncle Jesse, the Story of Jesse Knight—Miner, Industrialist, Philanthropist* (Salt Lake City: LDS Church History Library), 69–70.
72. Ibid., 70.
73. Richard H. Peterson, *Bonanza Rich, Lifestyles of the Western*

Mining Entrepreneurs (Moscow: University of Idaho Press, 1991), 49.

74. J. Frederic Templeman, *Oral History,* interviewed by Clinton D. Christensen (Salt Lake City: The James Moyle Oral History Program, Archives Division, Historical Department, The Church of Jesus Christ of Latter-day Saints), 10–11.
75. Kraut, *A Gift of Dreams,* 124.
76. Emelius Berg, *Juvenile Instructor* 31 (1 June 1896): 343.
77. "A String of Pearls for Those Who Have Intelligence to Appreciate Them," *The Young Woman's Journal*, 1:211.
78. Ibid., 211–13.
79. "About Dreams," *The Millennial Star*, 28:502.
80. Ibid., 502–3.
81. *Links of Forever*, 138–39.
82. *Spiritual Experiences in the Twentieth Century Like Those of Nephi,* research paper for Brigham Young University, Provo, Utah (copy on file at Salt Lake City: LDS Church History Library, 1974), 9.
83. Melvin S. Tagg, *The Life of Edward James Wood, Church Patriot* (copy on file at Salt Lake City: LDS Church History Library, 1959), 23.
84. Ibid., 23.
85. Ibid., 23–24.
86. Ibid., 22–24.

Chapter 4

1. Spencer W. Kimball, in Conference Reports of The Church of Jesus Christ of Latter-day Saints (Salt Lake City: The Church of Jesus Christ of Latter-day Saints, 1898 to present), October 1966, 25.
2. Heber C. Kimball, in *Journal of Discourses,* 26 vols. (London: Latter-day Saints' Book Depot, 1854–86), 3:112.
3. *The Millennial Star*, 26:293.
4. John Taylor, in *Journal of Discourses*, 14:189.
5. *BYU Studies* 33, no. 1 (1993), 57.
6. Ibid., 57.
7. Rebecca Rosetta Peterson Bean, talk delivered at a Salt Lake City fireside, fall 1964, as quoted by Frederick W. Babbel in *To Him That Believeth* (Salt Lake City: Bookcraft, 1982), 61–63.

8. Anson Call, *Autobiography of Anson Call*, unpublished manuscript (Provo, Utah: BYU Library, Special Collections), 6–7.
9. James A. Little, *Jacob Hamblin, Fifth Book of the Faith-Promoting Series* (Salt Lake City: Juvenile Instructor Office, 1881), 13.
10. Ibid., 11–13.
11. *Treasures in Heaven, Fifteenth Book of the Faith Promoting Series,* comp. Geo. C. Lambert (Salt Lake City: Geo. C. Lambert, 1914), 22.
12. Ibid., 21–22.
13. Ibid.
14. Norma Clark Larsen, *His Everlasting Love* (Bountiful: Horizon, 1977), 103–4.
15. Lucy Mack Smith, *The History of Joseph Smith by His Mother, Lucy Mack Smith* (Salt Lake City: Stevens & Wallis, Inc., 1945), 43.
16. Ibid.
17. Ibid., 42–45.
18. Antonia Flores, as quoted by Leon R. Hartshorn in *Remarkable Stories from the Lives of Latter-day Saint Women* (Salt Lake City: Deseret Book, 1975), 2:87.
19. Ibid., 87–88.
20. *Helpful Visions, The Fourteenth Book of the Faith-Promoting Series* (Salt Lake City: Juvenile Instructor Office, 1887), 30.
21. Ibid., 31.
22. Ibid., 32.
23. Ibid., 33.
24. Ibid., 30–34.
25. Ibid., 35–36.
26. Ibid., 38–39.
27. Ibid., 35–36, 38.
28. J. L. R., "A Mysterious Dog," *Juvenile Instructor* 19 (1 May 1884): 142.
29. *Early Scenes in Church History, Eighth Book of the Faith-Promoting Series* (Salt Lake City: Juvenile Instructor Office, 1882), 60.
30. Lula, "Lolie's Dream," *Juvenile Instructor* 26 (1 May 1891): 293.
31. Ibid., 293.
32. *Faith Like the Ancients, Vol. 2,* comp. N. B. Lundwall (Manti, Utah: Mountain Valley Publishers, 1968), 14.
33. Ibid.

34. Ibid., 14–15.
35. Ibid., 15.
36. Ibid., 12–16.
37. Andrew Jenson, *Latter-day Saint Biographical Encyclopedia,* Vol. 2 (Salt Lake City: Andrew Jenson History Company, 1914), 529.
38. Ibid., 530.
39. Ibid., 531.
40. Ibid., 528–31.
41. Helen Mar Whitney, "Some Serious Reflections," *Woman's Exponent* 17 (15 October 1888), 73.
42. *Visions of the Latter Days, No. 1* (Logan, Utah: Utah State University, Special Collections), 15.
43. Ibid.
44. Ibid., 13–19.
45. Carol Cornwall Madsen, *In Their Own Words, Women and the Story of Nauvoo* (Salt Lake City: Deseret Book, 1994), 195.
46. Ibid.
47. Ibid.
48. *Scraps of Biography, Tenth Book of the Faith-Promoting Series* (Salt Lake City: 1883), 69.
49. *Life Sketch and Experiences of Lorena A. Wilson*, Vol. 1, 1932 (Logan, Utah: Merrill Library, Utah State University, Special Collections), 34.
50. Michele R. Sorensen and David R. Willmore, *The Journey Beyond Life*, Vol. 1 (Orem, Utah: Family Affair Books, 1988), 113–16.
51. "Book of Mormon Responsible for Saving Youth's Life," *Idaho Falls Post Register*, summer 1966, as quoted by Jack K. Nielsen in *Spiritual Experiences in the Twentieth Century Like Those of Nephi* (1974), 6–7.
52. Cesar Guerra, "How Our Friends Blessed Us," *Ensign*, February 1975, 43.
53. Cora M. Pratt, "My Dream," *Juvenile Instructor* 28 (15 September 1893), 590.
54. Daniel Tyler, "A Significant Dream," *Juvenile Instructor*, 29:145–46.
55. Ibid., 145–47.

56. John M. Bohn, "Early Missionary Experiences," *Juvenile Instructor* 31 (1 April 1896), 205.
57. Ibid.
58. Ibid.
59. Ibid., 207.
60. Ibid.
61. Ibid.
62. Ibid., 208.
63. Ibid., 204–8.
64. Oscar McConkie Jr., *Angels* (Salt Lake City: Deseret Book, 1975), 110.
65. Ibid.
66. Heber J. Grant, *A Book of Remembrance, A Lesson Book for First Year Junior Genealogical Classes* (Salt Lake City: The Genealogical Society of Utah, 1936), 101.
67. Ibid., 101–2.

Chapter 5

1. *The Millennial Star,* 26:293.
2. Ibid.
3. Orson Pratt in *Journal of Discourses,* 26 vols. (London: Latter-day Saints' Book Depot, 1854–86), 25:144–45.
4. Ibid., 18:19.
5. Heber J. Grant, in Conference Reports of The Church of Jesus Christ of Latter-day Saints (Salt Lake City: The Church of Jesus Christ of Latter-day Saints, 1898 to present), October 1910, 119
6. Lexia Harris, "A Curious Conversion," *Juvenile Instructor* 41 (15 May 1906): 309.
5. Ibid., 309–10.
8. Milton R. Hunter, in Conference Report, October 1959, 30.
9. Ibid., 31.
10. Ibid.
11. Ibid.
12. Ibid., 31–32.
13. J. W. Crosby, "A Testimony," *Juvenile Instructor* 16 (1 July 1881): 154.
14. Ibid.

15. *Biography of David John* (Logan, Utah: Merrill Library, Utah State University, Leonard J. Arrington Collection), 81.
16. Ibid.
17. Walter G. Paul, "A Dream and Its Fulfillment," *The Millennial Star,* 68:175.
18. Ibid.
19. Ibid., 175–76.
20. *Cardon Family Biographies* (Logan, Utah: Merrill Library, Utah State University, Leonard J. Arrington Collection), 1–2.
21. Ibid.
22. Hannah Last Cornaby, *Autobiography and Poems* (Salt Lake City: LDS Church History Library), 30.
23. T. Lafayette Hatch, "A Remarkable Dream," *The Millennial Star*, 70:283.
24. *George H. Brimhall Diary*, as quoted by Joseph Heinerman in *Spirit World Manifestations* (Salt Lake City: Magazine Printing and Publishing, 1978), 250.
25. *Gems for the Young Folks, Fourth Book of the Faith-Promoting Series* (Salt Lake City: Juvenile Instructor Office, 1881), 62.
26. Ibid., 63–64.
27. Ibid., 62–64.
28. Ibid., 77.
29. Ibid., 77–78.
30. Carolyn Devitra Cruze Eyre, *Spears Family Information 2004* (Salt Lake City: LDS Church Archives), 43.
31. Ibid.
32. Ibid.
33. Gaston L. Braley, "A Remarkable Vision," ed. Isaac B. Ball, *Church News*, 3 November 1934, 2.
34. *Scraps of Biography, Tenth Book of the Faith-Promoting Series* (Salt Lake City: Juvenile Instructor Office, 1883), 24.
35. Ibid.
36. Ibid., 25.
37. Ibid.
38. Ibid., 26.
39. Ibid., 27.
40. Ibid., 52–53.

41. Jeremiah Stokes, *Modern Miracles* (Salt Lake City: Bookcraft, 1945), 120.
42. Ibid., 119–20.
43. *Heroines of Mormondom, Second Book of the Noble Women's Lives Series* (Salt Lake City, Juvenile Instructor Office: LDS Church History Library), 1884, 44.
44. Ibid., 45.
45. Ibid., 47.
46. Ibid., 49.
47. Ibid., 50.
48. Jens Hansen, "Emigrant Pioneers," *An Enduring Legacy* (Salt Lake City: Daughters of Utah Pioneers, 1982), 5:231.
49. Melvin S. Tagg, "The Life of Edward James Wood," master's thesis, Brigham Young University (Salt Lake City: LDS Church History Library, 1959), 108.
50. *Faith and Courage, LDS Stories of Faith, Courage and Conversion,* comp. members of Hunter 19th Ward, Salt Lake Hunter Stake (Salt Lake City: LDS Church History Library, 1983), 59.
51. Tagg, "The Life of Edward James Wood," 87.
52. Harold E. Card Jr., as quoted in *Faith Like the Ancients, Vol. 2,* N. B. Lundwall (Manti, Utah: Mountain Valley Publishers, 1968), 27.
53. Ibid., 27–28.
54. W. J. Kohlberg, *Improvement Era*, 9:573.
55. Ibid.
56. Ibid.
57. Jack E. Jarrard, "Gospel Proves Great Help in Officer's Work," *Church News*, 28 August 1971, 12.
58. David Robert Roberts, *Book of Remembrance of David D. and Cedy Davies, Davis Natives of Merthyr Tydfil, Glamorganshire, Wales, and Their Family Including* . . . (Salt Lake City: LDS Church History Library), 133.
59. Ibid.
60. David White Rogers, as quoted in *Heroines of the Restoration*, ed. Barbara B. Smith and Blythe Darlyn Thatcher (Salt Lake City: Bookcraft, 1997), 155.
61. Ibid.

62. *Lives of Our Leaders: Character Sketches of Living Presidents and Apostles of The Church of Jesus Christ of Latter-day Saints* (Salt Lake City: The Deseret News, 1901), 230.
63. Ibid.
64. Ogden Wedlund Kraut, *The Gift of Dreams* (Salt Lake City, LDS Church History Library), 51.
65. Ibid., 52.
66. Soren Rasmus Nielsen, *Temple record book and autobiographical sketch* [ca. 1888–1898] (Salt Lake City: LDS Church Archives), 1–2.
67. Thomas C. Haddon, *Writings* [ca. 1882] (Salt Lake City: LDS Church Archives), 7.
68. Ibid.
69. *Spirit World Experiences* (Salt Lake City: LDS Church History Library), 47–48.
70. Ibid., 49–50.
71. Ibid., 51.
72. Ibid., 47–52.
73. Milton R. Hunter, in Conference Report, 6 April 1972, 36.
74. James Forman Turpin, *Pioneer Ancestors of Edward James Turpin 1997* (Salt Lake City: LDS Church Archives), 37.
75. Ibid., 38.
76. Ibid., 39.
77. Ibid.
78. J. M. S., *The Millennial Star*, 79:4–5.
79. Ibid., 11–12.
80. Ibid., 13.
81. Mark E. Petersen, "The Gift of the Holy Ghost," *The New Era*, September 1978, 4.
82. Lucy Mack Smith, *The History of Joseph Smith by His Mother, Lucy Mack Smith* (Salt Lake City: Stevens & Wallis, Inc., 1945), 47.
83. Ibid., 48–49
84. Ibid., 49.
85. Ibid.
86. Ibid., 50.
87. Ann Booth, *Wilford Woodruff's Journal, 1833–1898 Typescript, Vol. 1*, ed. Scott G. Kenney (Midvale, Utah: Signature Books), 475–76.

88. Ibid., 476.
89. Ibid., 77.

Chapter 6

1. Wilford Woodruff, in *Journal of Discourses,* 26 vols. (London: Latter-day Saints' Book Depot, 1854–86), 22:333.
2. Ibid.
3. Orson Pratt, in *Journal of Discourses,* 25:145.
4. Wilford Woodruff, as quoted by Joseph Fielding Smith in *Answers to Gospel Questions,* 5 vols. (Salt Lake City: Deseret Book, 1958), 2:47.
5. Carlos H. Amado, in Conference Reports of The Church of Jesus Christ of Latter-day Saints (Salt Lake City: The Church of Jesus Christ of Latter-day Saints, 1898 to present), April 2002, 95.
6. Bryant S. Hinckley, *The Faith of Our Pioneer Fathers* (Salt Lake City: Bookcraft, 1956), 225–26.
7. Joseph Anderson, *Prophets of the Living God,* Brigham Young University Speeches of the Year, 29 July 1969, 4–5.
8. Ibid., 6.
9. *Fragments of Experience, Sixth Book of the Faith-Promoting Series* (Salt Lake City: Juvenile Instructor Office, 1882), 78.
10. Ibid., 78–79.
11. Ibid., 79.
12. Ibid.
13. Ibid., 79–80.
14. Ibid., 80.
15. Ibid., 81.
16. Ibid., 23.
17. Ibid., 232–24.
18. *Gems for the Young Folks, Fourth Book of the Faith-Promoting Series* (Salt Lake City: Juvenile Instructor Office, 1881), 54–58.
19. Andrew Jenson, *Latter-day Saint Biographical Encyclopedia, Vol. 1* (Salt Lake City: The Andrew Jenson History Company, 1901), 44.
20. *A String of Pearls, Second Book of the Faith-Promoting Series*, 2d ed. (Salt Lake City: Juvenile Instructor Office, 1882), 72–73.
21. "Early Reminiscences," *Juvenile Instructor* 18 (15 February 1883): 52.

22. Ibid.
23. Amanda W. Anderson, *Dreams, 1934* (Salt Lake City: LDS Church Archives).
24. George C. Lambert comp., *Precious Memories, Sixteenth Book of the Faith Promoting Series* (Salt Lake City: George C. Lambert, 1914), 36.
25. Ibid., 37.
26. Ibid., 38–39.
27. Ibid., 39.
28. Ibid., 36–40.
29. *Early Scenes in Church History, Eighth Book of the Faith-Promoting Series* (Salt Lake City: Juvenile Instructor Office, 1882), 94.
30. "A Dream," *The Millennial Star*, 1:133.
31. Ibid.
32. Ibid., 1:134.
33. *Labors in the Vineyard, Twelfth Book of the Faith-Promoting Series* (Salt Lake City: Juvenile Instructor Office, 1884), 15.
34. Ibid., 16.
35. *Labors in the Vineyard, Twelfth Book of the Faith-Promoting Series* (Salt Lake City: Juvenile Instructor Office, 1884), 15–16.
36. Jeremiah Stokes, *Modern Miracles* (Salt Lake City: Bookcraft, 1945), 52–53.
37. Ibid., 53.
38. Ibid.
39. Ibid., 53–54.
40. John Henry Evans, *Charles Coulson Rich, Pioneer Builder of the West* (New York: Macmillan, 1936), 38–39.
41. Ibid., 39–40.
42. Ibid., 38.
43. *Biographical Record of Martha Cragun Cox*, unpublished manuscript, 232, as quoted by Joseph Heinerman, *Spirit World Manifestations* (Salt Lake City: Magazine Printing and Publishing, 1978), 125–26.
44. M. F. Cowley, "Fulfillment of Dreams," *Improvement Era*, 2:265.
45. Ibid.
46. Ibid., 2:266.
47. Evan Molbourne Greene, *Papers [ca. 184–]–1882* (Salt Lake City: LDS Church Archives), 26–27.

48. Ibid., 27–29.
49. Ibid., 29–30.
50. Johannes Hasler, *From Switzerland to Utah, Arthur D. Hasler's grandparents* (Salt Lake City: LDS Church History Library), 27–28.
51. Mephibosheth Sirrine, *Visions of the Latter Days, Book 2* (Logan, Utah: Merrill Library, USU Special Collections), 1–2.
52. Ibid., 1–3.
53. *Diary of Frederick William Hurst* (Salt Lake City: LDS Church Historical Library), 205–7
54. Add–Caput–Ville, "Remarkable Dreams," *The Contributor*, 5:411.
55. Ibid., 411–13.
56. James A. Little, *Jacob Hamblin* (Salt Lake City: Bookcraft, 1969), 83, 89–90.
57. *The Forefather Quest, A Lesson Book for Third-Year Junior Genealogical Classes* (Salt Lake City: Genealogical Society of Utah, 1937), 31.
58. Ibid.
59. Ibid., 31–32.
60. Joseph Smith, *History of The Church of Jesus Christ of Latter-day Saints,* ed. B. H. Roberts, 2d ed. rev., 7 vols. (Salt Lake City: The Church of Jesus Christ of Latter-day Saints, 1932–51), 1:101.
61. *Journal of John Sims Carter: 1797–1834* (Logan, Utah: Merrill Library, USU Special Collections).
62. "A Dream," *The Millennial Star*, 13:123.
63. Ibid.
64. *The Millennial Star*, 9:266–67.
65. Oliver Boardman Huntington, *Diary and Reminiscences, 1843 June 1900 January* (Salt Lake City: LDS Church Archives), 164.
66. Ibid., 164.

Index

A

B

C

G

H

I

J

K

L

M

N

O

P

R

S.

W

Y

Z

About the Author

Marlene Bateman Sullivan was born in Salt Lake City and grew up in Sandy, Utah. She graduated from the University of Utah with a bachelor's degree in English. She is a member of the Bountiful Utah Orchard Stake, currently serving as her ward's welfare specialist and a visiting teacher.

Marlene has been published extensively in various magazines and newspapers. Her first book, *Latter-day Saint Heroes and Heroines,* is a collection of true stories relating stories about people who risked their lives to defend the gospel. The sequel, *Latter-day Saint Heroes and Heroines Volume 2,* was published in 2003. Her first book published by Horizon, *And There Were Angels among Them,* consists of documented accounts of angelic visits in early LDS Church history. Her second book with Horizon was *Visits from Beyond the Veil,* another unique collection of authenticated angelic experiences in LDS history.

In June 1974, she married Kelly R. Sullivan. They are the parents of seven children. Her hobbies are gardening, card making, and reading. She and her husband reside in North Salt Lake.